APEX
— LEGENDS™ —
OVERTIME

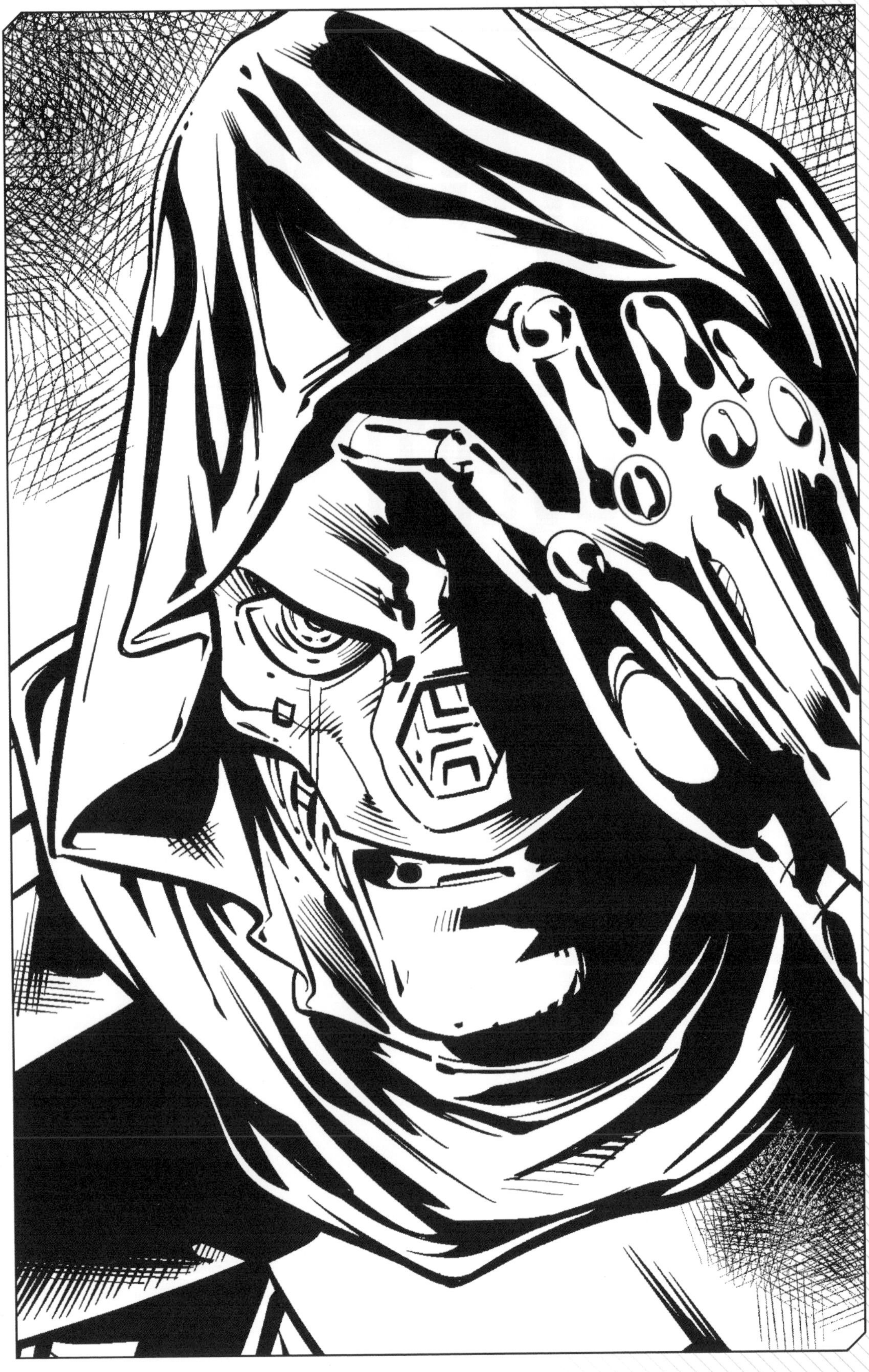

APEX
— LEGENDS™ —
OVERTIME

>>

WRITTEN BY	JESSE STERN
STORY BY	JESSE STERN
	TOM CASIELLO
	MANNY HAGOPIAN
PENCILS BY	NEIL EDWARDS
INKS BY	KEITH CHAMPAGNE
COLORS BY	ANTONIO FABELA
LETTERS BY	NATE PIEKOS
COVER BY	BENGAL &
	DAVID NAKAYAMA

DARK HORSE BOOKS

PRESIDENT AND PUBLISHER
MIKE RICHARDSON

EDITOR
SPENCER CUSHING

ASSISTANT EDITOR
KONNER KNUDSEN

DESIGNER
SKYLER WEISSENFLUH

DIGITAL ART TECHNICIAN
ALLYSON HALLER

Special Thanks: Audrey Wojtowick, Erin Gums, Jason Torfin, Jung Park, Ashley Reed, Amanda Doiron, Sam Gill, Kevin Lee, Josh Mohan, Mohammad Alavi, Pete Scarborough, Christina Kim, Steve Fukuda, Vince Zampella, Chad Grenier, and Jason McCord of Respawn Entertainment

Neil Hankerson Executive Vice President · Tom Weddle Chief Financial Officer · Dale LaFountain Chief Information Officer · Tim Wiesch Vice President of Licensing · Matt Parkinson Vice President of Marketing · Vanessa Todd-Holmes Vice President of Production and Scheduling · Mark Bernardi Vice President of Book Trade and Digital Sales Randy Lahrman Vice President of Product Development · Ken Lizzi General Counsel · Dave Marshall Editor in Chief Davey Estrada Editorial Director · Chris Warner Senior Books Editor · Cary Grazzini Director of Specialty Projects Lia Ribacchi Art Director · Matt Dryer Director of Digital Art and Prepress · Michael Gombos Senior Director of Licensed Publications · Kari Yadro Director of Custom Programs · Kari Torson Director of International Licensing

ComicShopLocator.com

This volume collects issues #1 through #4 of the Dark Horse comic book series *Apex Legends: Overtime*.

Published by Dark Horse Books
A division of Dark Horse Comics LLC
10956 SE Main Street
Milwaukie, OR 97222

DarkHorse.com

Electronic Arts

First edition: June 2022
ISBN 978-1-50672-211-5
eBook ISBN 978-1-50672-212-2

10 9 8 7 6 5 4 3 2 1
Printed in China

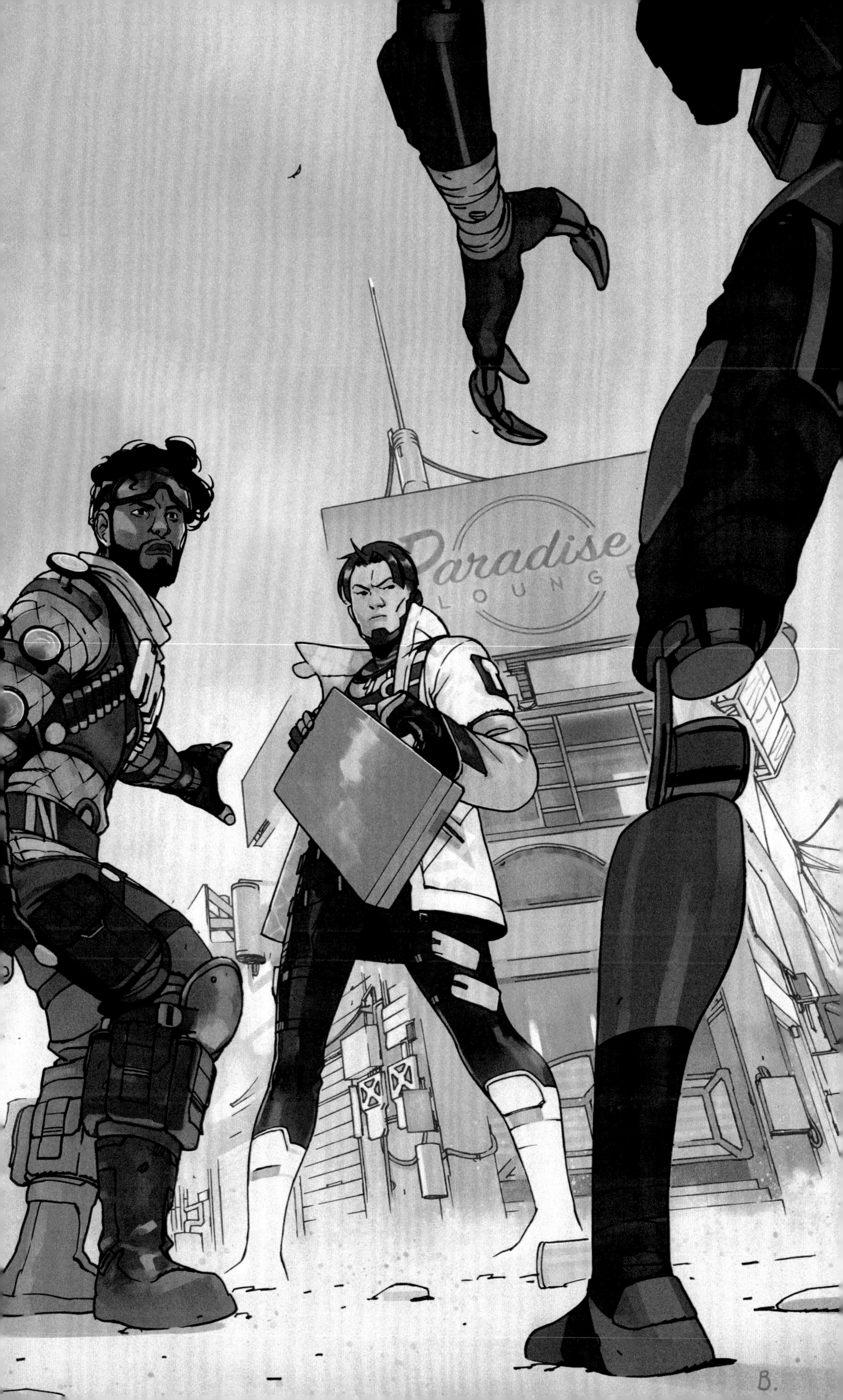
Paradise
B.

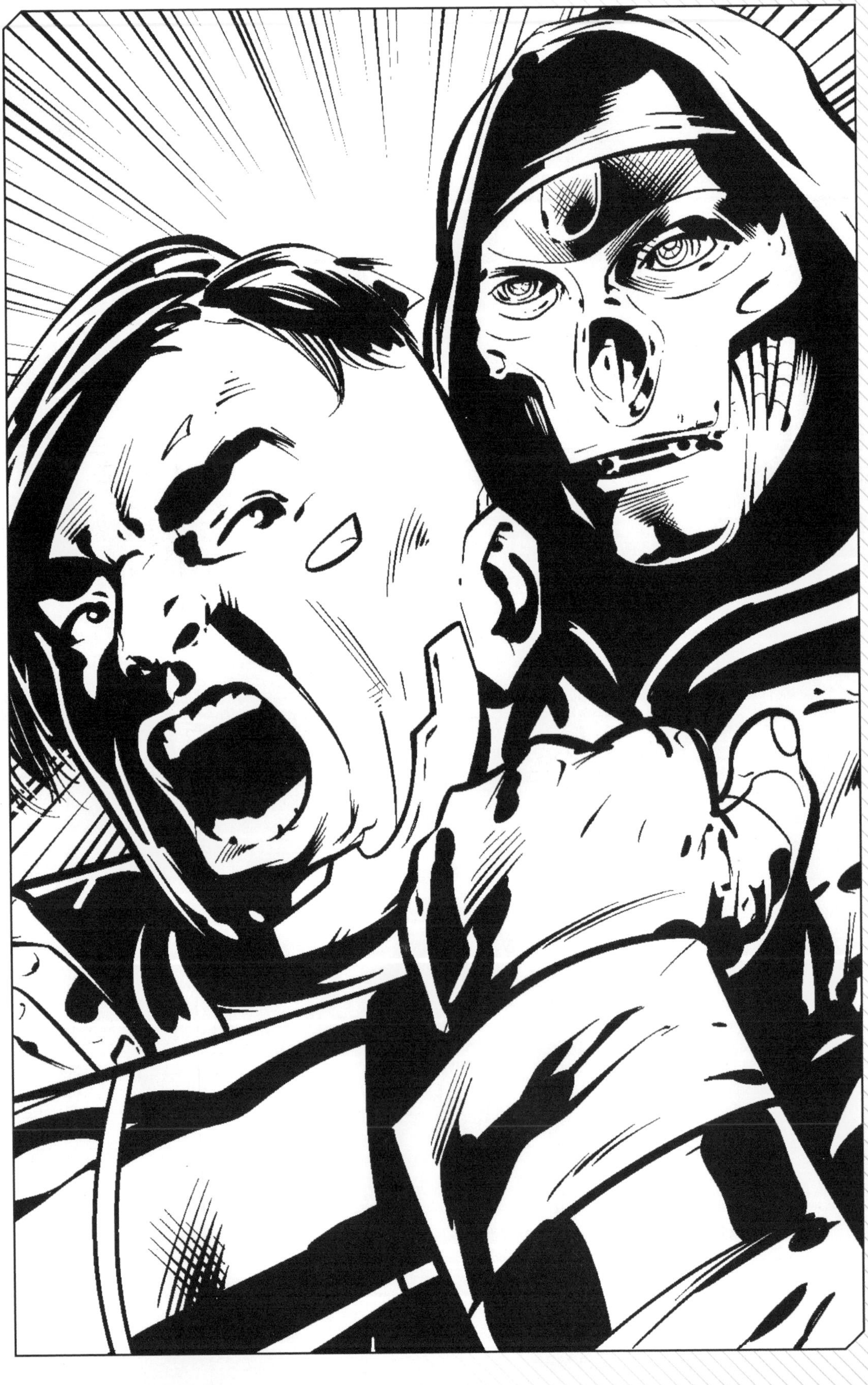

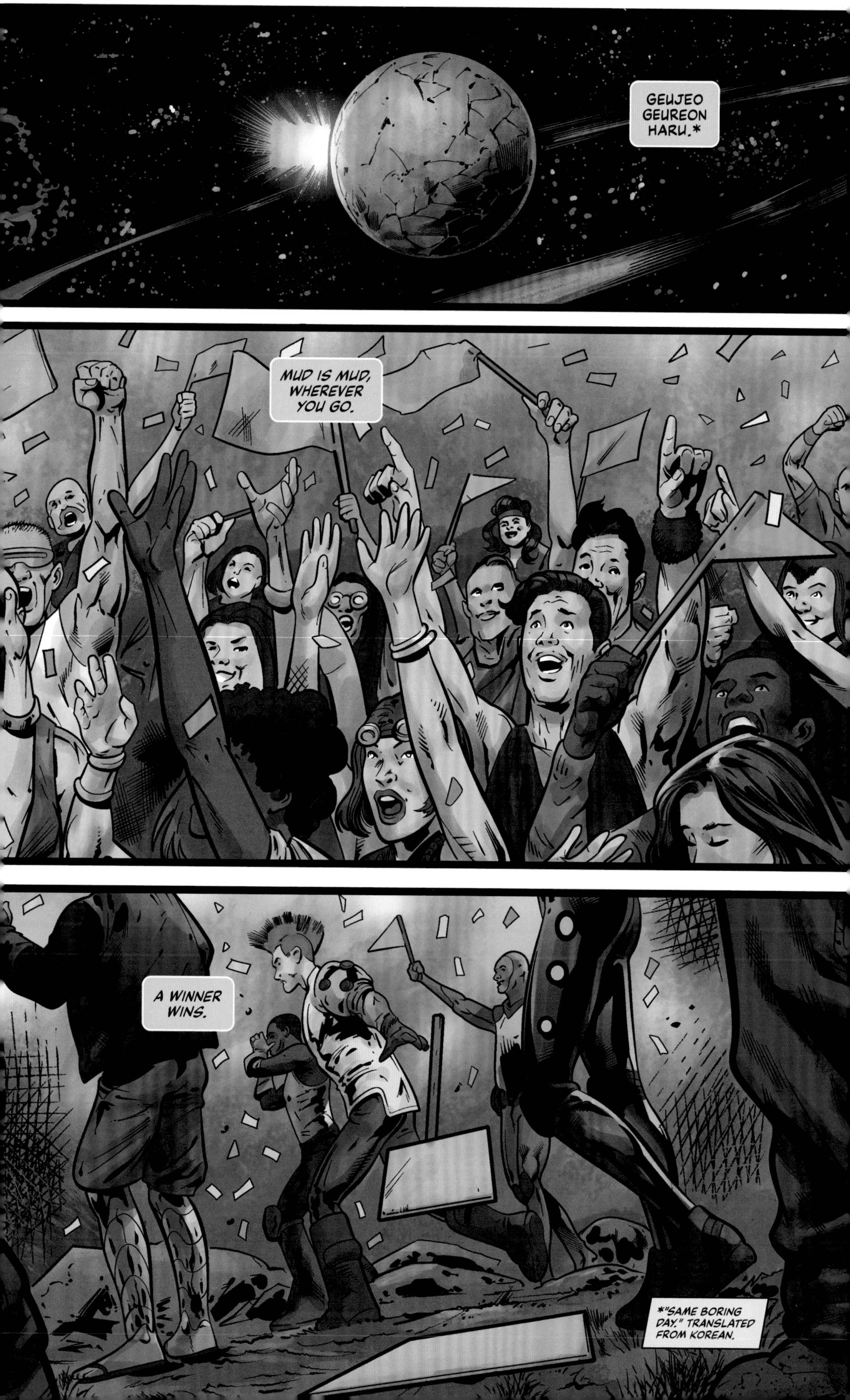
GEUJEO GEUREON HARU.*
MUD IS MUD, WHEREVER YOU GO.
A WINNER WINS.
*"SAME BORING DAY." TRANSLATED FROM KOREAN.

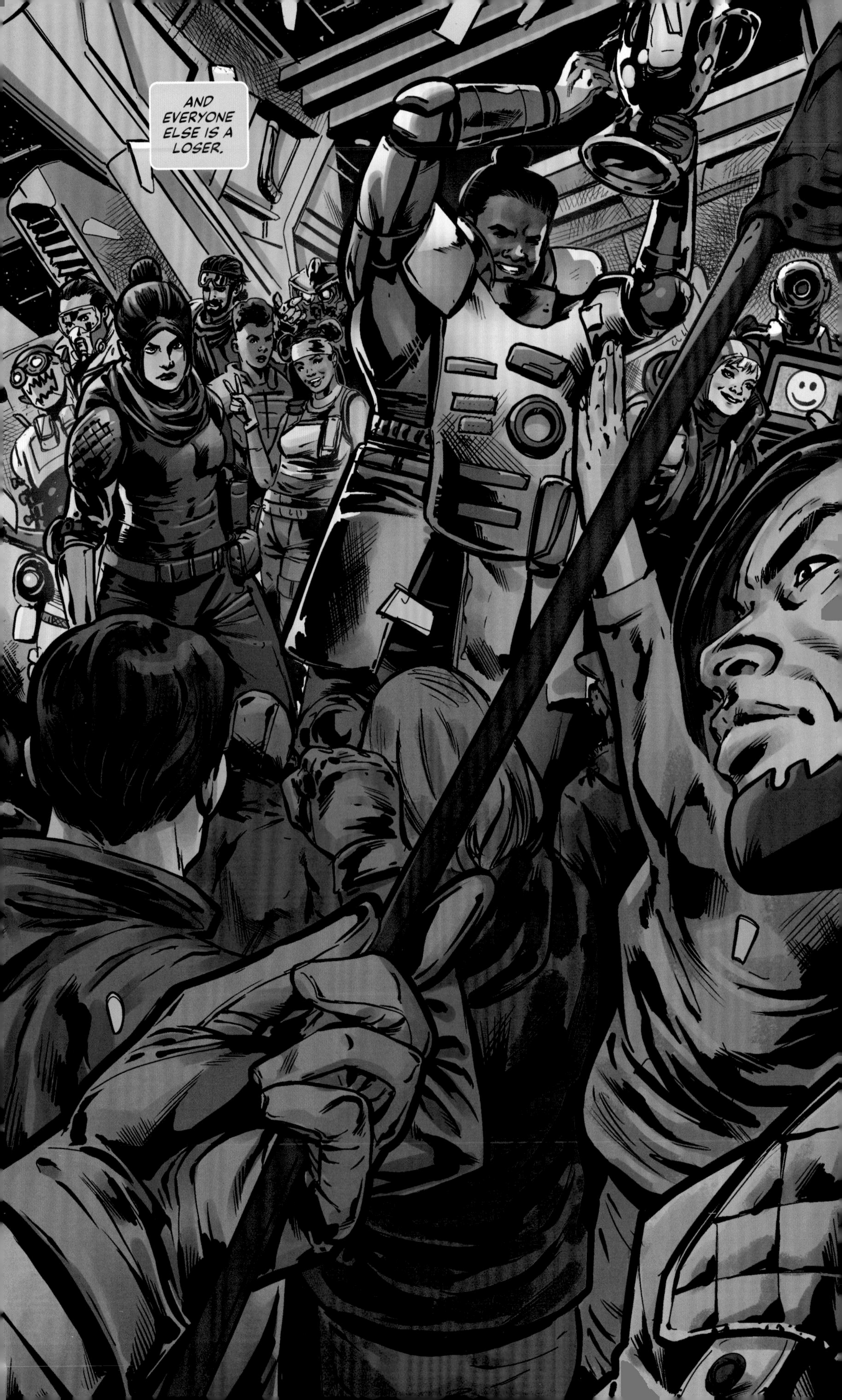
AND EVERYONE ELSE IS A LOSER.

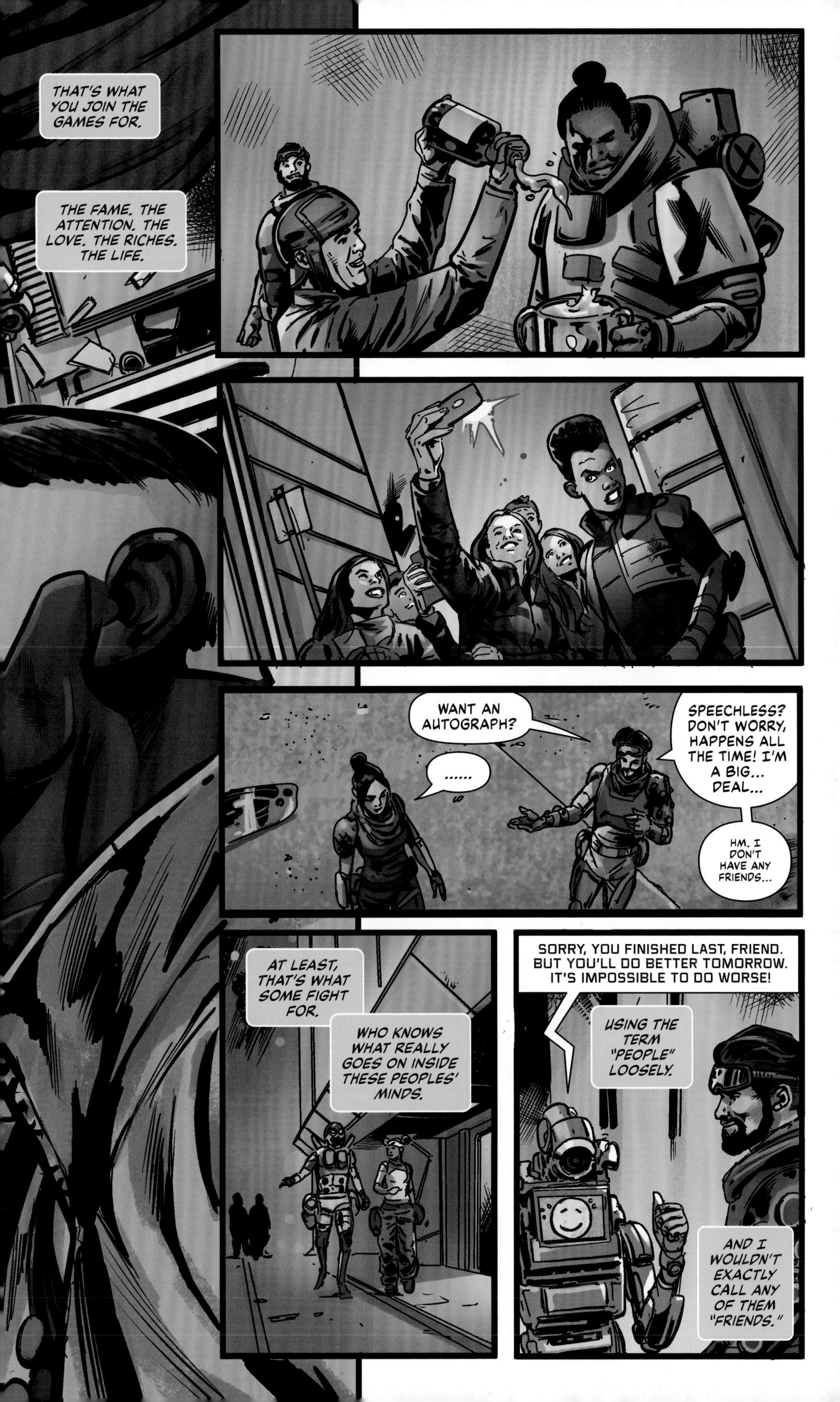
THAT'S WHAT YOU JOIN THE GAMES FOR.
THE FAME. THE ATTENTION. THE LOVE. THE RICHES. THE LIFE.
WANT AN AUTOGRAPH?
......
SPEECHLESS? DON'T WORRY, HAPPENS ALL THE TIME! I'M A BIG... DEAL...
HM. I DON'T HAVE ANY FRIENDS...
AT LEAST, THAT'S WHAT SOME FIGHT FOR.
WHO KNOWS WHAT REALLY GOES ON INSIDE THESE PEOPLES' MINDS.
SORRY, YOU FINISHED LAST, FRIEND. BUT YOU'LL DO BETTER TOMORROW. IT'S IMPOSSIBLE TO DO WORSE!
USING THE TERM "PEOPLE" LOOSELY.
AND I WOULDN'T EXACTLY CALL ANY OF THEM "FRIENDS."

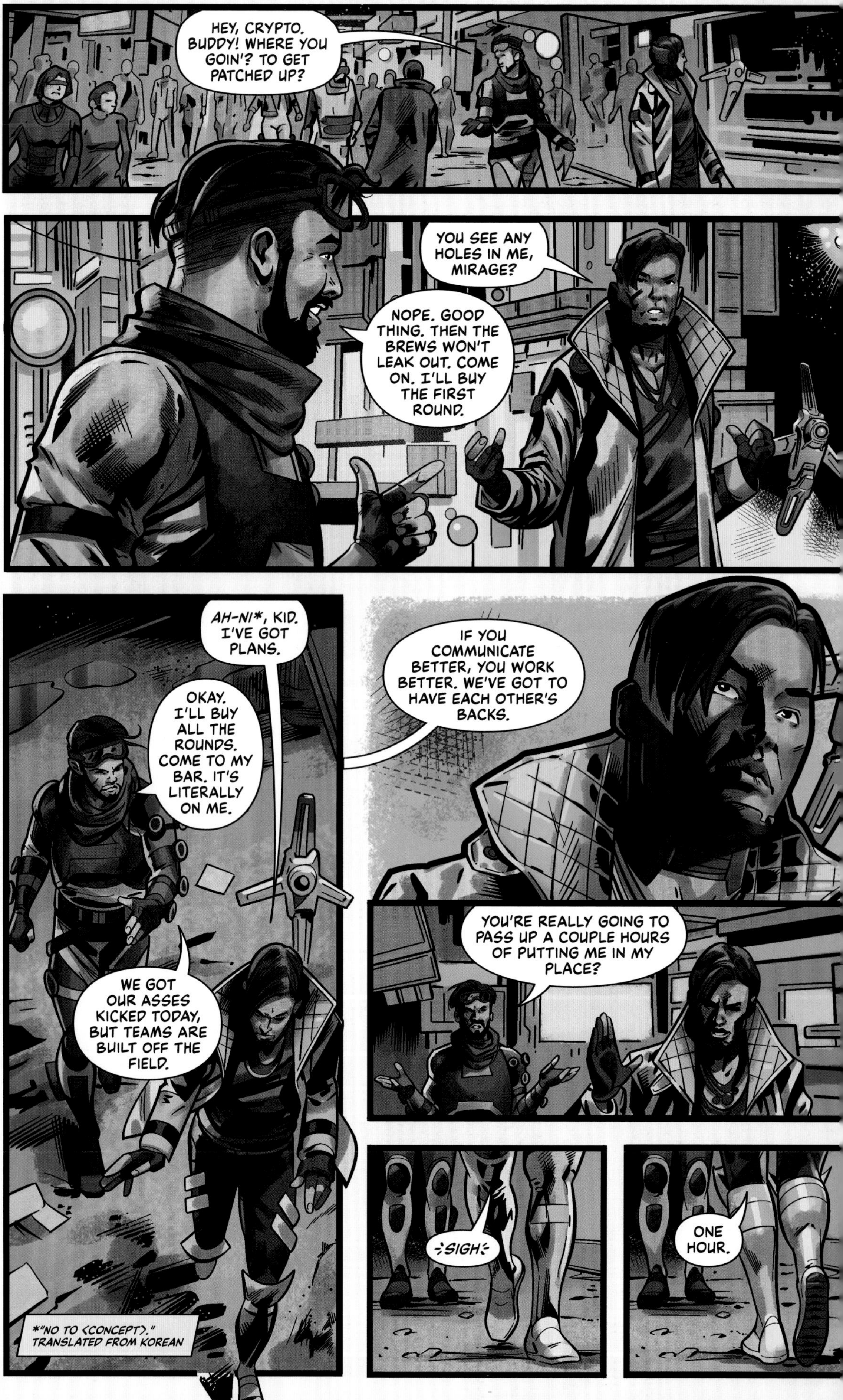
HEY, CRYPTO. BUDDY! WHERE YOU GOIN'? TO GET PATCHED UP?
YOU SEE ANY HOLES IN ME, MIRAGE?
NOPE. GOOD THING. THEN THE BREWS WON'T LEAK OUT. COME ON. I'LL BUY THE FIRST ROUND.
AH-NI*, KID. I'VE GOT PLANS.
OKAY. I'LL BUY ALL THE ROUNDS. COME TO MY BAR. IT'S LITERALLY ON ME.
WE GOT OUR ASSES KICKED TODAY, BUT TEAMS ARE BUILT OFF THE FIELD.
*"NO TO <CONCEPT>." TRANSLATED FROM KOREAN
IF YOU COMMUNICATE BETTER, YOU WORK BETTER. WE'VE GOT TO HAVE EACH OTHER'S BACKS.
YOU'RE REALLY GOING TO PASS UP A COUPLE HOURS OF PUTTING ME IN MY PLACE?
-SIGH-
ONE HOUR.

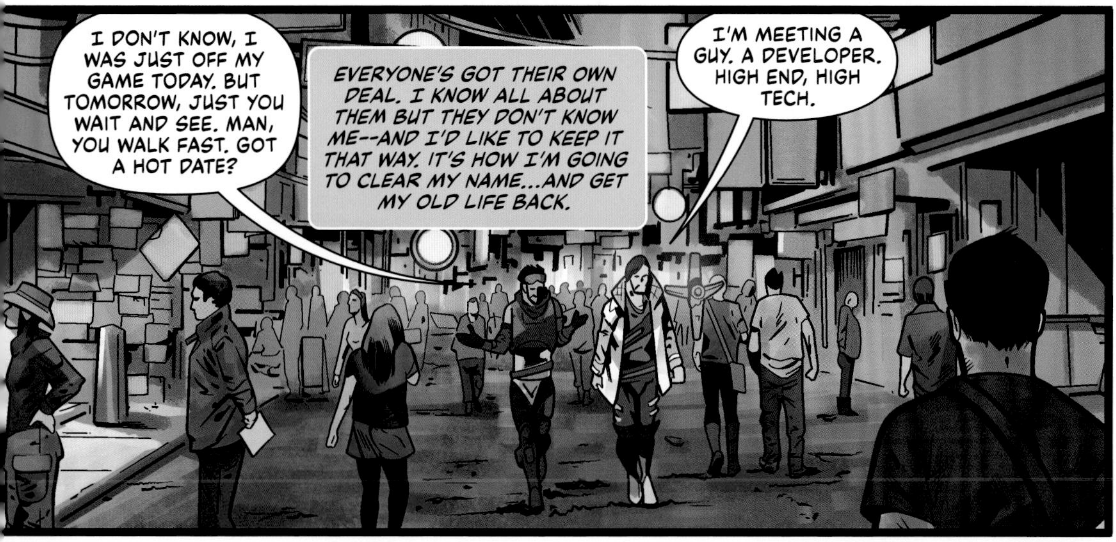
I DON'T KNOW, I WAS JUST OFF MY GAME TODAY. BUT TOMORROW, JUST YOU WAIT AND SEE. MAN, YOU WALK FAST. GOT A HOT DATE?
EVERYONE'S GOT THEIR OWN DEAL. I KNOW ALL ABOUT THEM BUT THEY DON'T KNOW ME--AND I'D LIKE TO KEEP IT THAT WAY. IT'S HOW I'M GOING TO CLEAR MY NAME...AND GET MY OLD LIFE BACK.
I'M MEETING A GUY. A DEVELOPER. HIGH END, HIGH TECH.

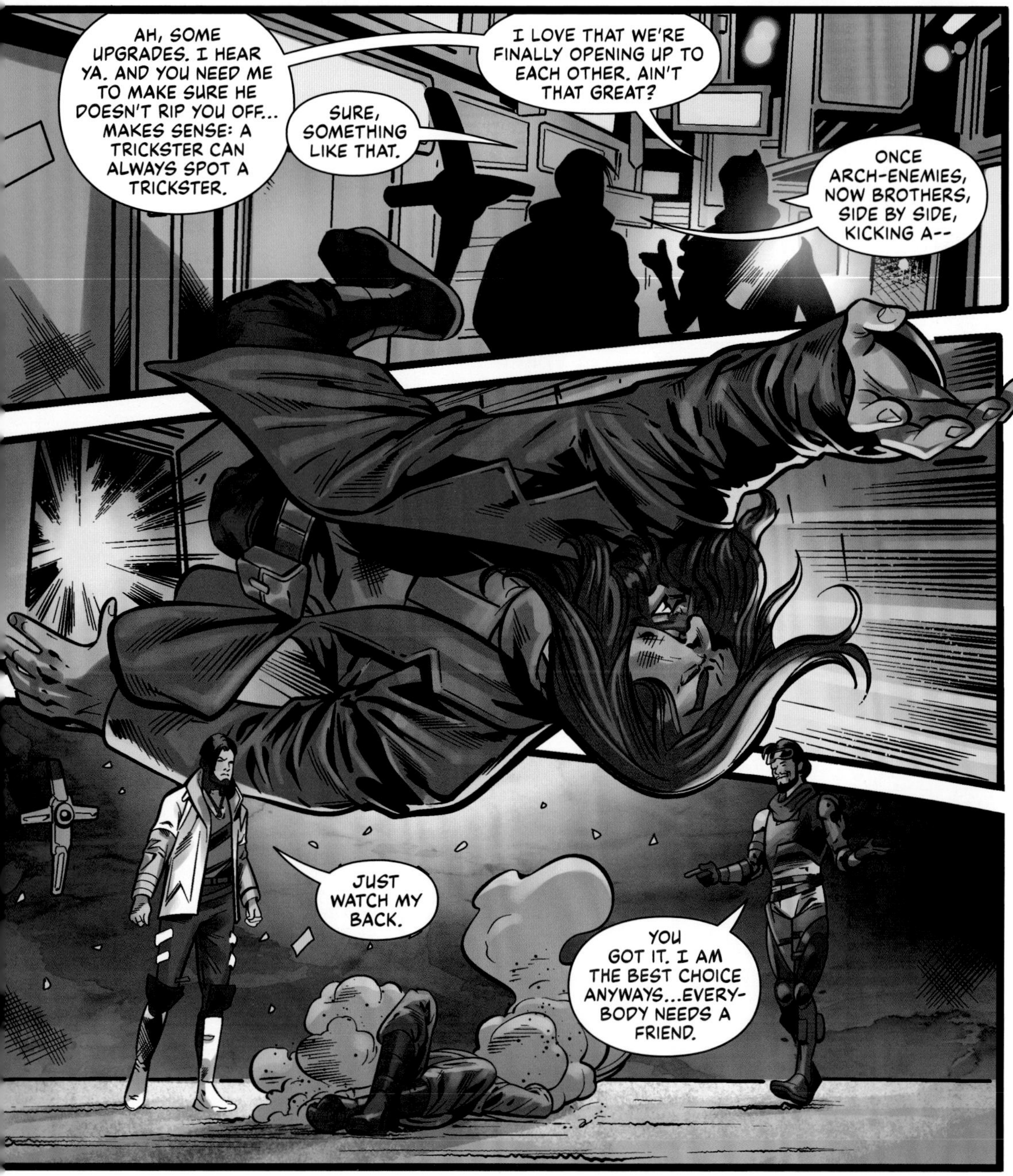
AH, SOME UPGRADES. I HEAR YA. AND YOU NEED ME TO MAKE SURE HE DOESN'T RIP YOU OFF... MAKES SENSE: A TRICKSTER CAN ALWAYS SPOT A TRICKSTER.
SURE, SOMETHING LIKE THAT.
I LOVE THAT WE'RE FINALLY OPENING UP TO EACH OTHER. AIN'T THAT GREAT?
ONCE ARCH-ENEMIES, NOW BROTHERS, SIDE BY SIDE, KICKING A--
JUST WATCH MY BACK.
YOU GOT IT. I AM THE BEST CHOICE ANYWAYS...EVERY-BODY NEEDS A FRIEND.

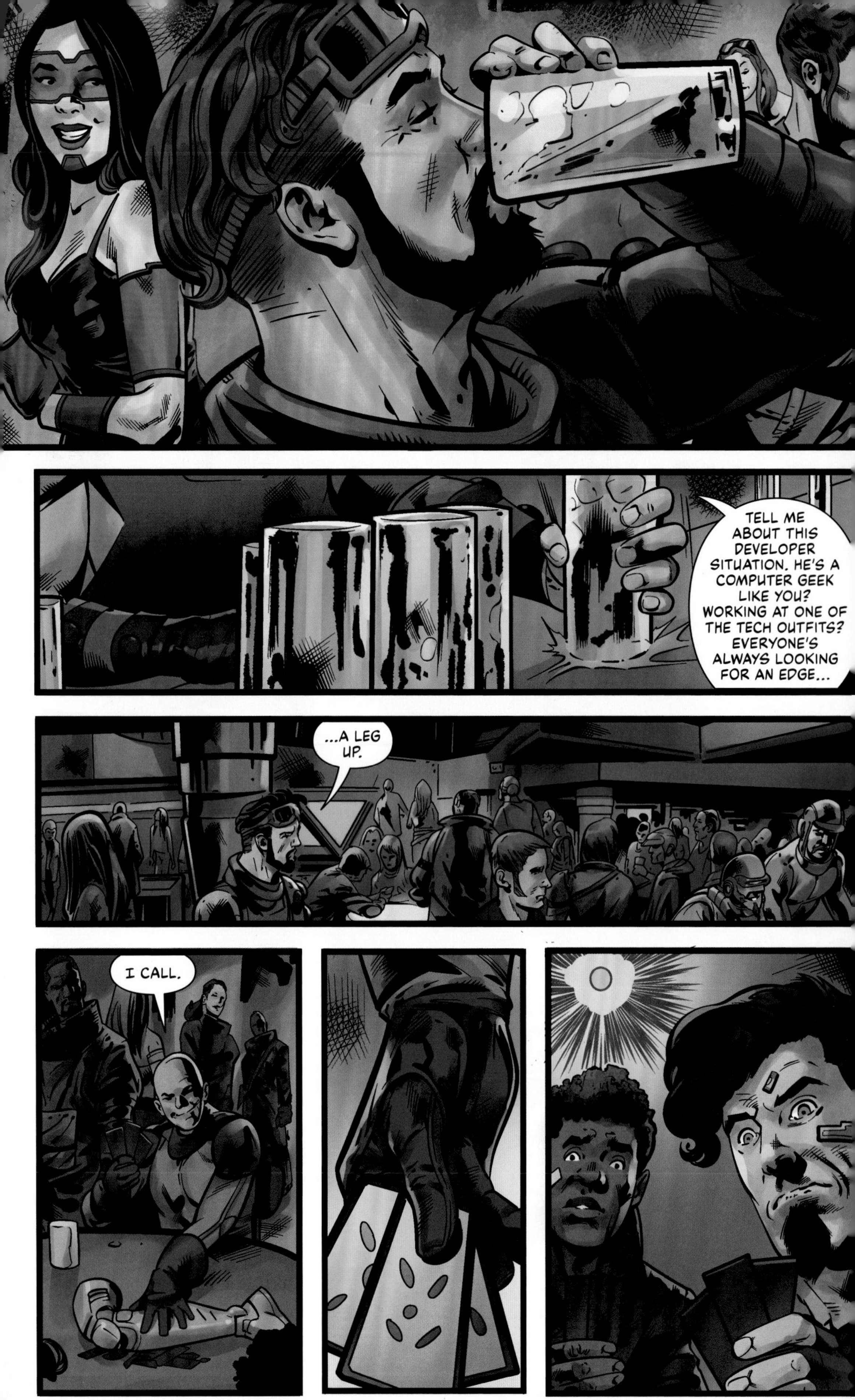
TELL ME ABOUT THIS DEVELOPER SITUATION. HE'S A COMPUTER GEEK LIKE YOU? WORKING AT ONE OF THE TECH OUTFITS? EVERYONE'S ALWAYS LOOKING FOR AN EDGE...
...A LEG UP.
I CALL.

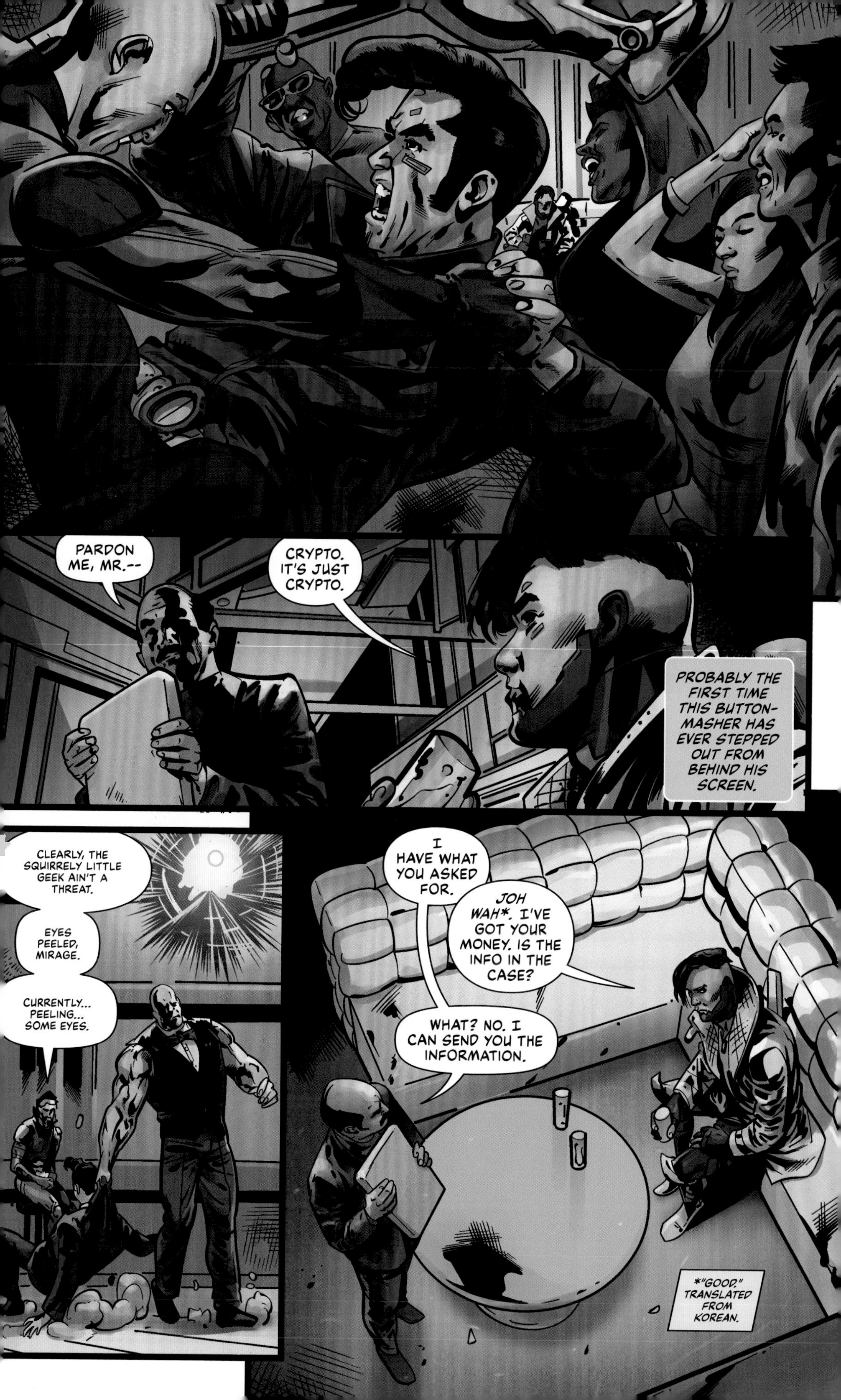
PARDON ME, MR.--
CRYPTO. IT'S JUST CRYPTO.
PROBABLY THE FIRST TIME THIS BUTTON-MASHER HAS EVER STEPPED OUT FROM BEHIND HIS SCREEN.
CLEARLY, THE SQUIRRELY LITTLE GEEK AIN'T A THREAT.
EYES PEELED, MIRAGE.
CURRENTLY... PEELING... SOME EYES.
I HAVE WHAT YOU ASKED FOR.
JOH WAH*. I'VE GOT YOUR MONEY. IS THE INFO IN THE CASE?
WHAT? NO. I CAN SEND YOU THE INFORMATION.
*"GOOD." TRANSLATED FROM KOREAN.

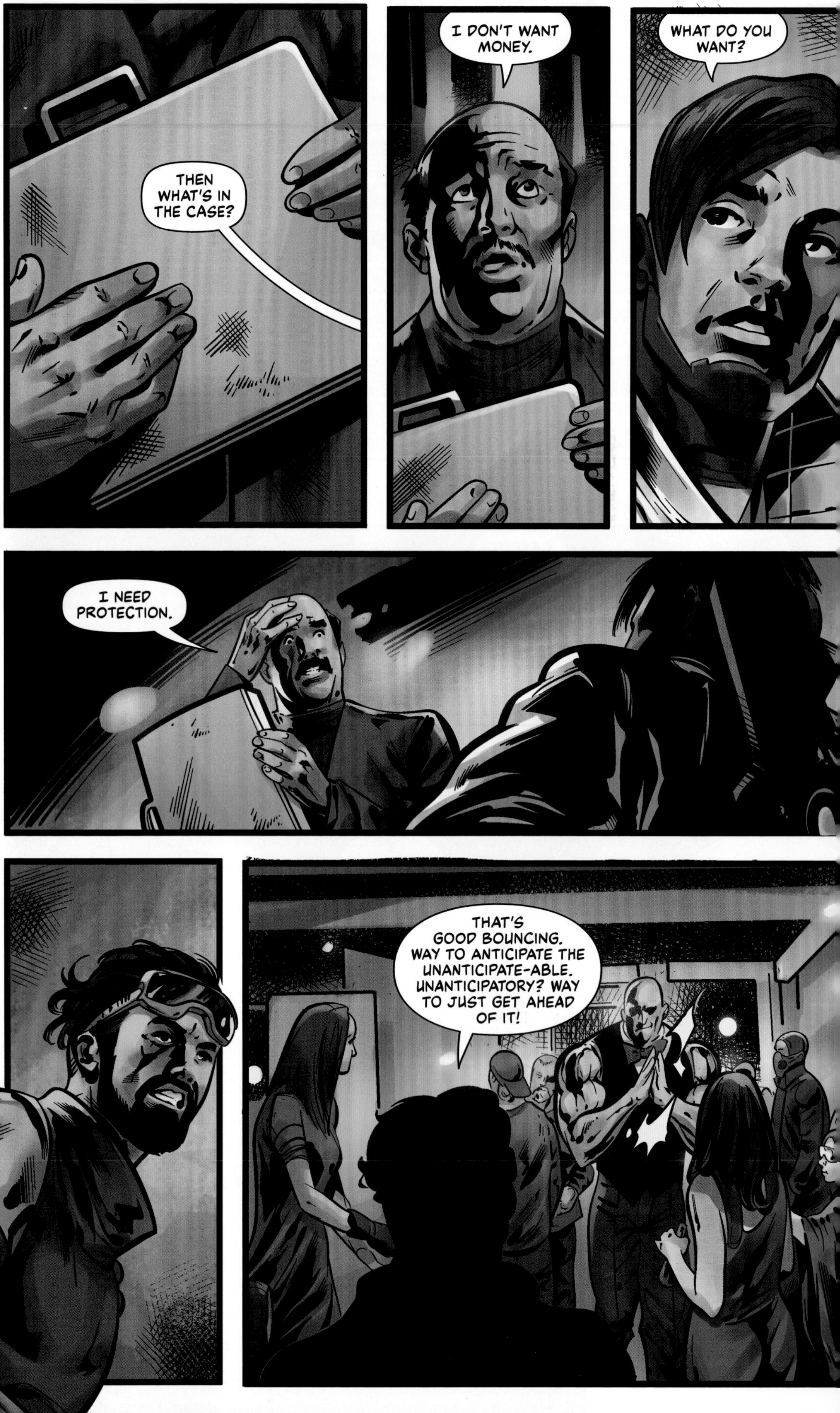
THEN WHAT'S IN THE CASE?
I DON'T WANT MONEY.
WHAT DO YOU WANT?
I NEED PROTECTION.
THAT'S GOOD BOUNCING. WAY TO ANTICIPATE THE UNANTICIPATE-ABLE. UNANTICIPATORY? WAY TO JUST GET AHEAD OF IT!

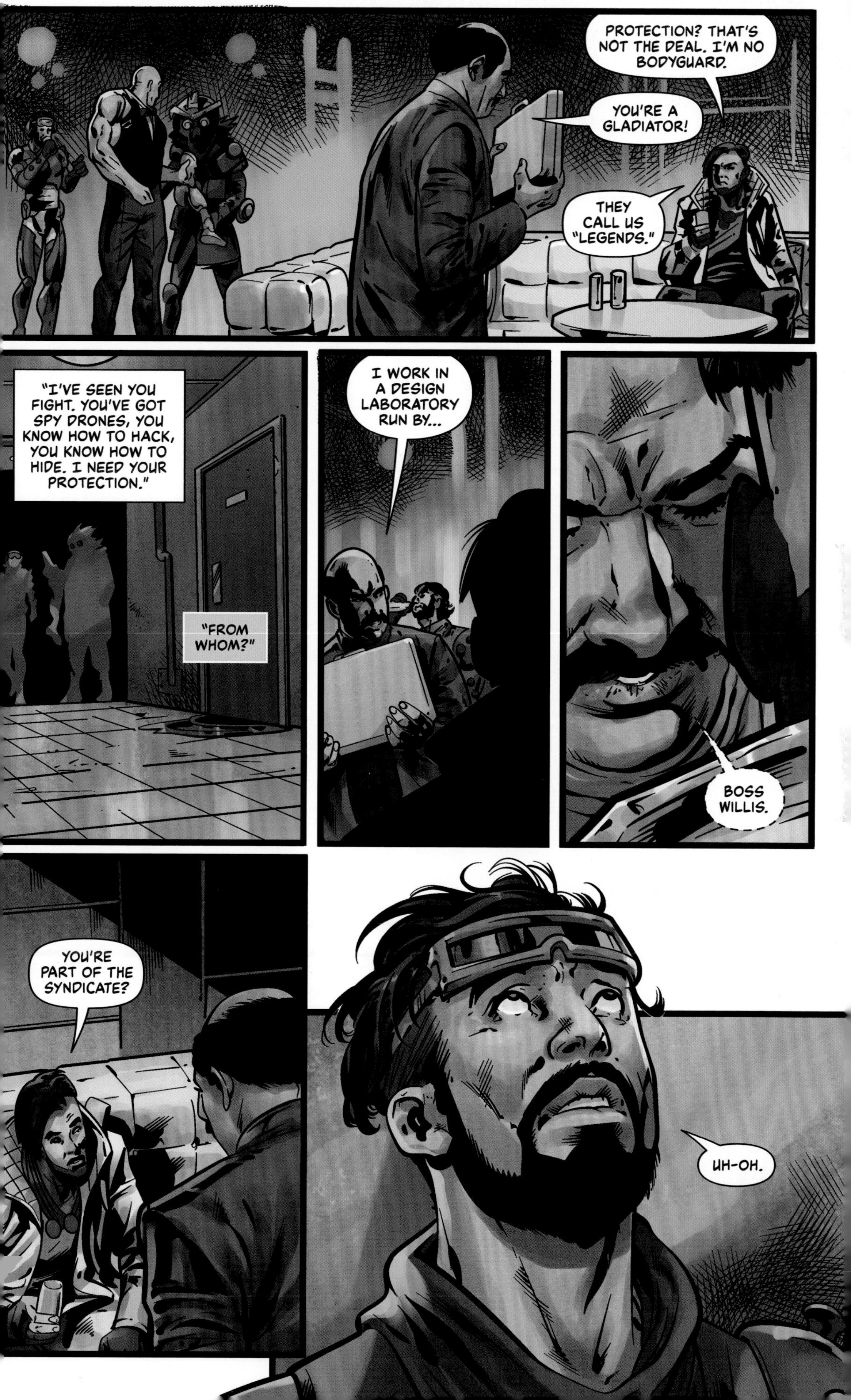
PROTECTION? THAT'S NOT THE DEAL. I'M NO BODYGUARD.
YOU'RE A GLADIATOR!
THEY CALL US "LEGENDS."
"I'VE SEEN YOU FIGHT. YOU'VE GOT SPY DRONES, YOU KNOW HOW TO HACK, YOU KNOW HOW TO HIDE. I NEED YOUR PROTECTION."
"FROM WHOM?"
I WORK IN A DESIGN LABORATORY RUN BY...
BOSS WILLIS.
YOU'RE PART OF THE SYNDICATE?
UH-OH.

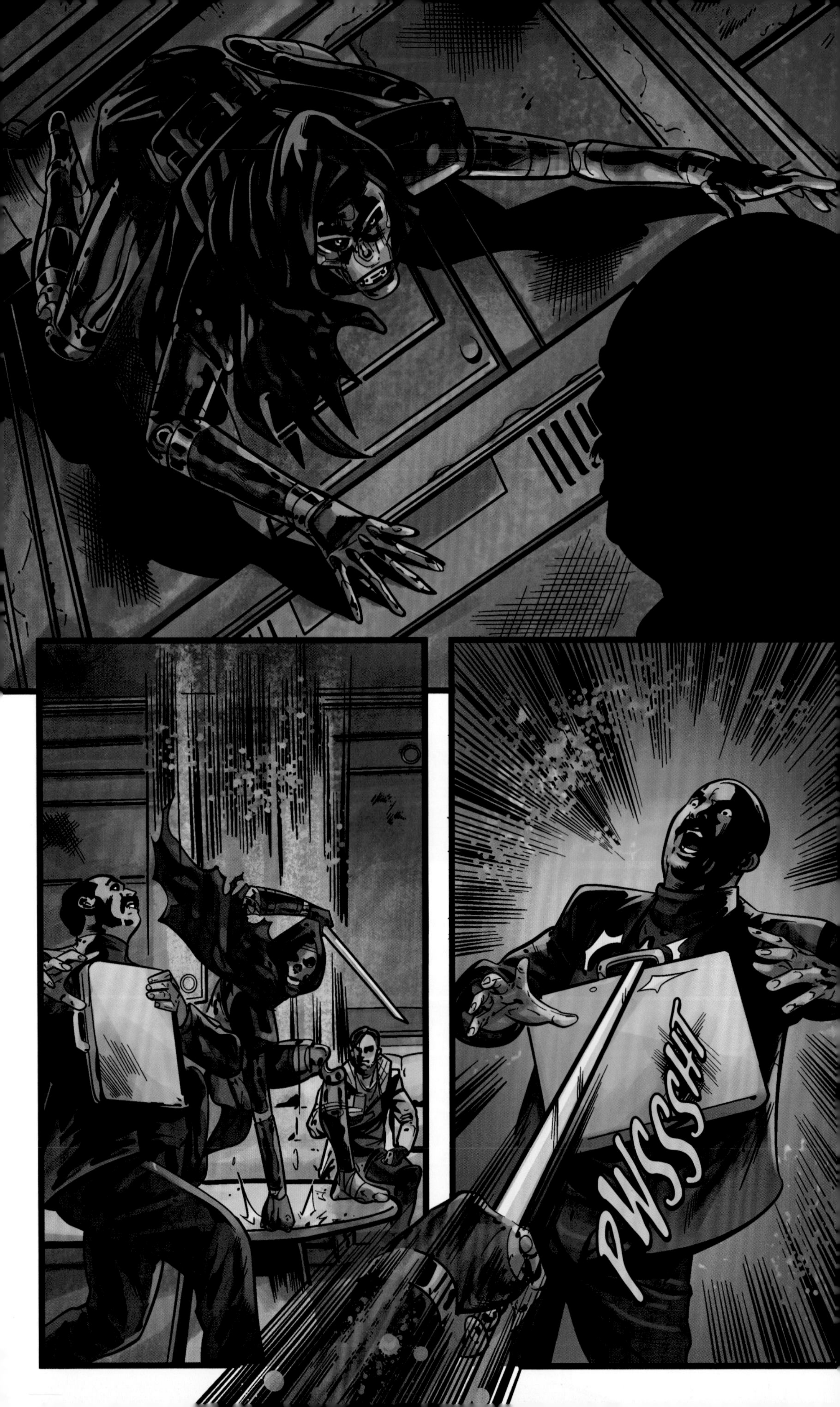
PWSSSHT

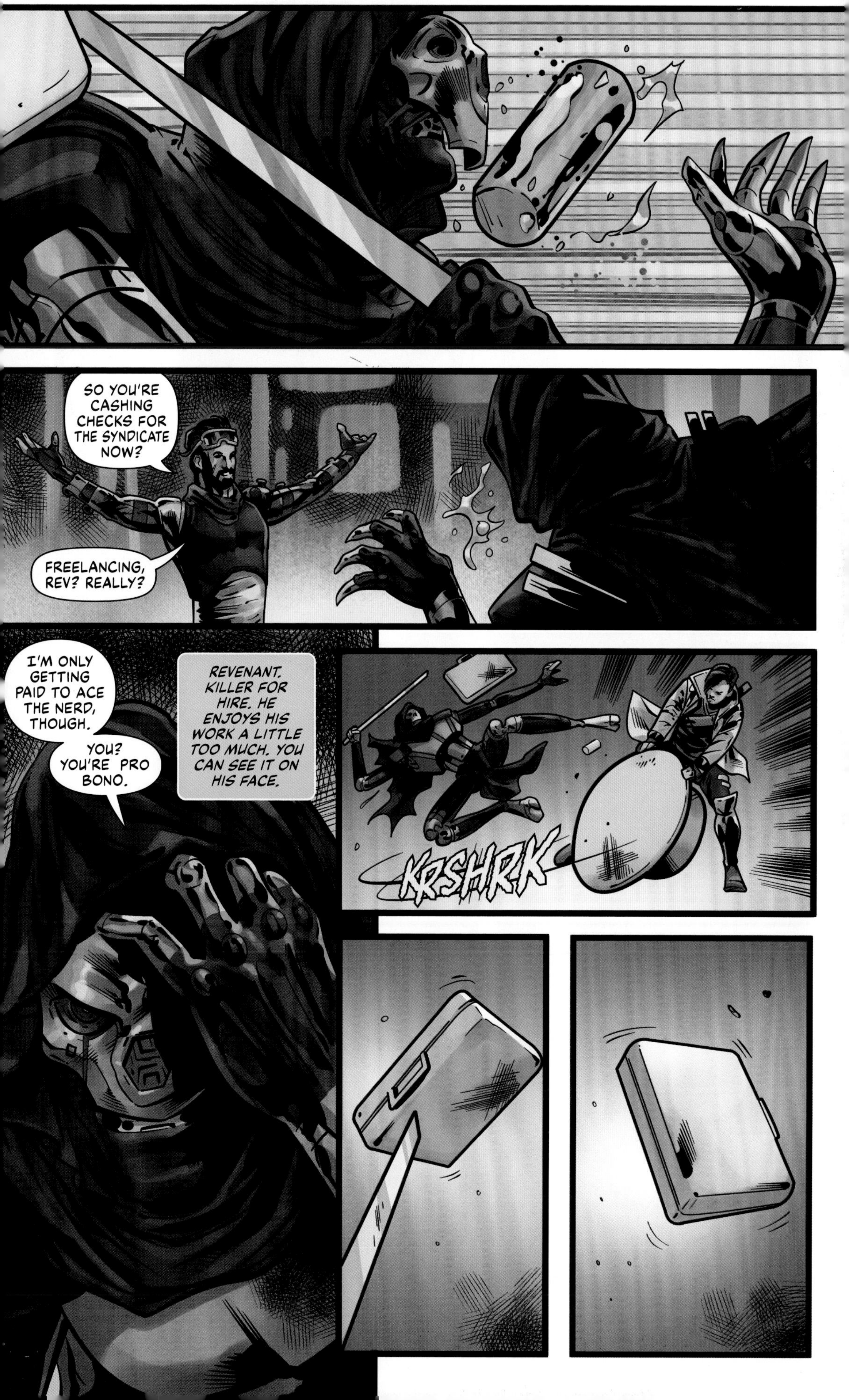

SO YOU'RE CASHING CHECKS FOR THE SYNDICATE NOW?
FREELANCING, REV? REALLY?
I'M ONLY GETTING PAID TO ACE THE NERD, THOUGH.
YOU? YOU'RE PRO BONO.
REVENANT. KILLER FOR HIRE. HE ENJOYS HIS WORK A LITTLE TOO MUCH. YOU CAN SEE IT ON HIS FACE.
KRSHRK

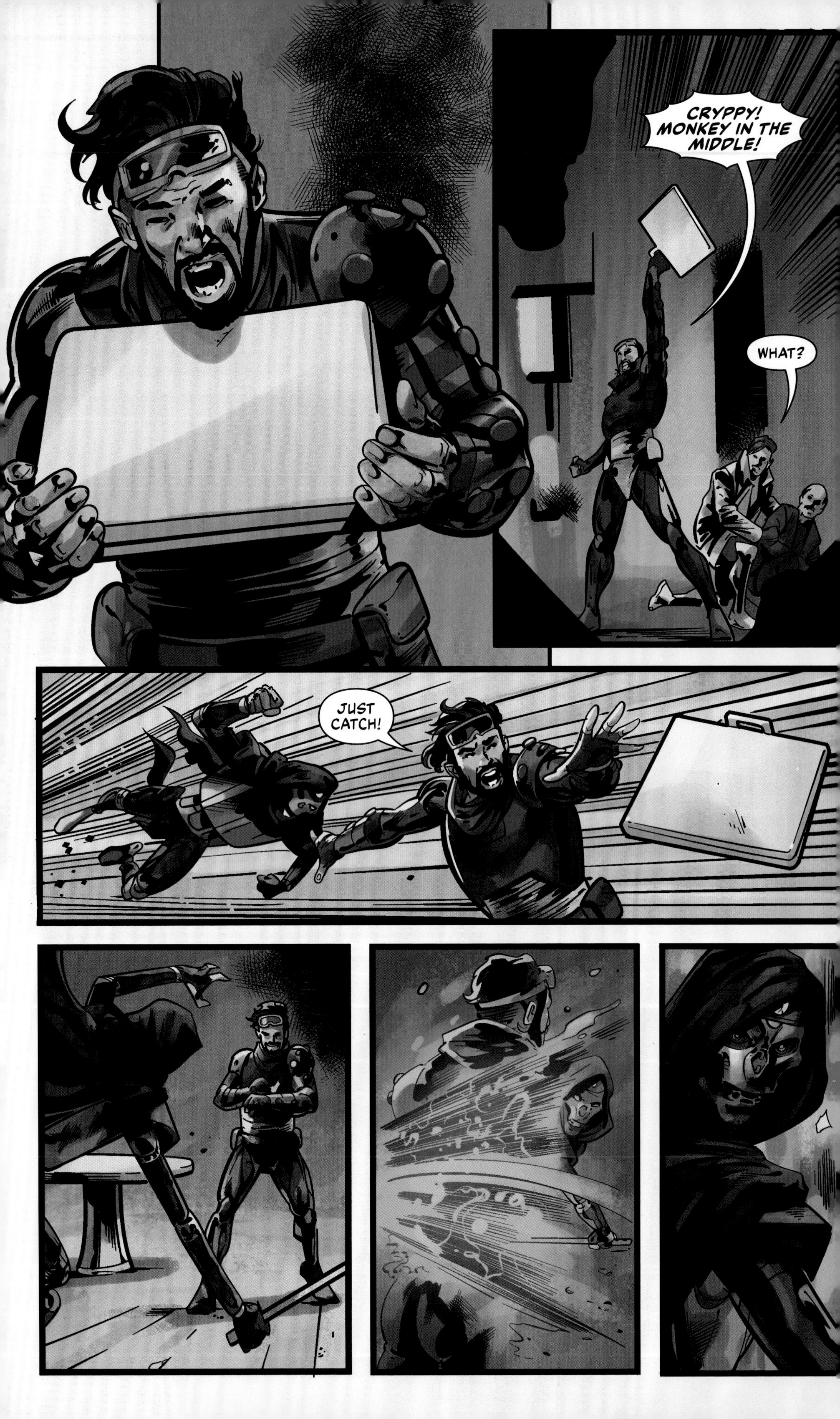
CRYPPY! MONKEY IN THE MIDDLE!
WHAT?
JUST CATCH!

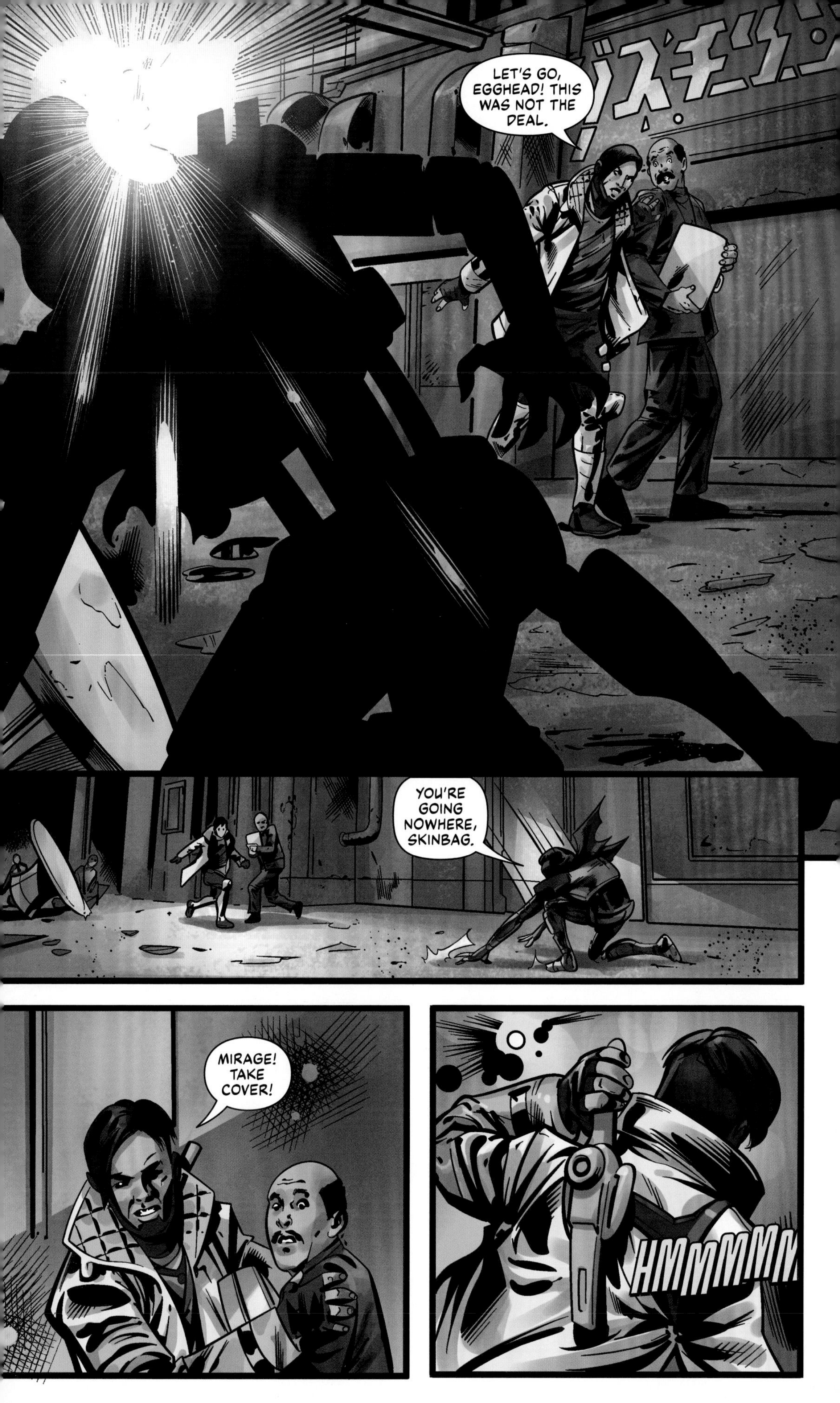

LET'S GO, EGGHEAD! THIS WAS NOT THE DEAL.
YOU'RE GOING NOWHERE, SKINBAG.
MIRAGE! TAKE COVER!
HMMMMM

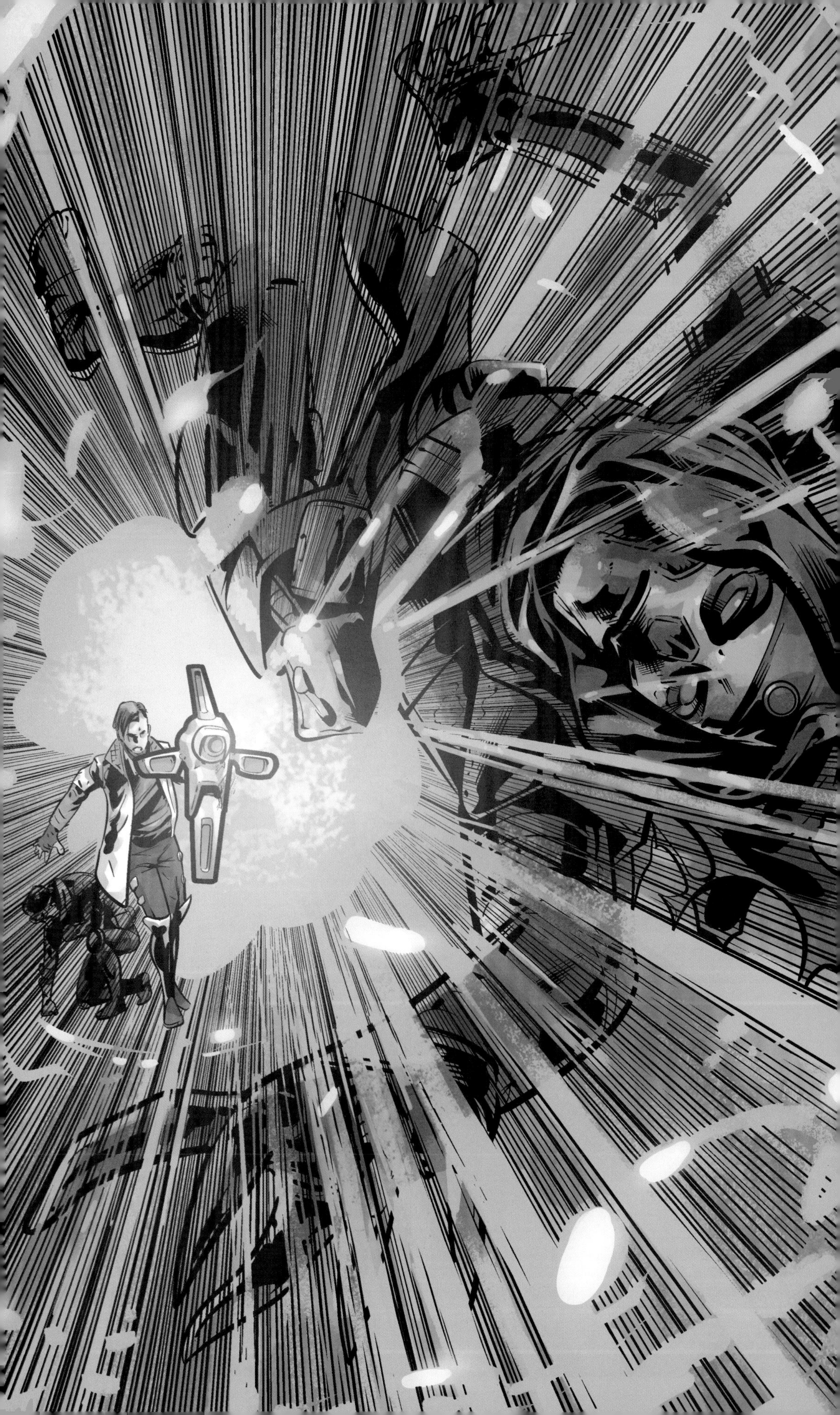

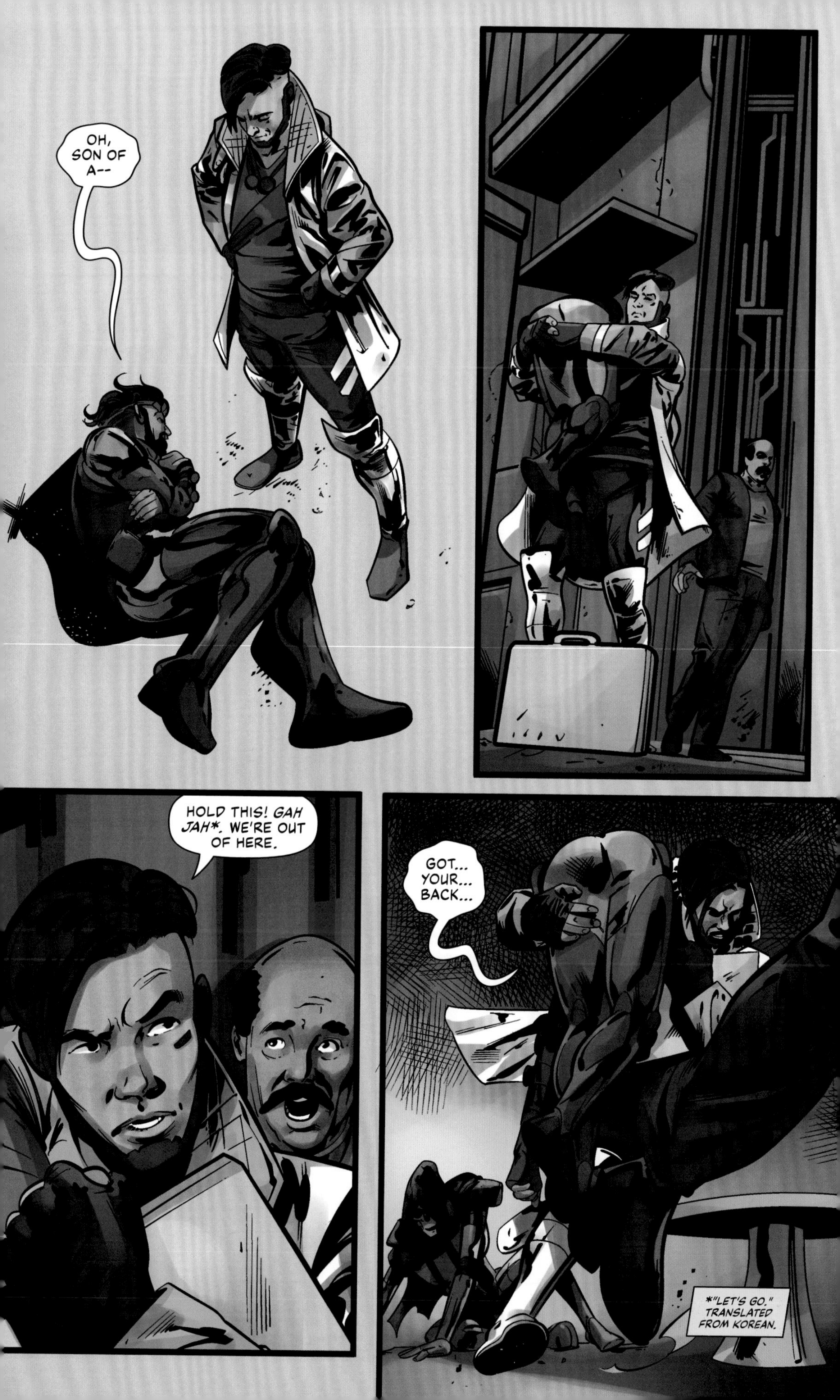

OH, SON OF A--
HOLD THIS! *GAH JAH**. WE'RE OUT OF HERE.
GOT... YOUR... BACK...
*"LET'S GO." TRANSLATED FROM KOREAN.

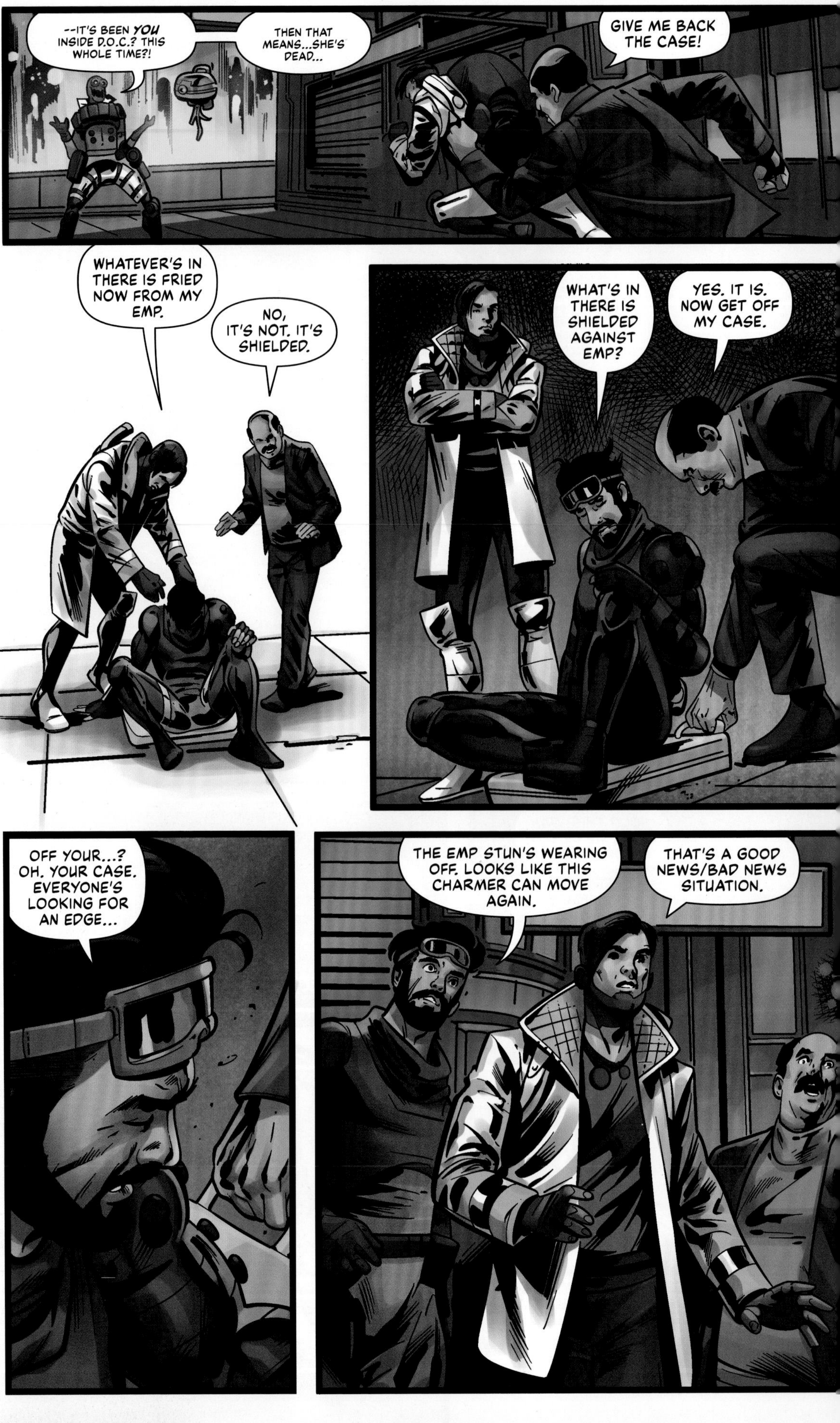

--IT'S BEEN YOU INSIDE D.O.C.? THIS WHOLE TIME?!
THEN THAT MEANS...SHE'S DEAD...
GIVE ME BACK THE CASE!
WHATEVER'S IN THERE IS FRIED NOW FROM MY EMP.
NO, IT'S NOT. IT'S SHIELDED.
WHAT'S IN THERE IS SHIELDED AGAINST EMP?
YES. IT IS. NOW GET OFF MY CASE.
OFF YOUR...? OH. YOUR CASE. EVERYONE'S LOOKING FOR AN EDGE...
THE EMP STUN'S WEARING OFF. LOOKS LIKE THIS CHARMER CAN MOVE AGAIN.
THAT'S A GOOD NEWS/BAD NEWS SITUATION.

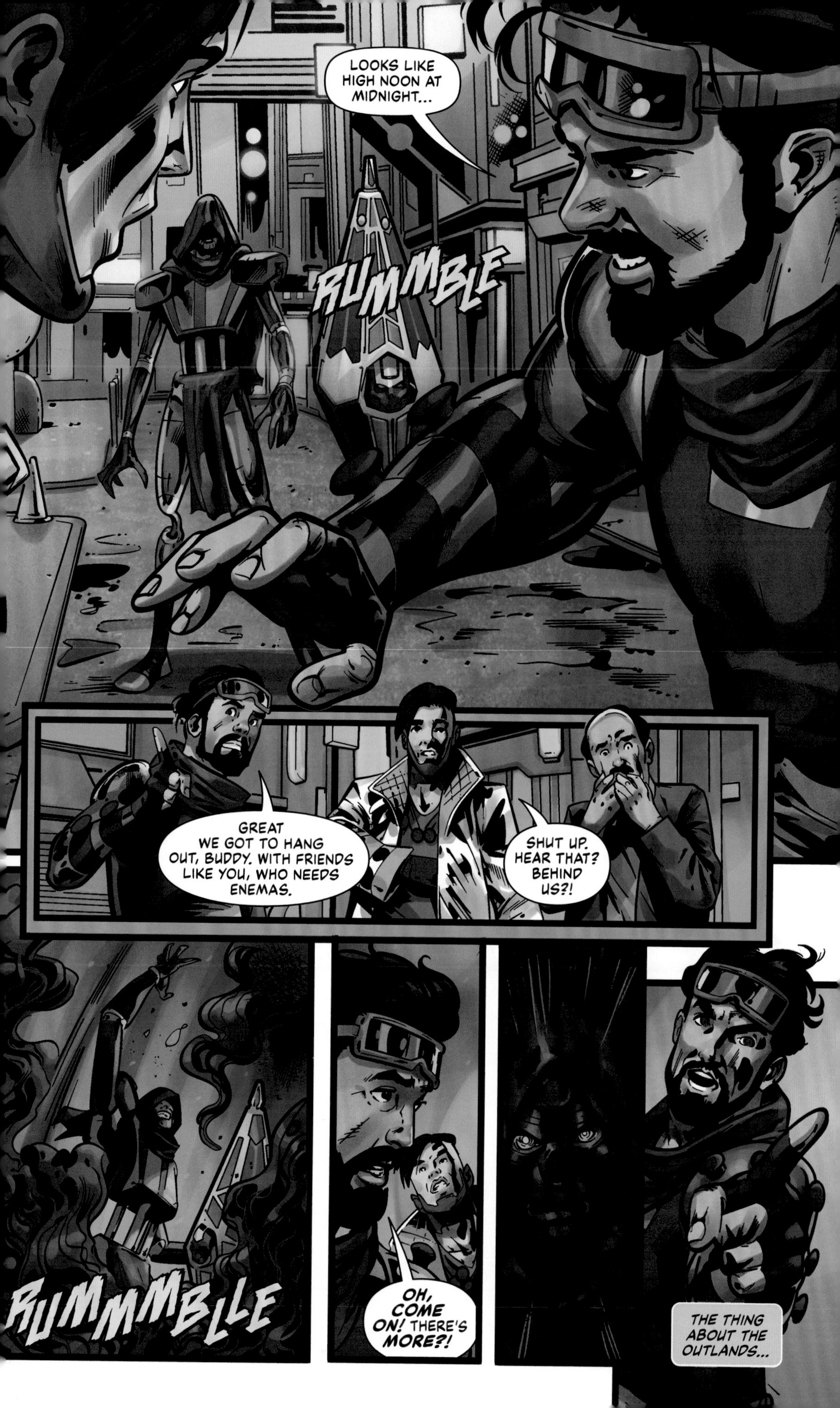
LOOKS LIKE HIGH NOON AT MIDNIGHT...
RUMMBLE
GREAT WE GOT TO HANG OUT, BUDDY. WITH FRIENDS LIKE YOU, WHO NEEDS ENEMAS.
SHUT UP. HEAR THAT? BEHIND US?!
RUMMMMBLLE
OH, COME ON! THERE'S MORE?!
THE THING ABOUT THE OUTLANDS...

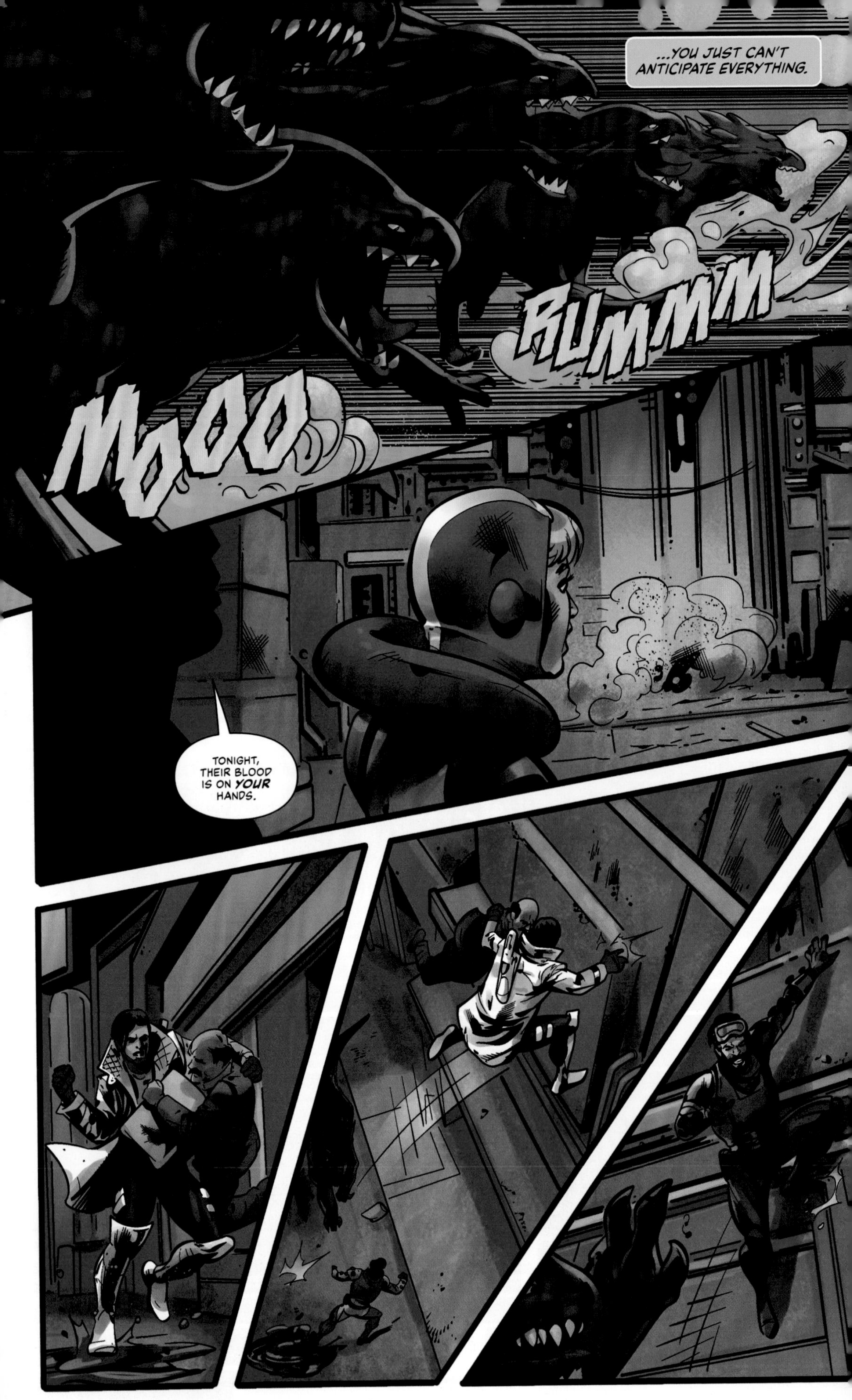
...YOU JUST CAN'T ANTICIPATE EVERYTHING.
RUMMM
MOOO
TONIGHT, THEIR BLOOD IS ON YOUR HANDS.

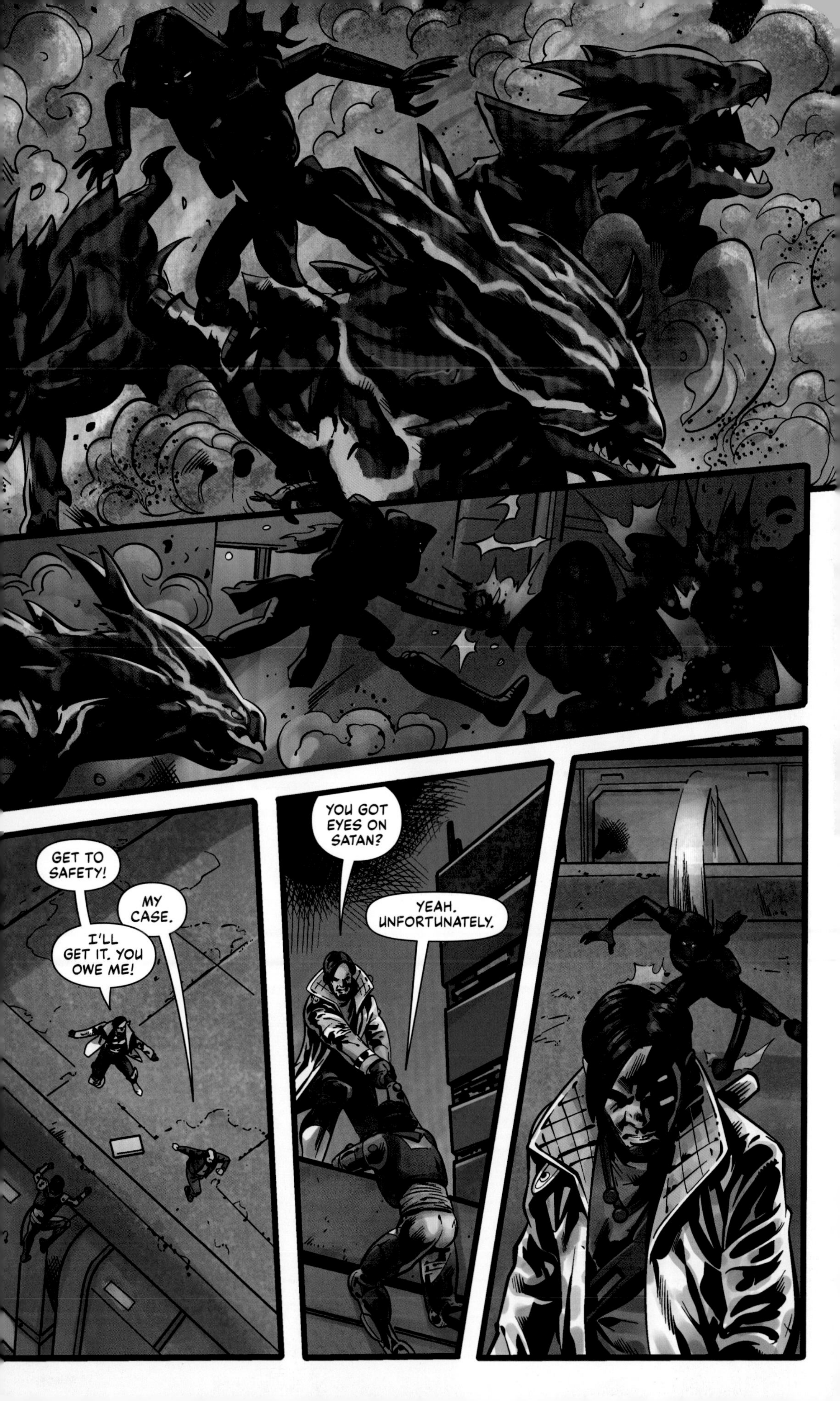
GET TO SAFETY!
MY CASE.
I'LL GET IT. YOU OWE ME!
YOU GOT EYES ON SATAN?
YEAH. UNFORTUNATELY.

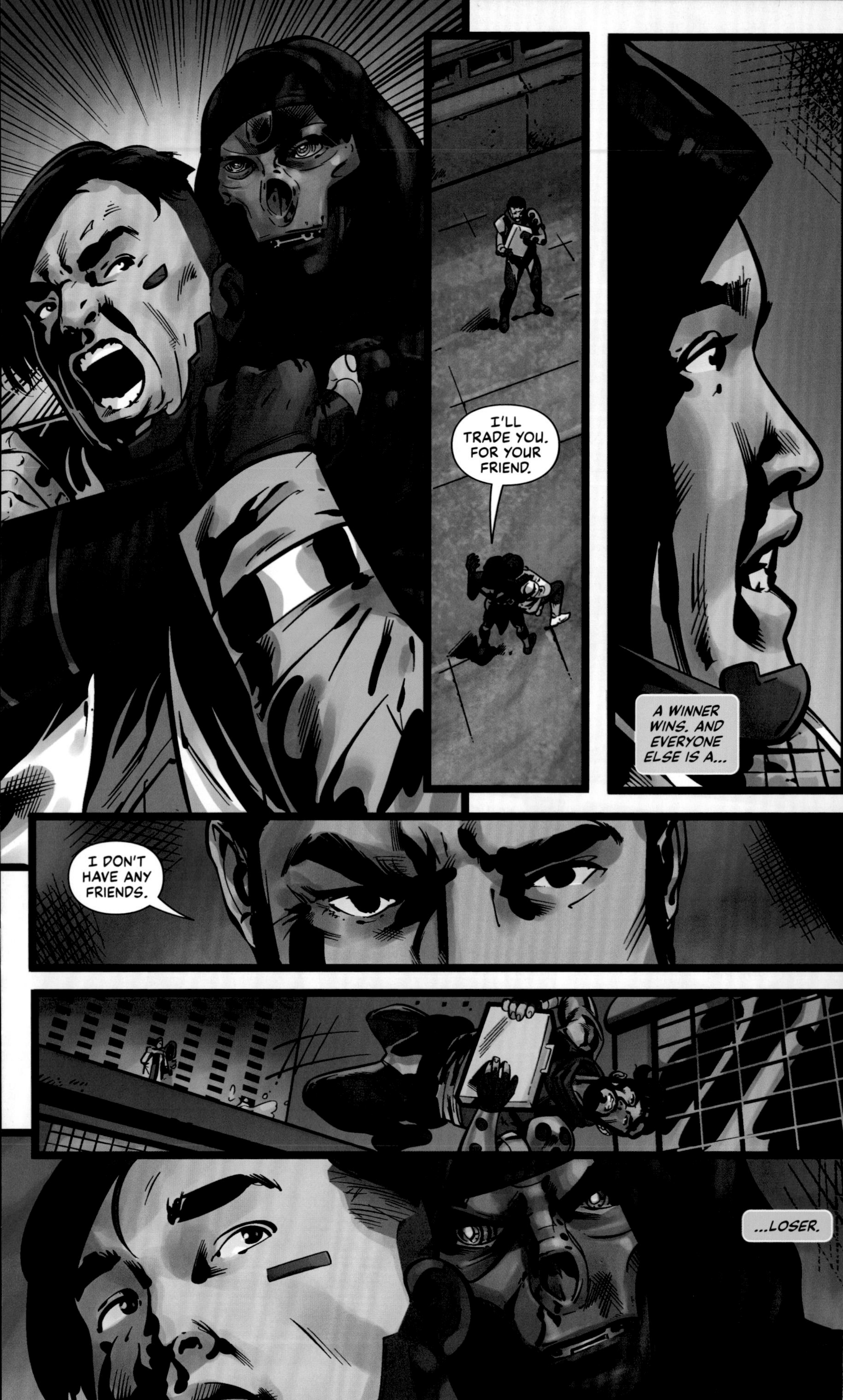
I'LL TRADE YOU. FOR YOUR FRIEND.
A WINNER WINS. AND EVERYONE ELSE IS A...
I DON'T HAVE ANY FRIENDS.
...LOSER.

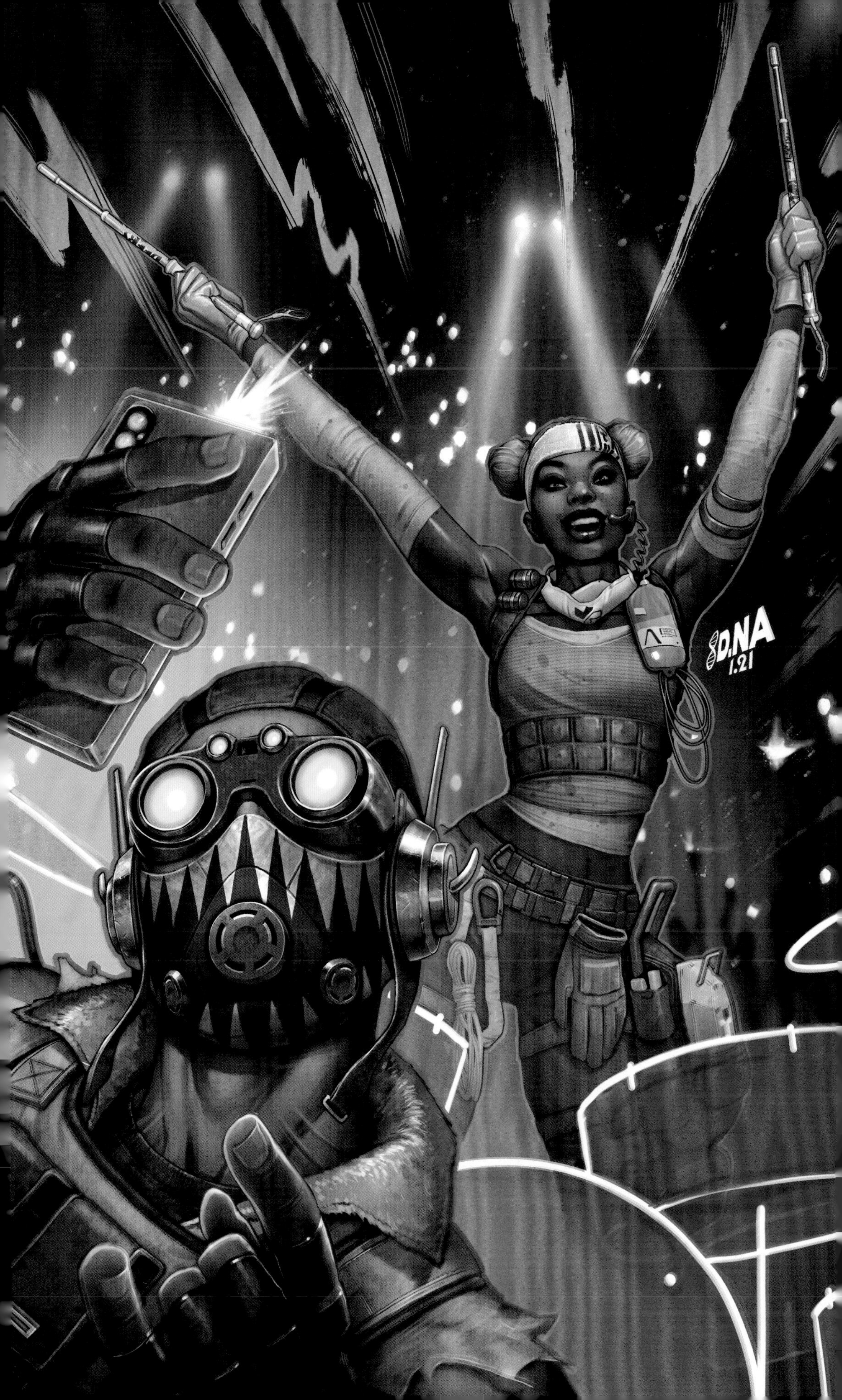
D.NA
1.21

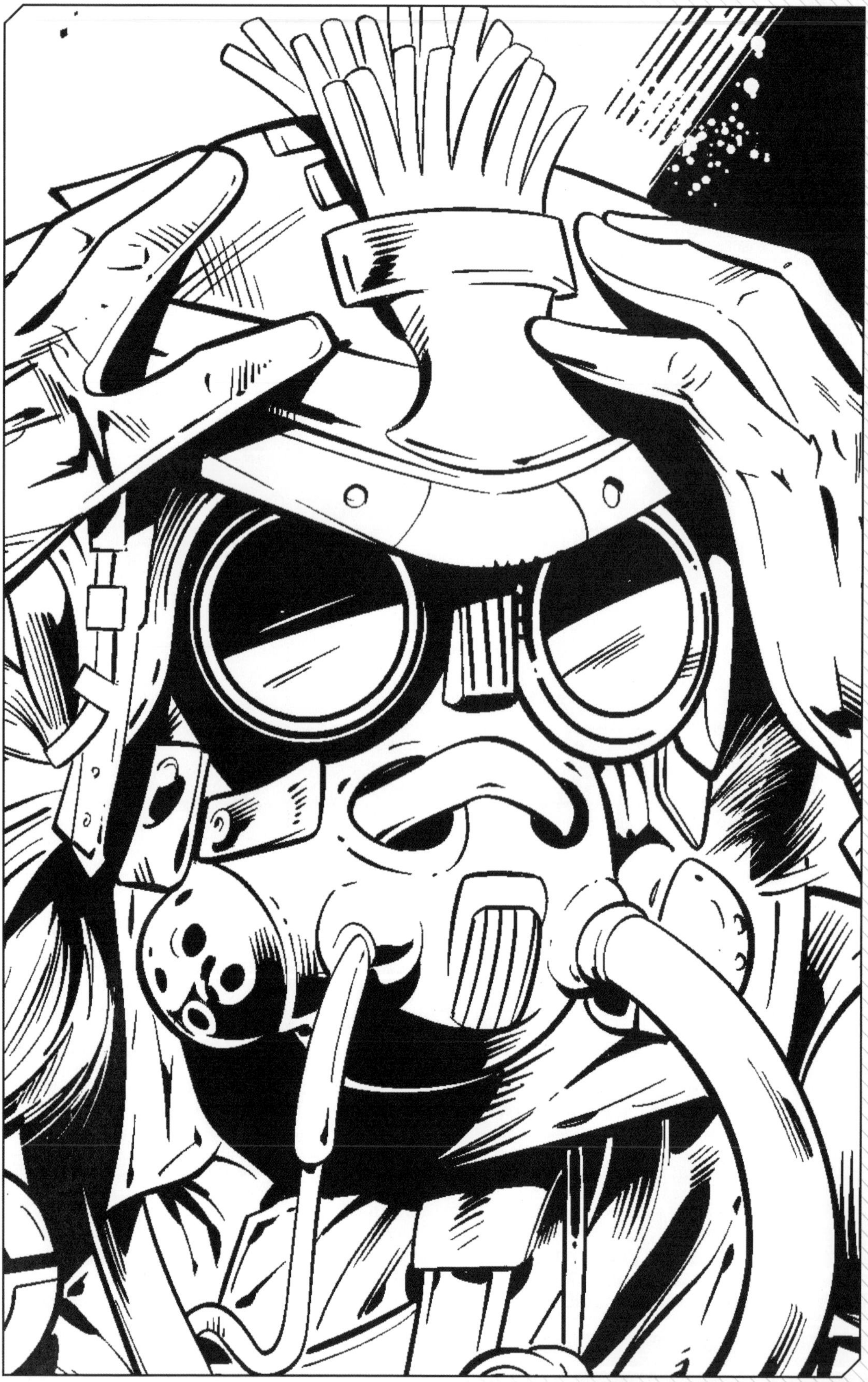

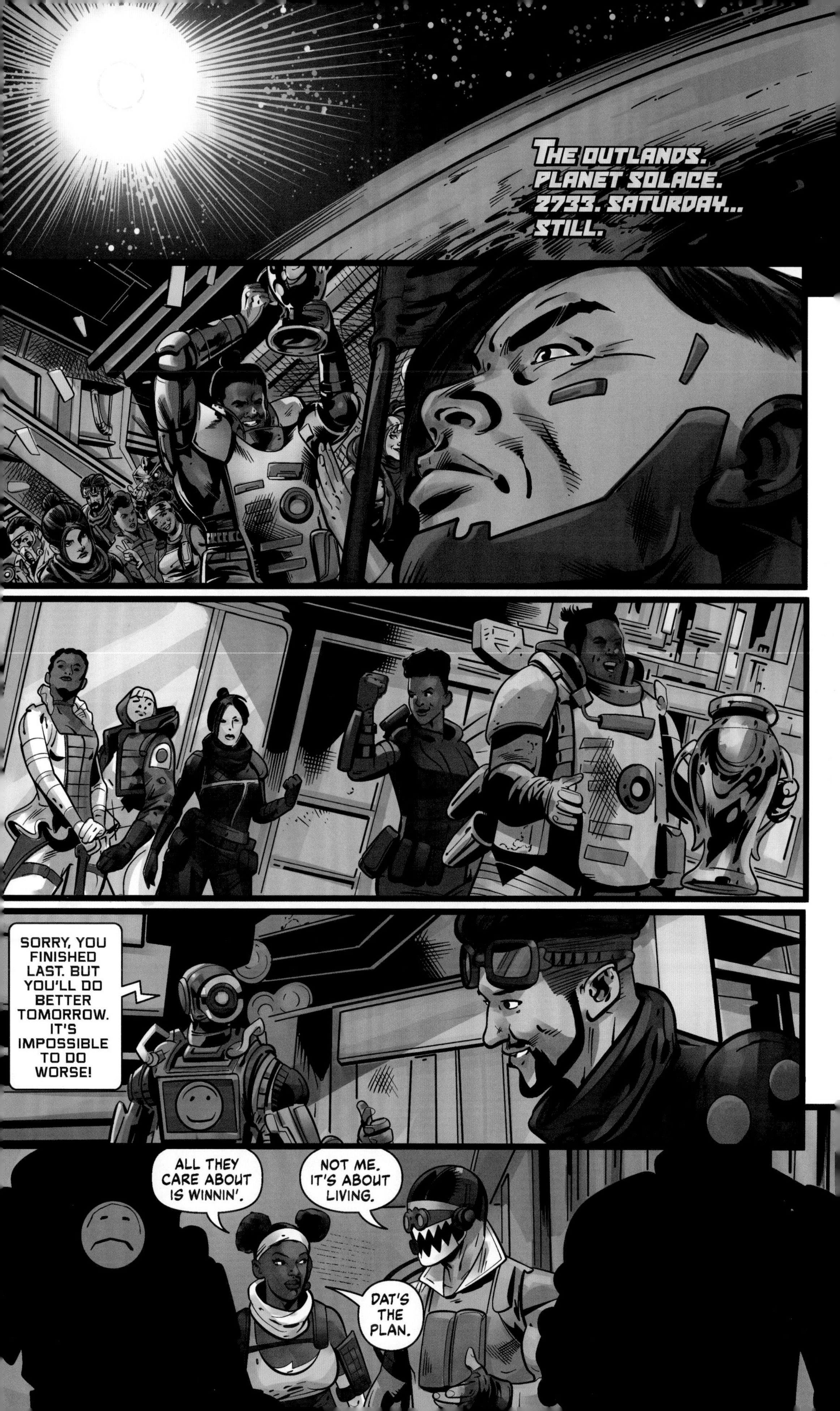
THE OUTLANDS. PLANET SOLACE. 2733. SATURDAY... STILL.
SORRY, YOU FINISHED LAST. BUT YOU'LL DO BETTER TOMORROW. IT'S IMPOSSIBLE TO DO WORSE!
ALL THEY CARE ABOUT IS WINNIN'.
NOT ME. IT'S ABOUT LIVING.
DAT'S THE PLAN.

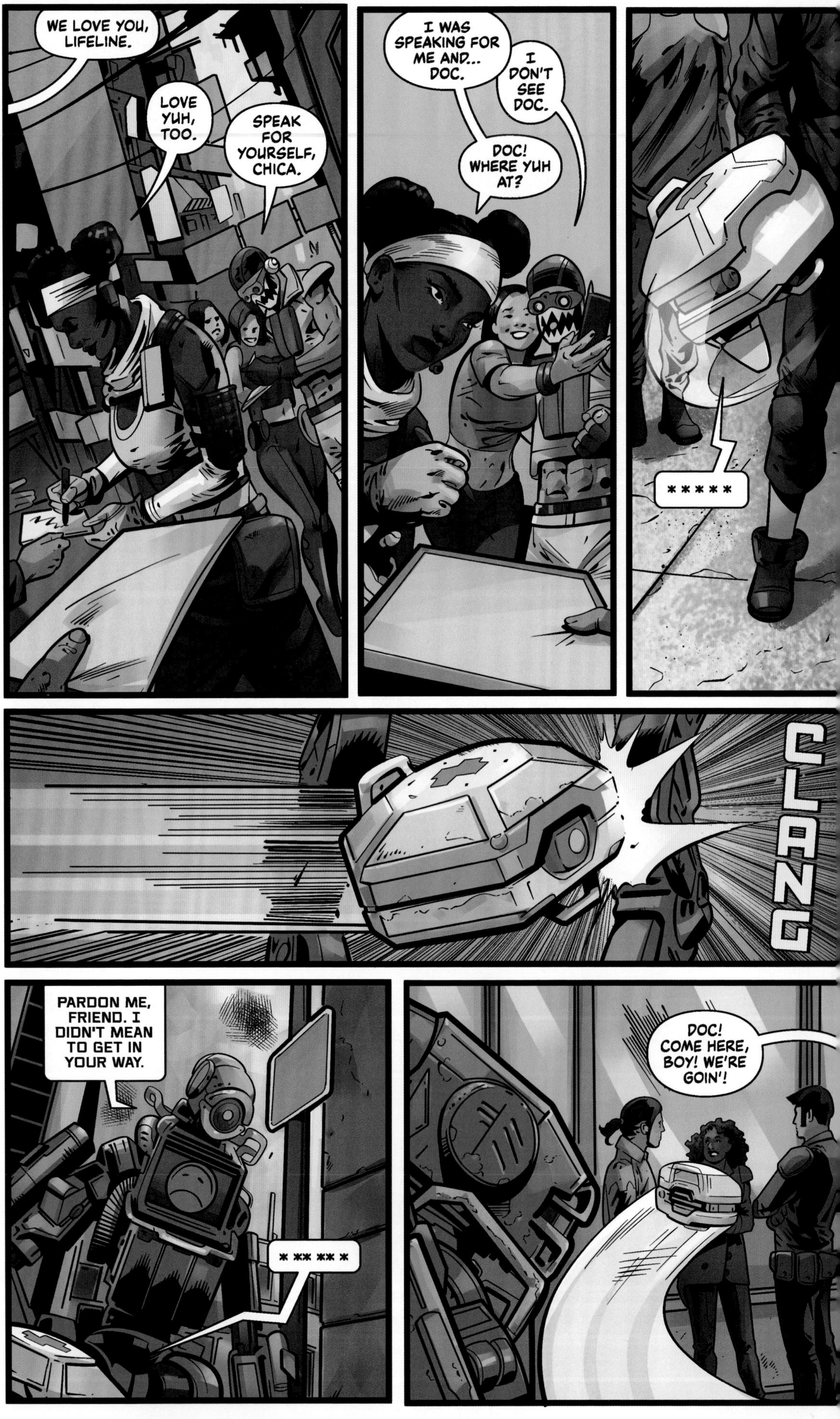
WE LOVE YOU, LIFELINE.
LOVE YUH, TOO.
SPEAK FOR YOURSELF, CHICA.
I WAS SPEAKING FOR ME AND... DOC.
I DON'T SEE DOC.
DOC! WHERE YUH AT?
*****
CLANG
PARDON ME, FRIEND. I DIDN'T MEAN TO GET IN YOUR WAY.
* ** ** *
DOC! COME HERE, BOY! WE'RE GOIN'!

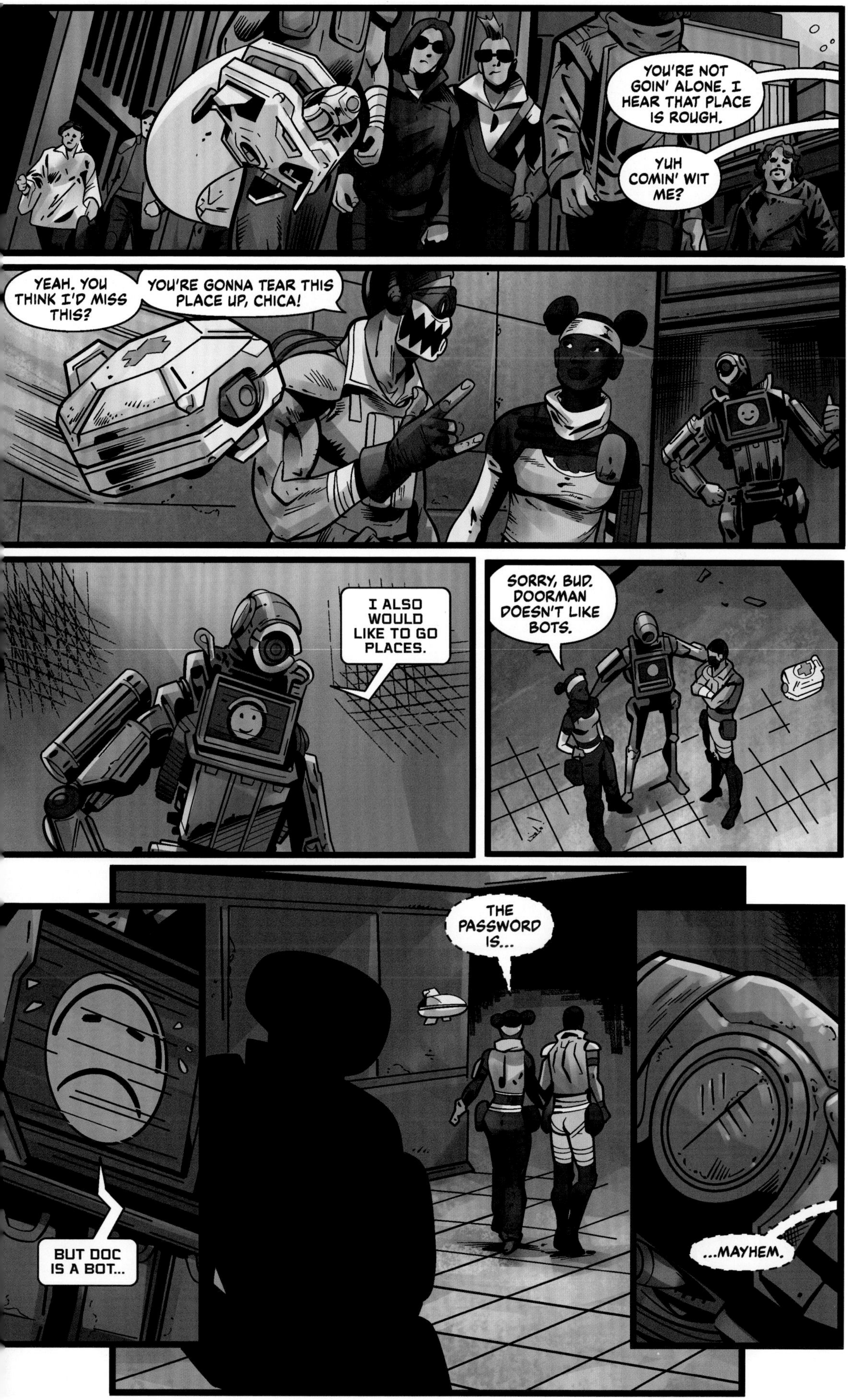
YOU'RE NOT GOIN' ALONE. I HEAR THAT PLACE IS ROUGH.
YUH COMIN' WIT ME?
YEAH. YOU THINK I'D MISS THIS?
YOU'RE GONNA TEAR THIS PLACE UP, CHICA!
I ALSO WOULD LIKE TO GO PLACES.
SORRY, BUD. DOORMAN DOESN'T LIKE BOTS.
BUT DOC IS A BOT...
THE PASSWORD IS...
...MAYHEM.

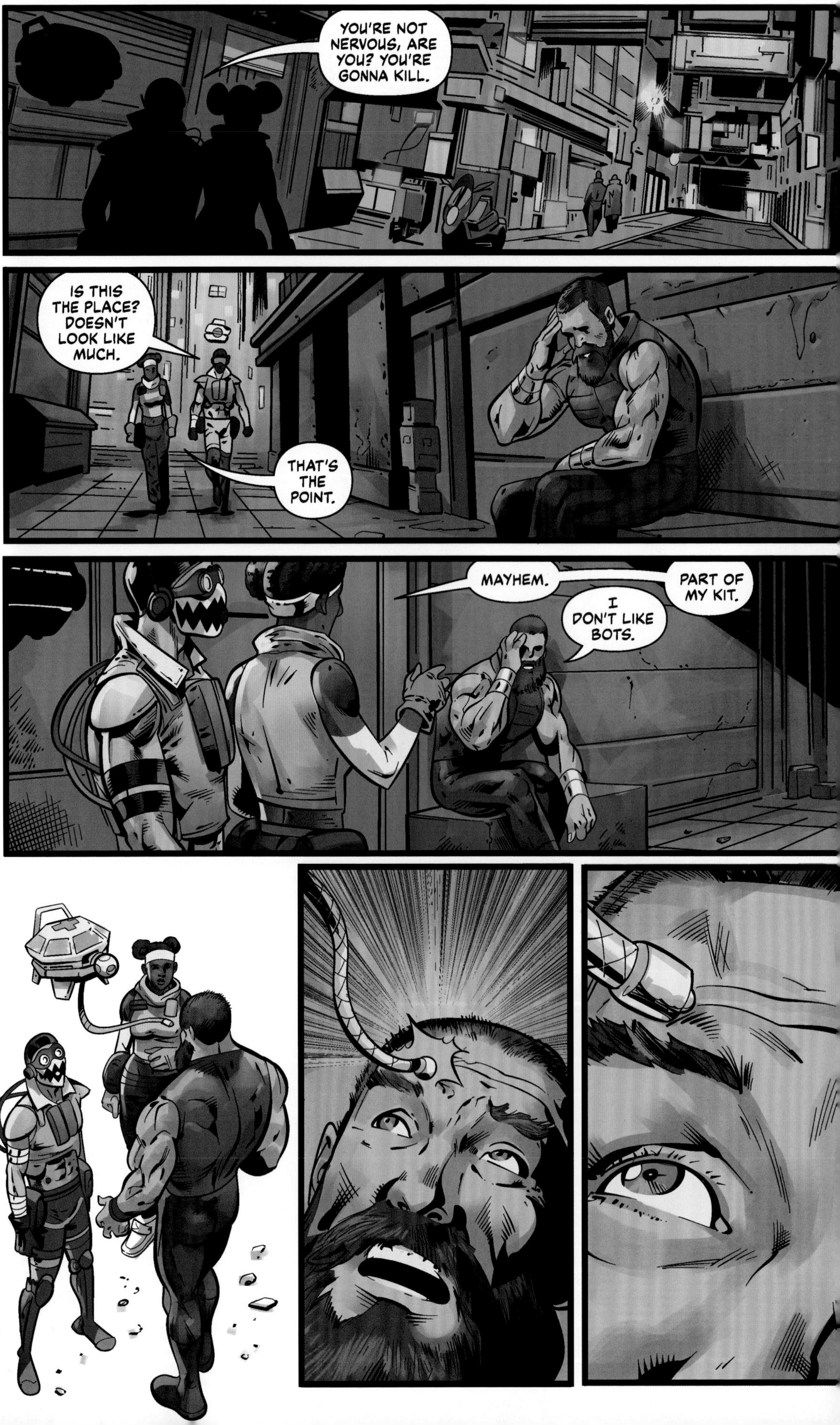

YOU'RE NOT NERVOUS, ARE YOU? YOU'RE GONNA KILL.
IS THIS THE PLACE? DOESN'T LOOK LIKE MUCH.
THAT'S THE POINT.
MAYHEM.
I DON'T LIKE BOTS.
PART OF MY KIT.

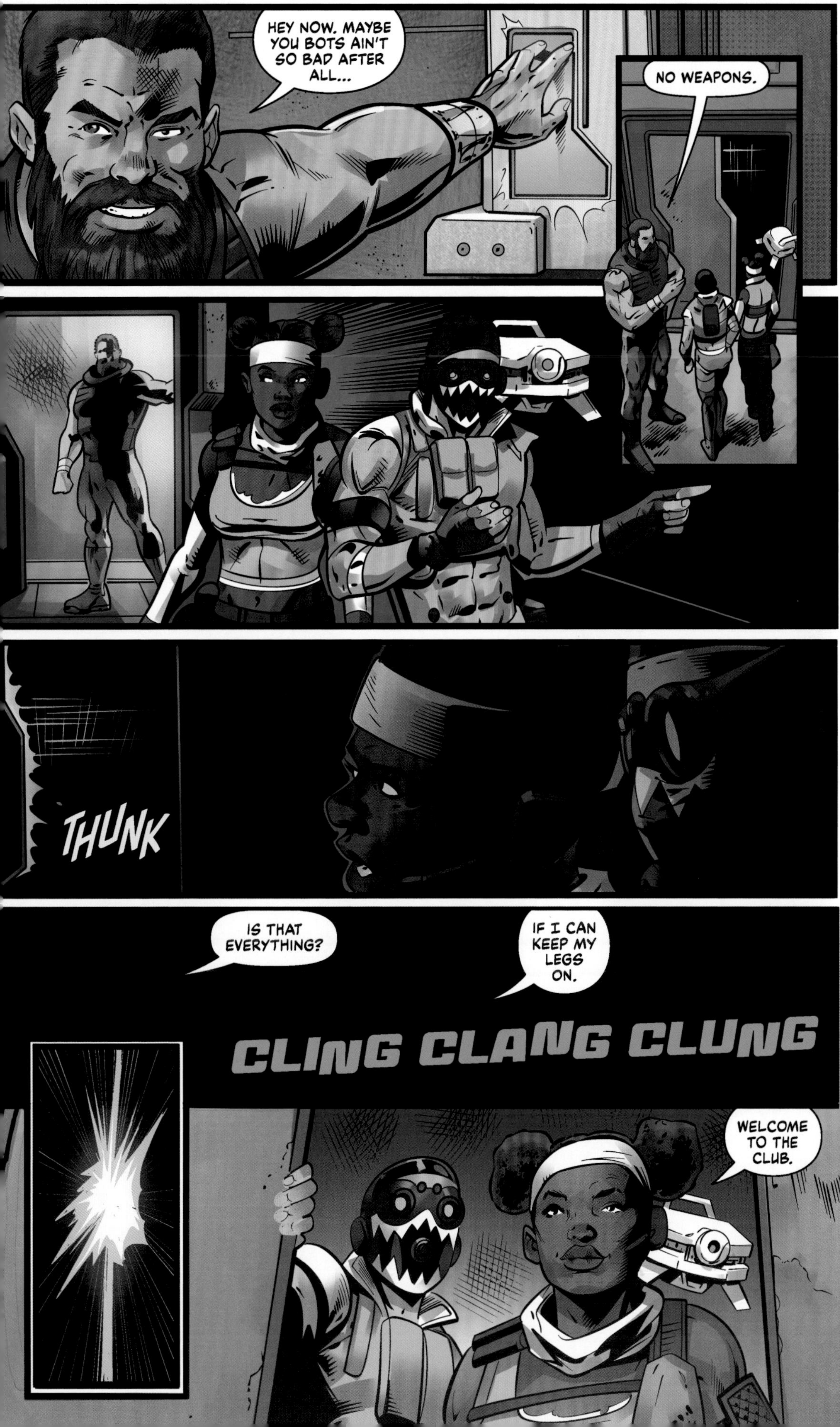
HEY NOW. MAYBE YOU BOTS AIN'T SO BAD AFTER ALL...
NO WEAPONS.
THUNK
IS THAT EVERYTHING?
IF I CAN KEEP MY LEGS ON.
CLING CLANG CLUNG
WELCOME TO THE CLUB.

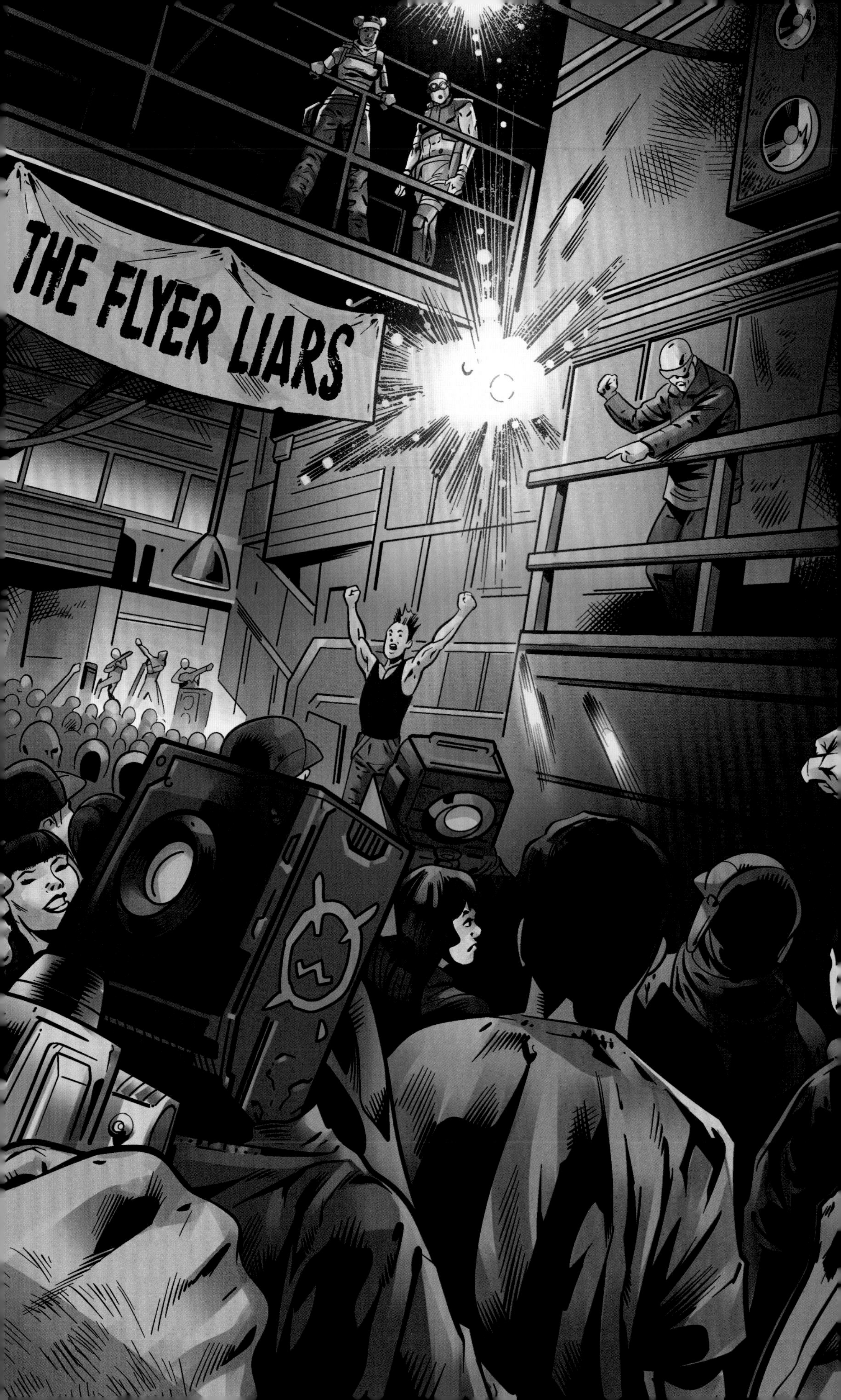
THE FLYER LIARS

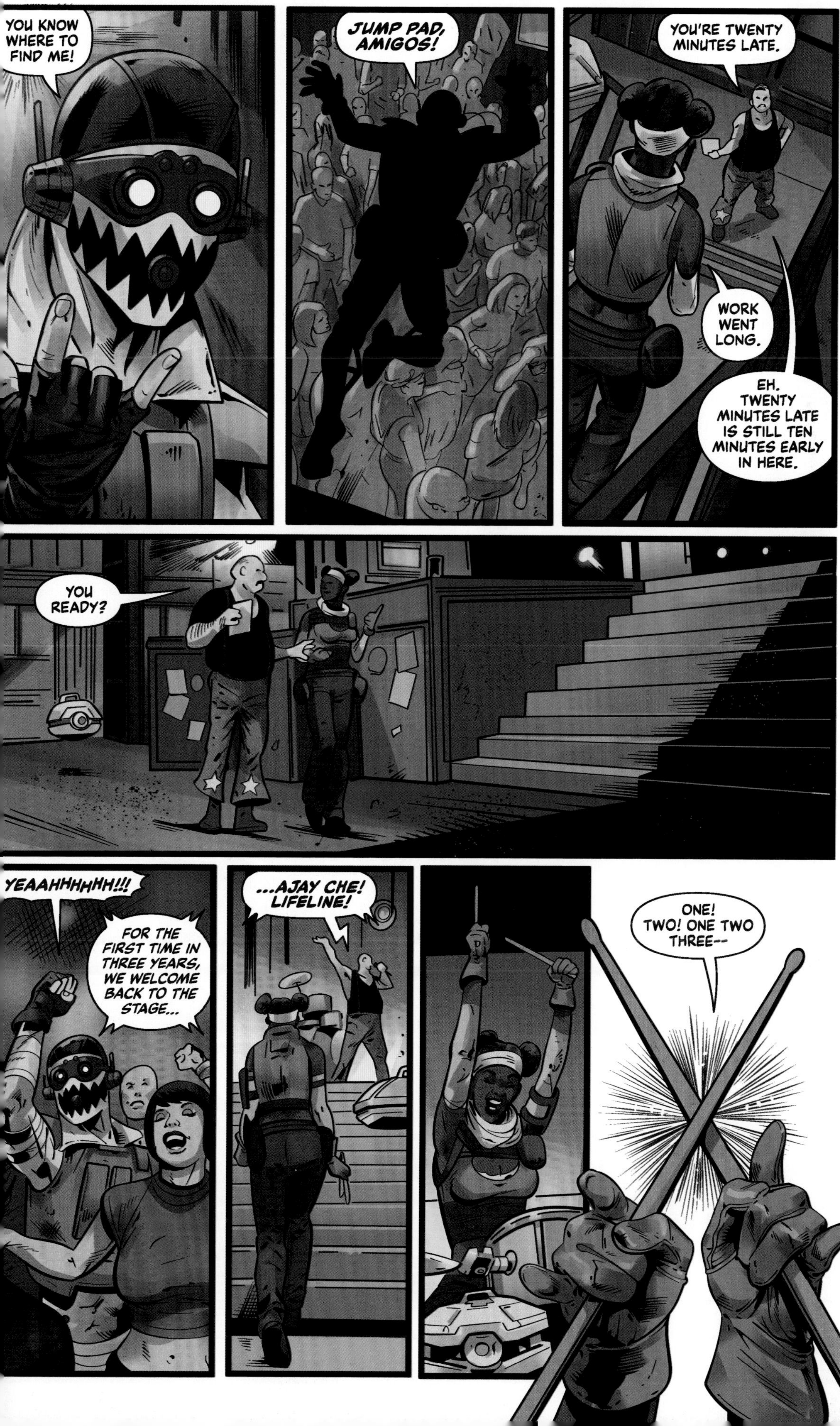

YOU KNOW WHERE TO FIND ME!
JUMP PAD, AMIGOS!
YOU'RE TWENTY MINUTES LATE.
WORK WENT LONG.
EH. TWENTY MINUTES LATE IS STILL TEN MINUTES EARLY IN HERE.
YOU READY?
YEAAHHHHHH!!!
FOR THE FIRST TIME IN THREE YEARS, WE WELCOME BACK TO THE STAGE...
...AJAY CHE! LIFELINE!
ONE! TWO! ONE TWO THREE--

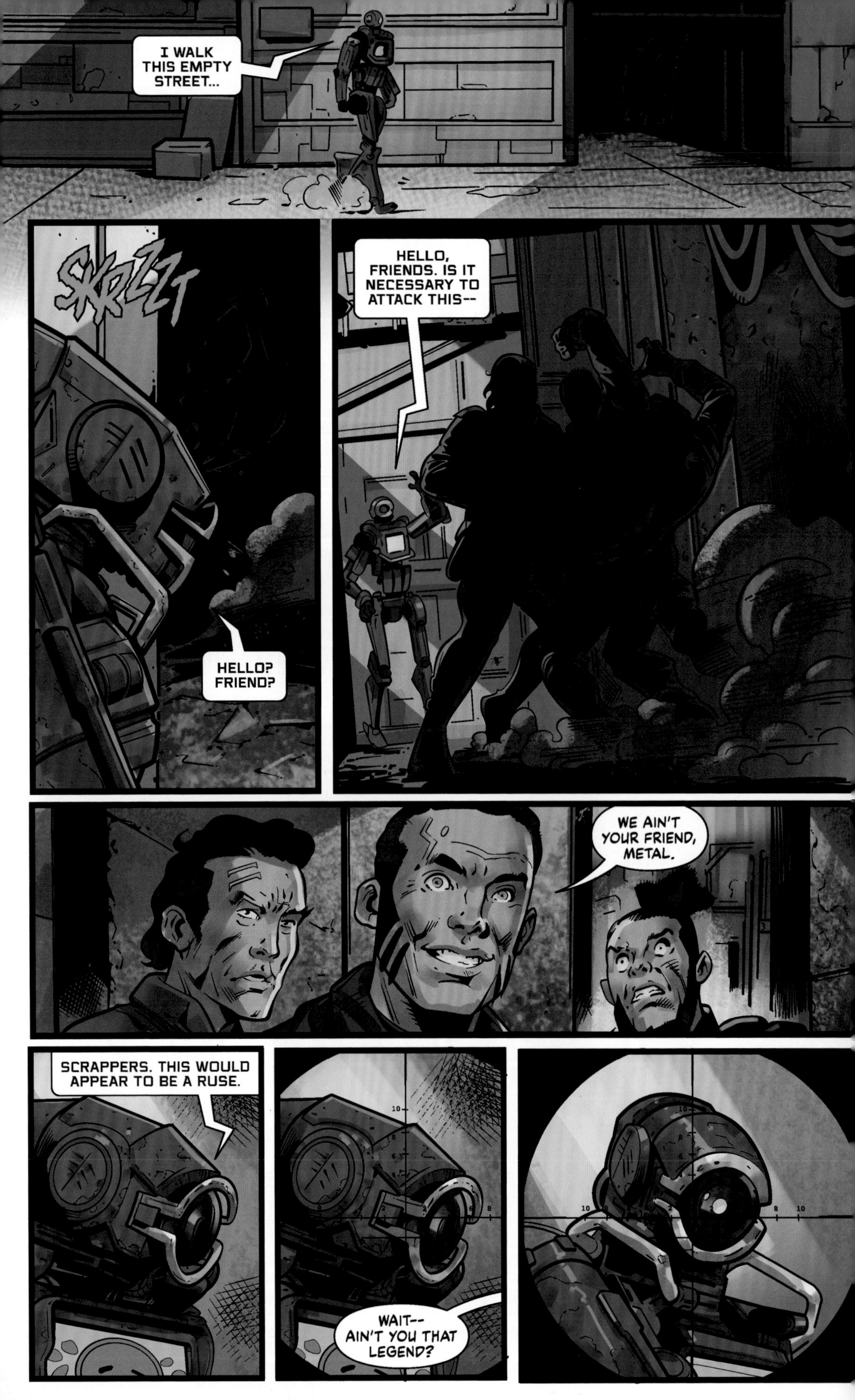
I WALK THIS EMPTY STREET...
SKRZZZT
HELLO? FRIEND?
HELLO, FRIENDS. IS IT NECESSARY TO ATTACK THIS--
WE AIN'T YOUR FRIEND, METAL.
SCRAPPERS. THIS WOULD APPEAR TO BE A RUSE.
WAIT-- AIN'T YOU THAT LEGEND?

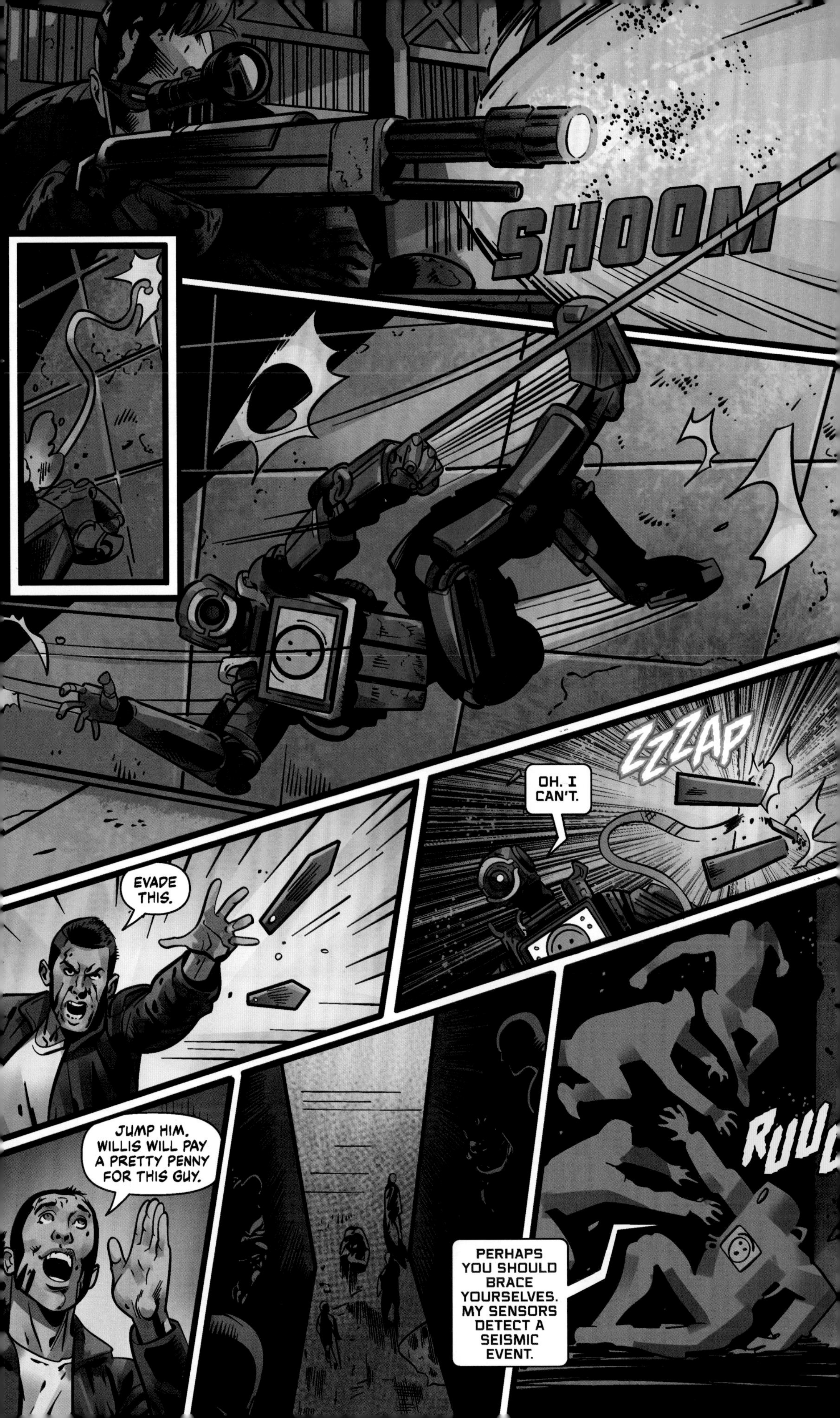
SHOOM
ZZZAP
OH. I CAN'T.
EVADE THIS.
JUMP HIM. WILLIS WILL PAY A PRETTY PENNY FOR THIS GUY.
RUUU
PERHAPS YOU SHOULD BRACE YOURSELVES. MY SENSORS DETECT A SEISMIC EVENT.

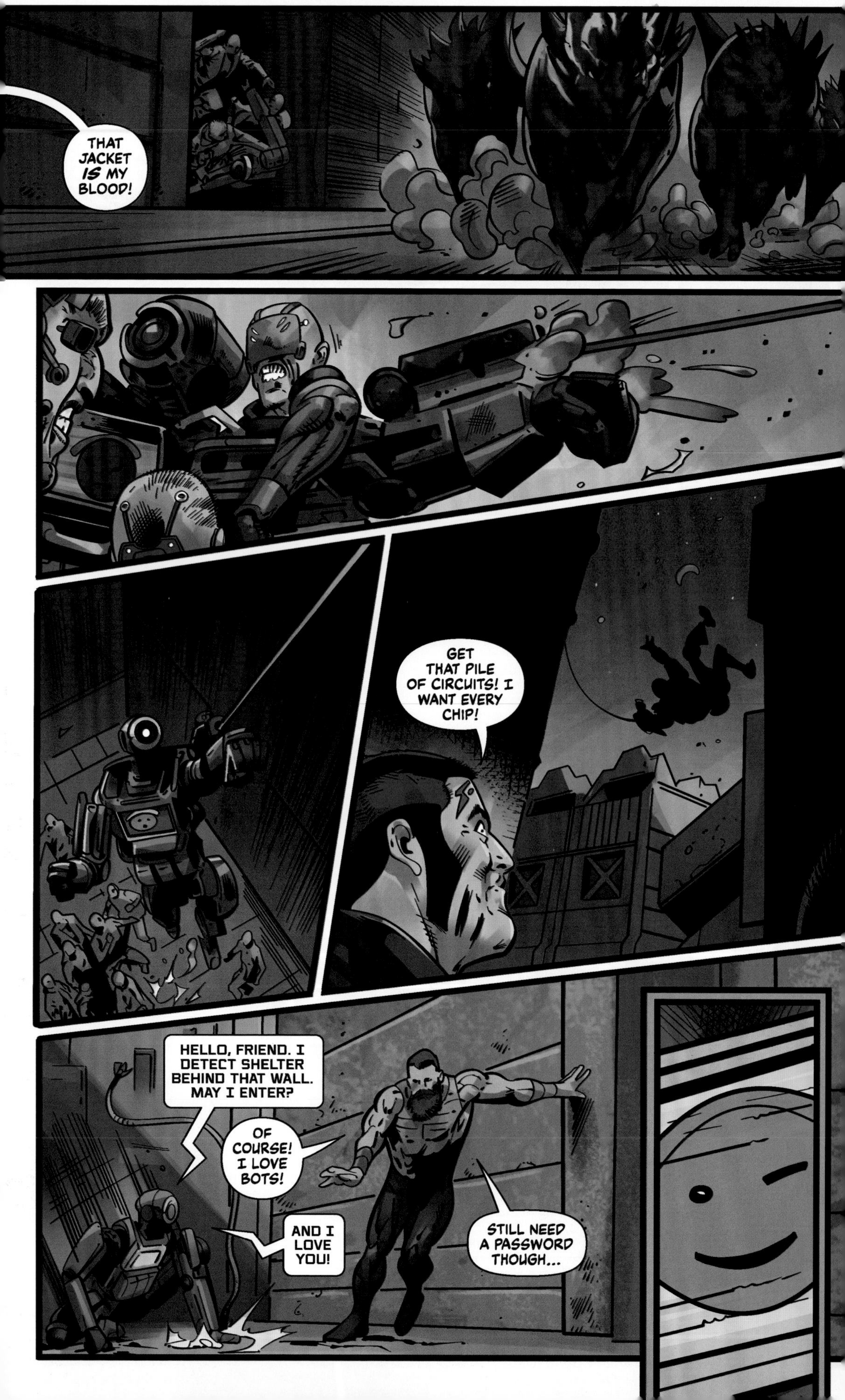
THAT JACKET *IS* MY BLOOD!
GET THAT PILE OF CIRCUITS! I WANT EVERY CHIP!
HELLO, FRIEND. I DETECT SHELTER BEHIND THAT WALL. MAY I ENTER?
OF COURSE! I LOVE BOTS!
AND I LOVE YOU!
STILL NEED A PASSWORD THOUGH...

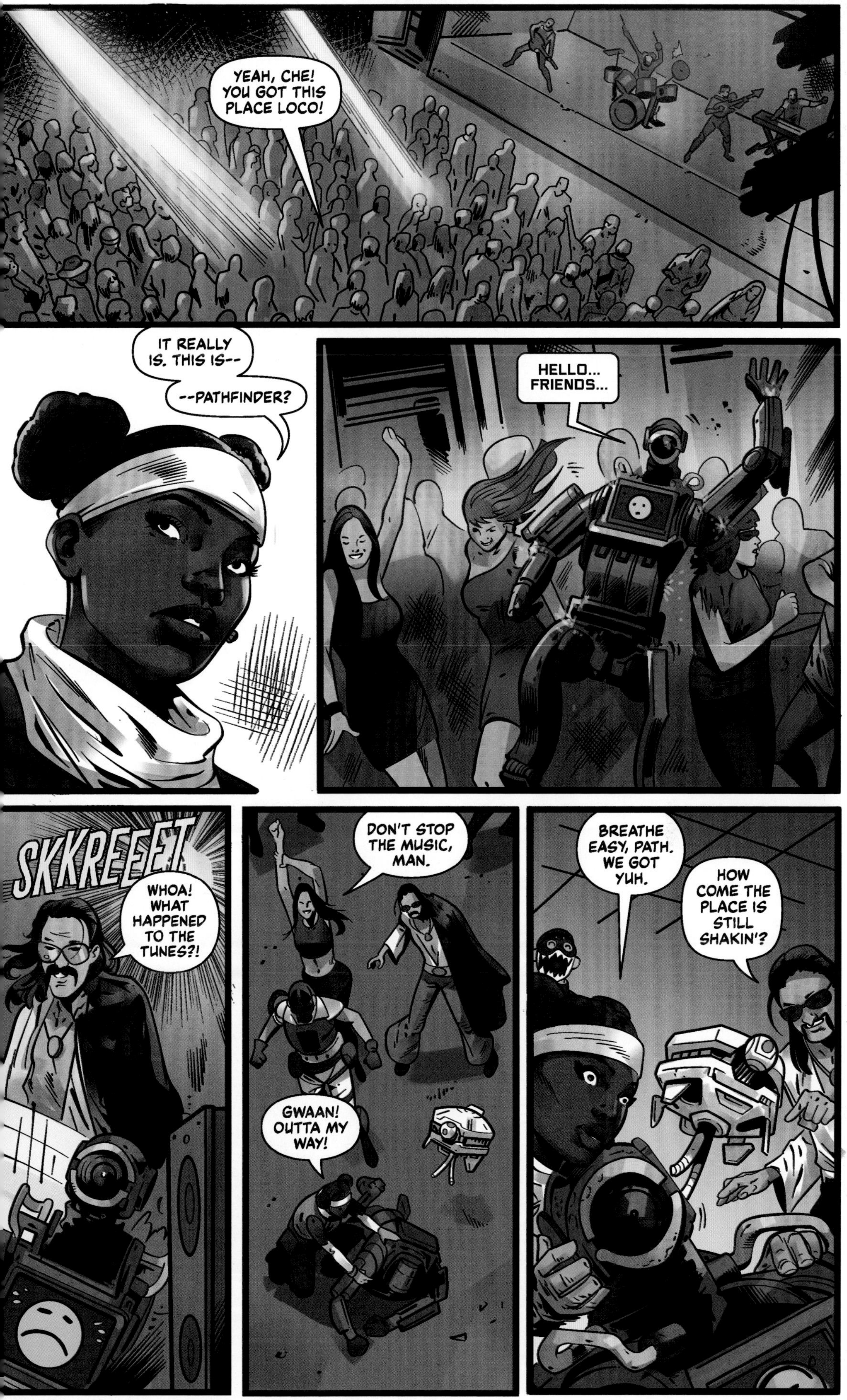
YEAH, CHE! YOU GOT THIS PLACE LOCO!
IT REALLY IS. THIS IS--
--PATHFINDER?
HELLO... FRIENDS...
SKKREEET
WHOA! WHAT HAPPENED TO THE TUNES?!
DON'T STOP THE MUSIC, MAN.
GWAAN! OUTTA MY WAY!
BREATHE EASY, PATH. WE GOT YUH.
HOW COME THE PLACE IS STILL SHAKIN'?

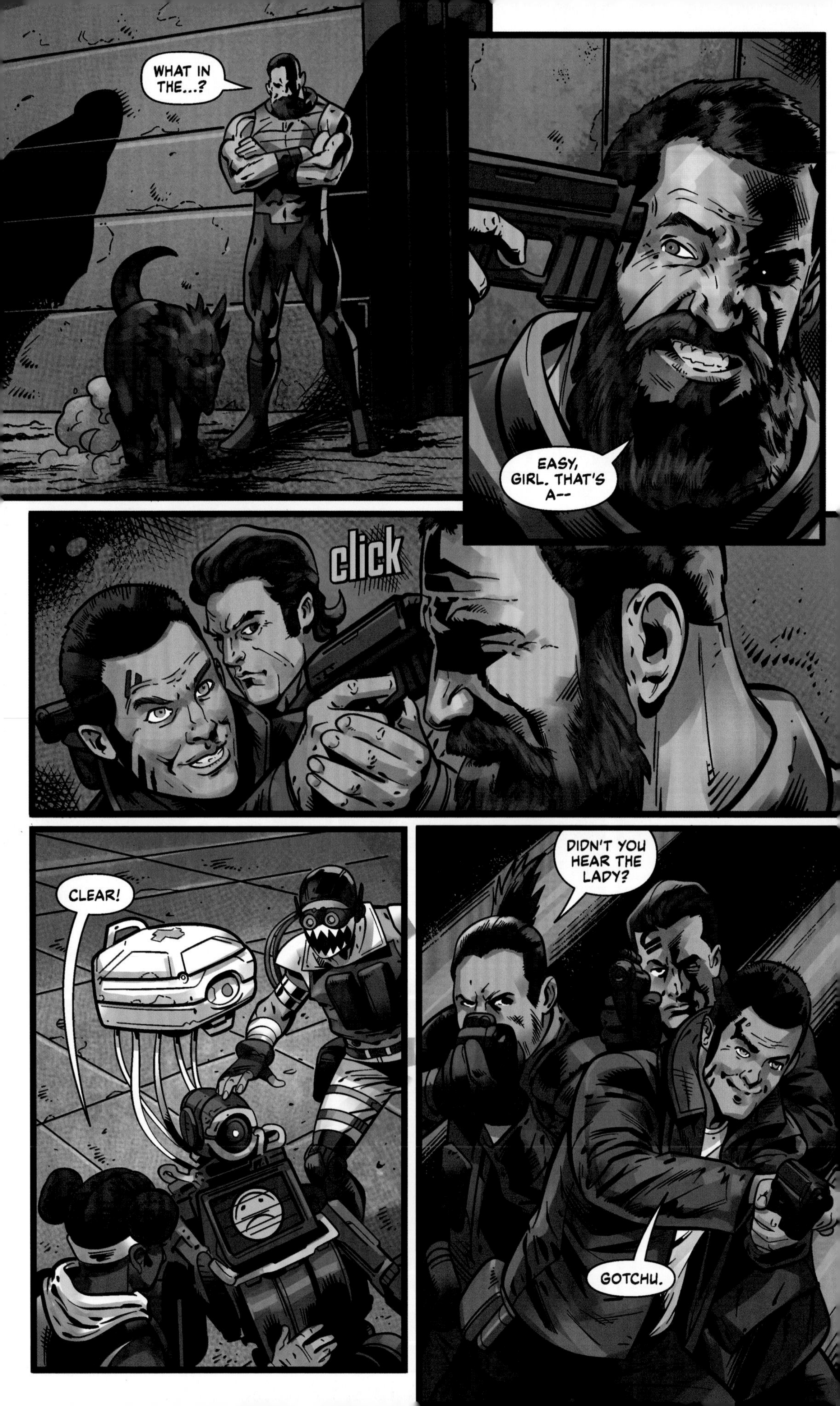
WHAT IN THE...?
EASY, GIRL. THAT'S A--
click
CLEAR!
DIDN'T YOU HEAR THE LADY?
GOTCHU.

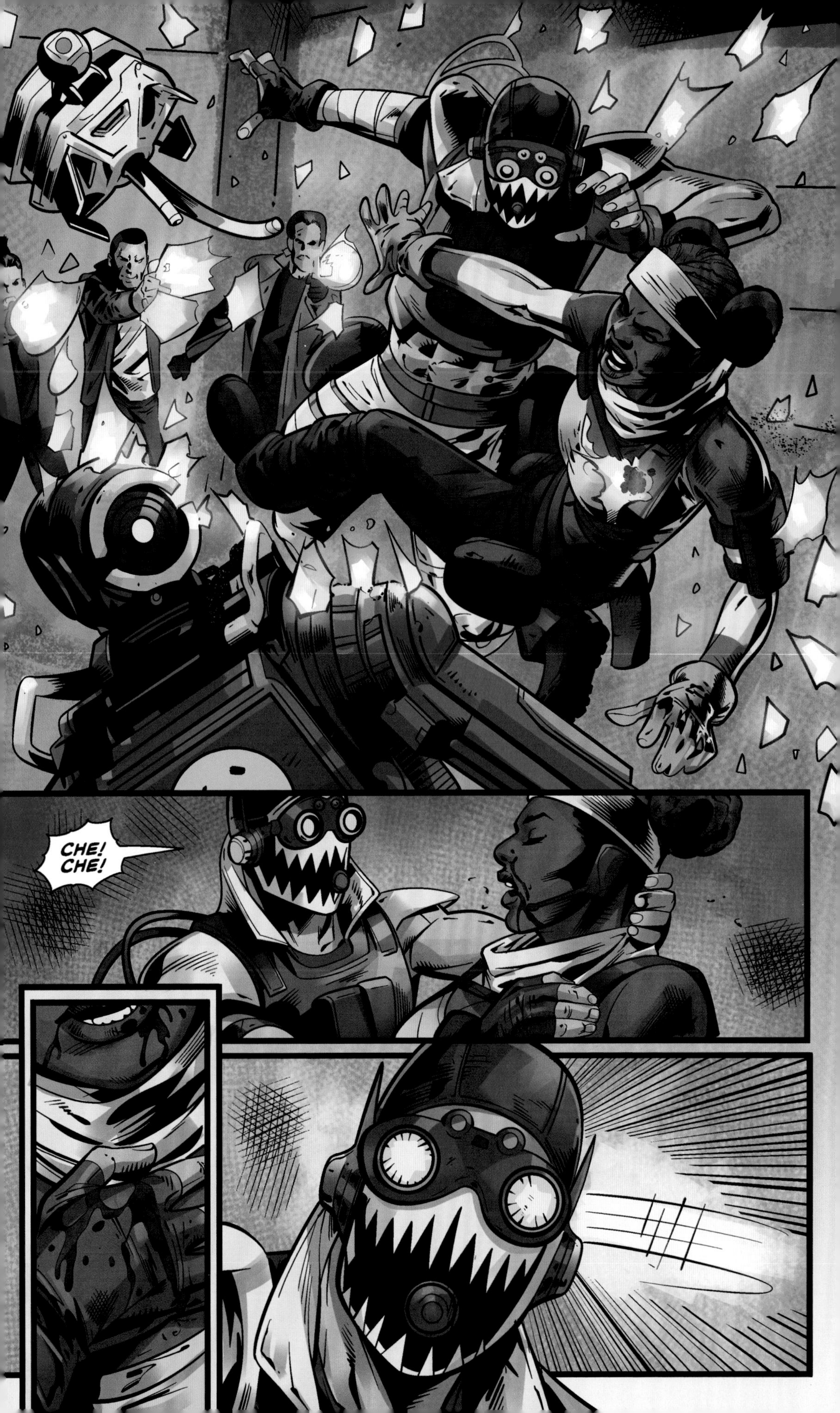
CHE! CHE!

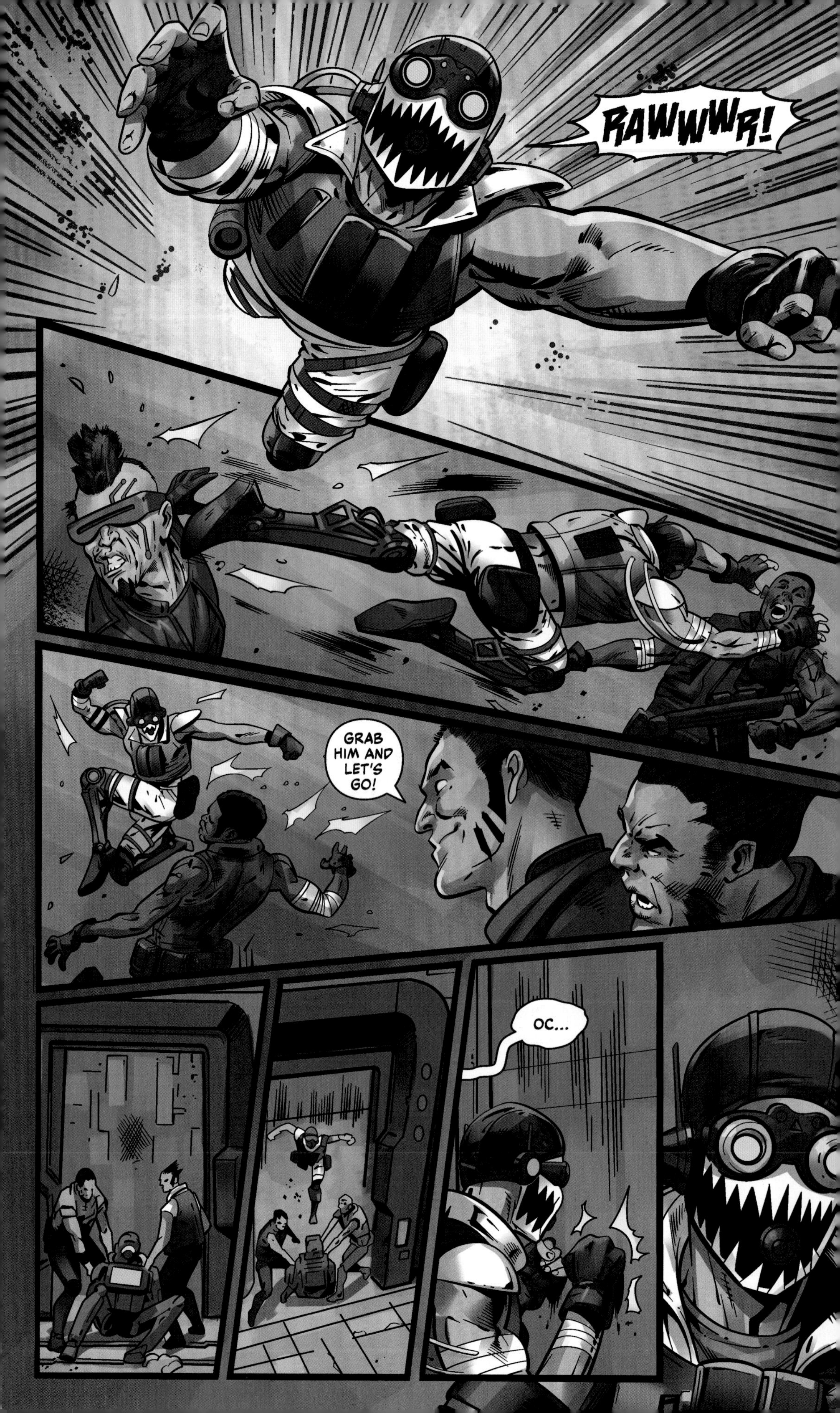
RAWWWR!
GRAB HIM AND LET'S GO!
OC...

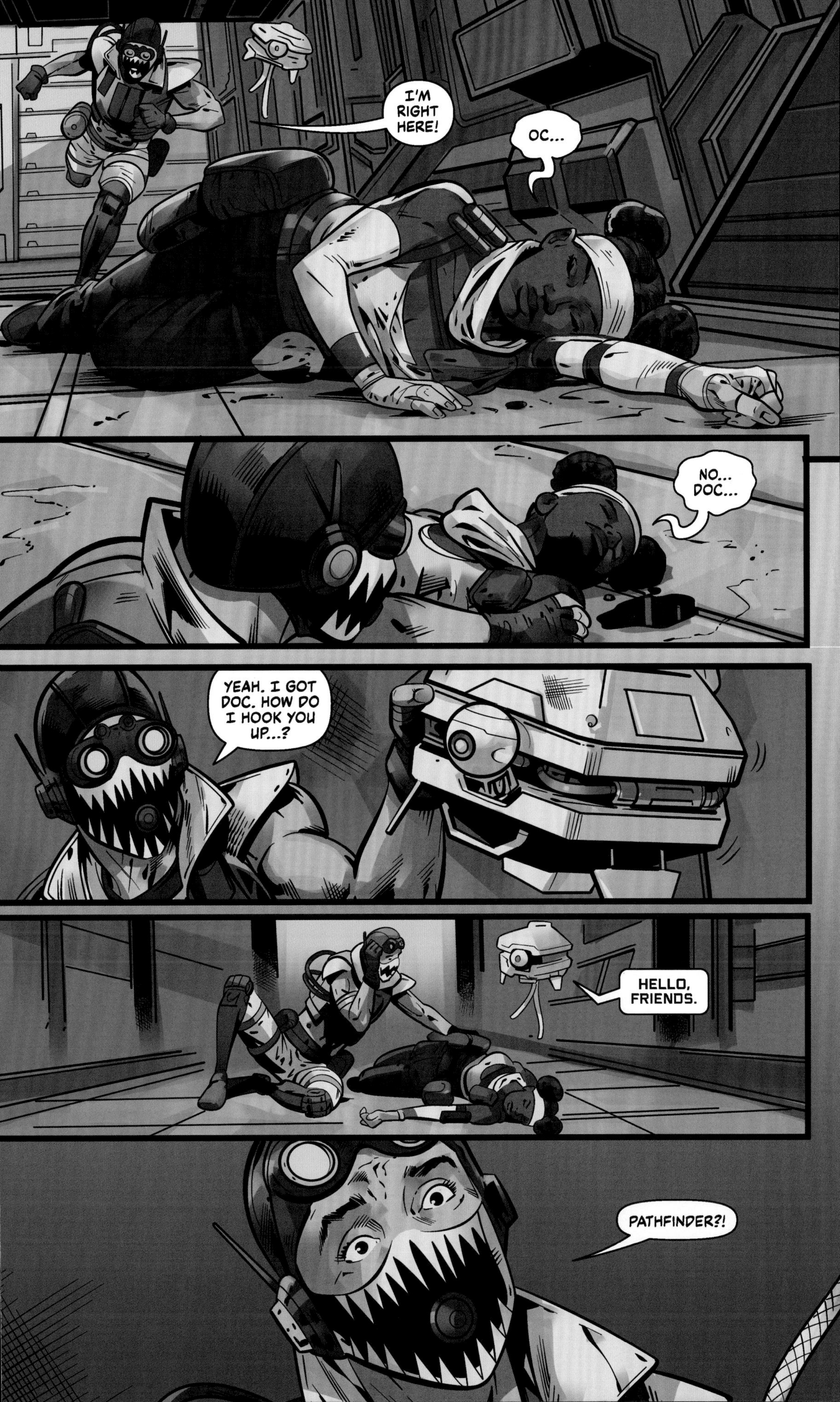
I'M RIGHT HERE!
OC...
NO... DOC...
YEAH. I GOT DOC. HOW DO I HOOK YOU UP...?
HELLO, FRIENDS.
PATHFINDER?!

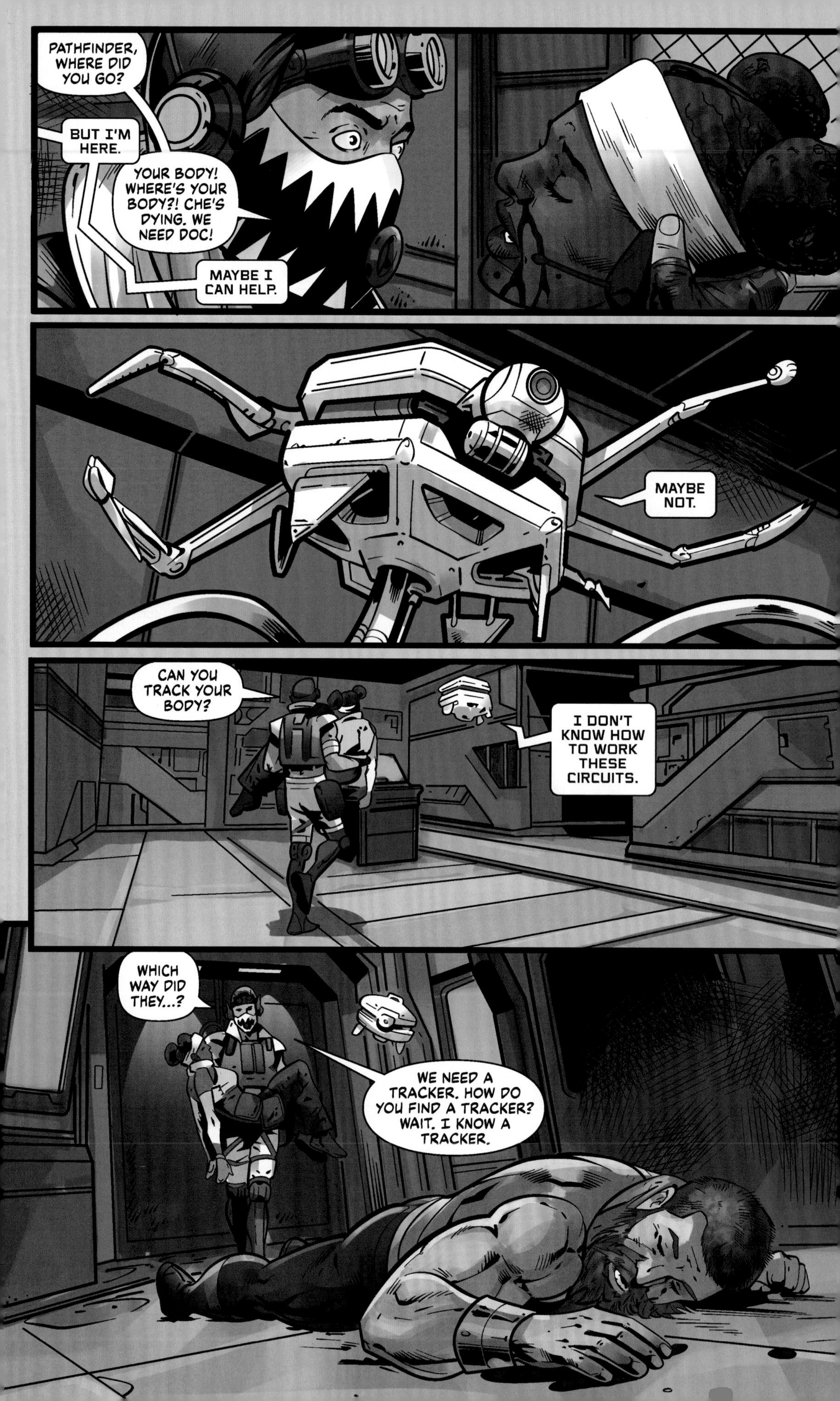
PATHFINDER, WHERE DID YOU GO?
BUT I'M HERE.
YOUR BODY! WHERE'S YOUR BODY?! CHE'S DYING. WE NEED DOC!
MAYBE I CAN HELP.
MAYBE NOT.
CAN YOU TRACK YOUR BODY?
I DON'T KNOW HOW TO WORK THESE CIRCUITS.
WHICH WAY DID THEY...?
WE NEED A TRACKER. HOW DO YOU FIND A TRACKER? WAIT. I KNOW A TRACKER.

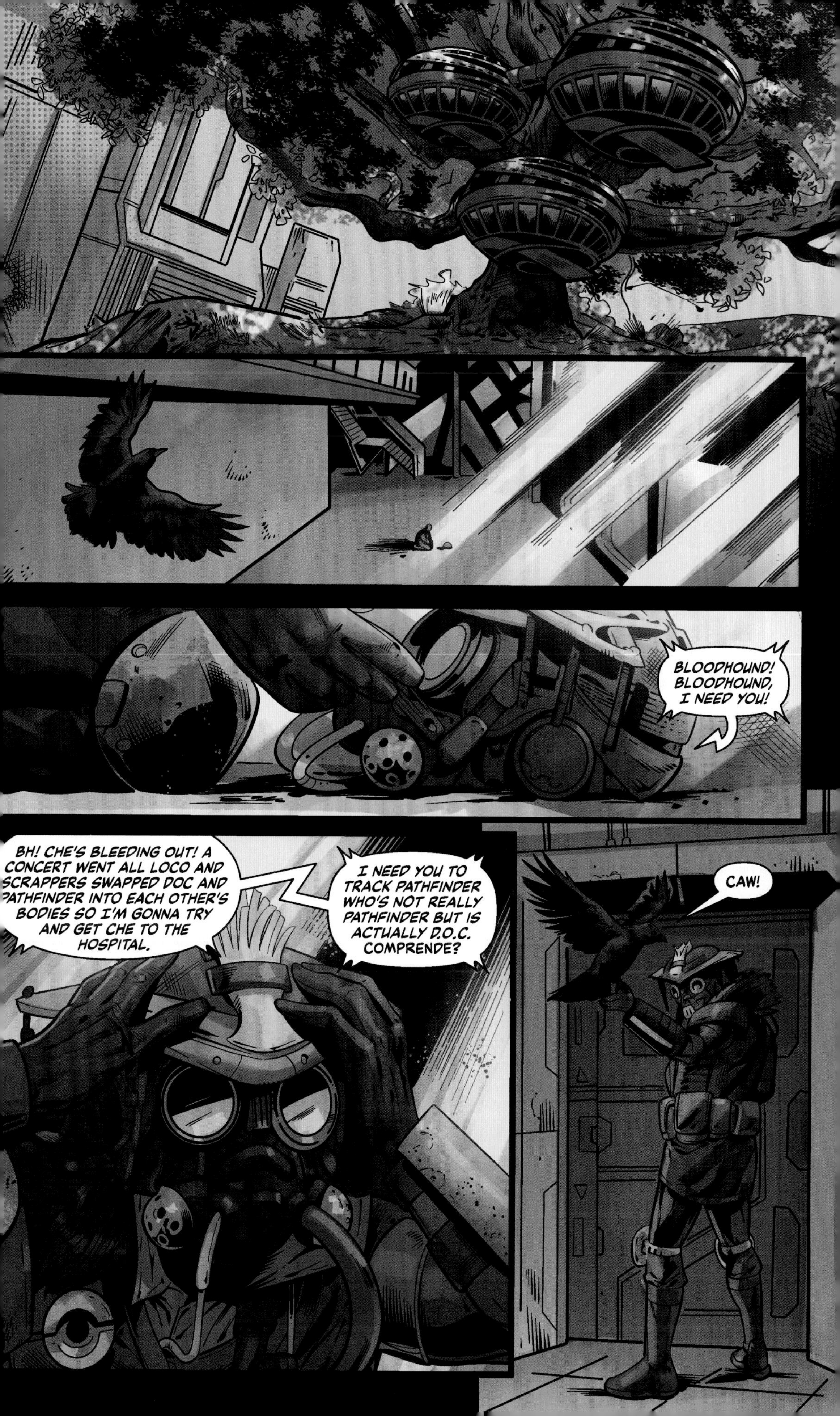
BLOODHOUND! BLOODHOUND, I NEED YOU!
BH! CHE'S BLEEDING OUT! A CONCERT WENT ALL LOCO AND SCRAPPERS SWAPPED DOC AND PATHFINDER INTO EACH OTHER'S BODIES SO I'M GONNA TRY AND GET CHE TO THE HOSPITAL.
I NEED YOU TO TRACK PATHFINDER WHO'S NOT REALLY PATHFINDER BUT IS ACTUALLY D.O.C. COMPRENDE?
CAW!

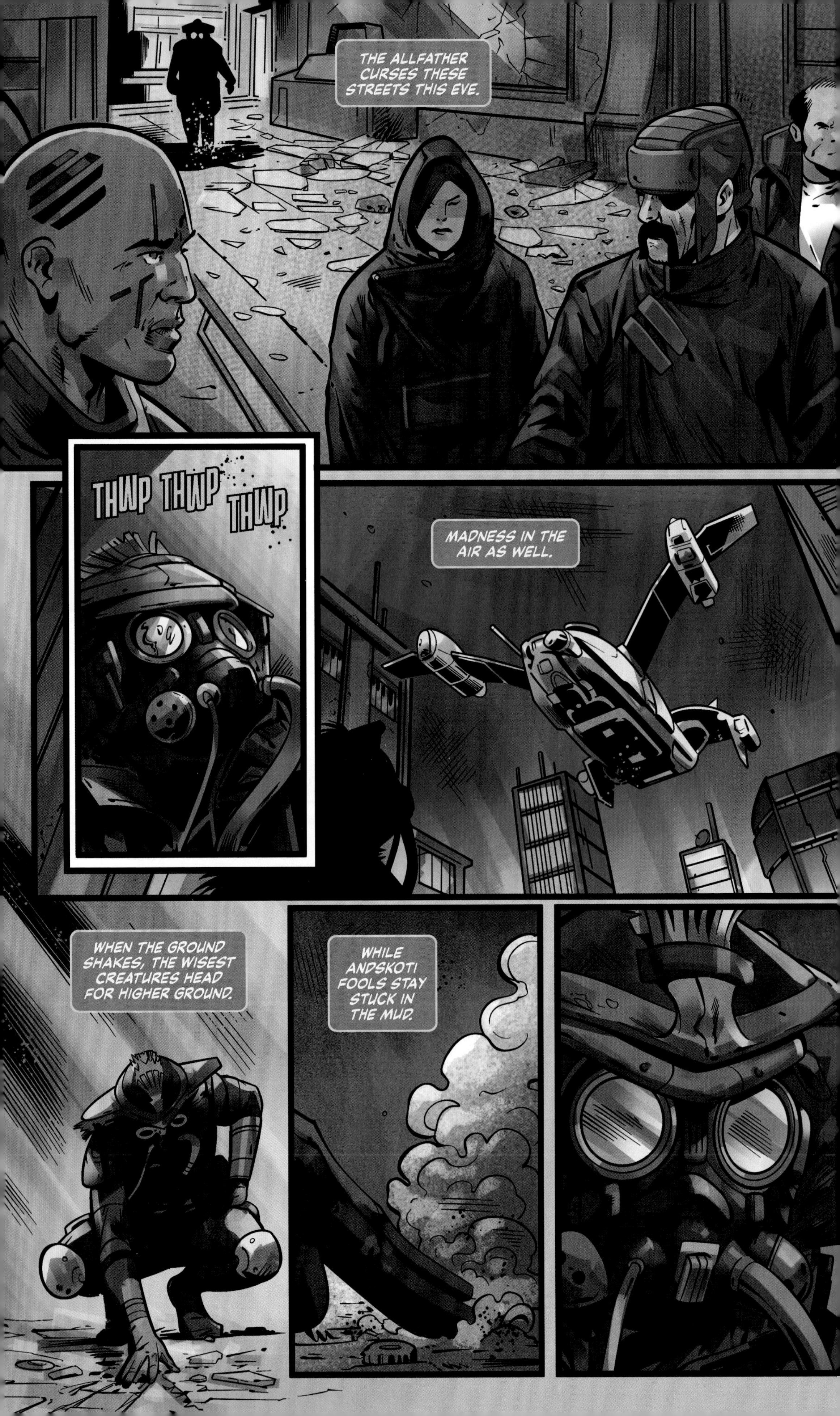
THE ALLFATHER CURSES THESE STREETS THIS EVE.
THWP THWP THWP
MADNESS IN THE AIR AS WELL.
WHEN THE GROUND SHAKES, THE WISEST CREATURES HEAD FOR HIGHER GROUND.
WHILE ANDSKOTI FOOLS STAY STUCK IN THE MUD.

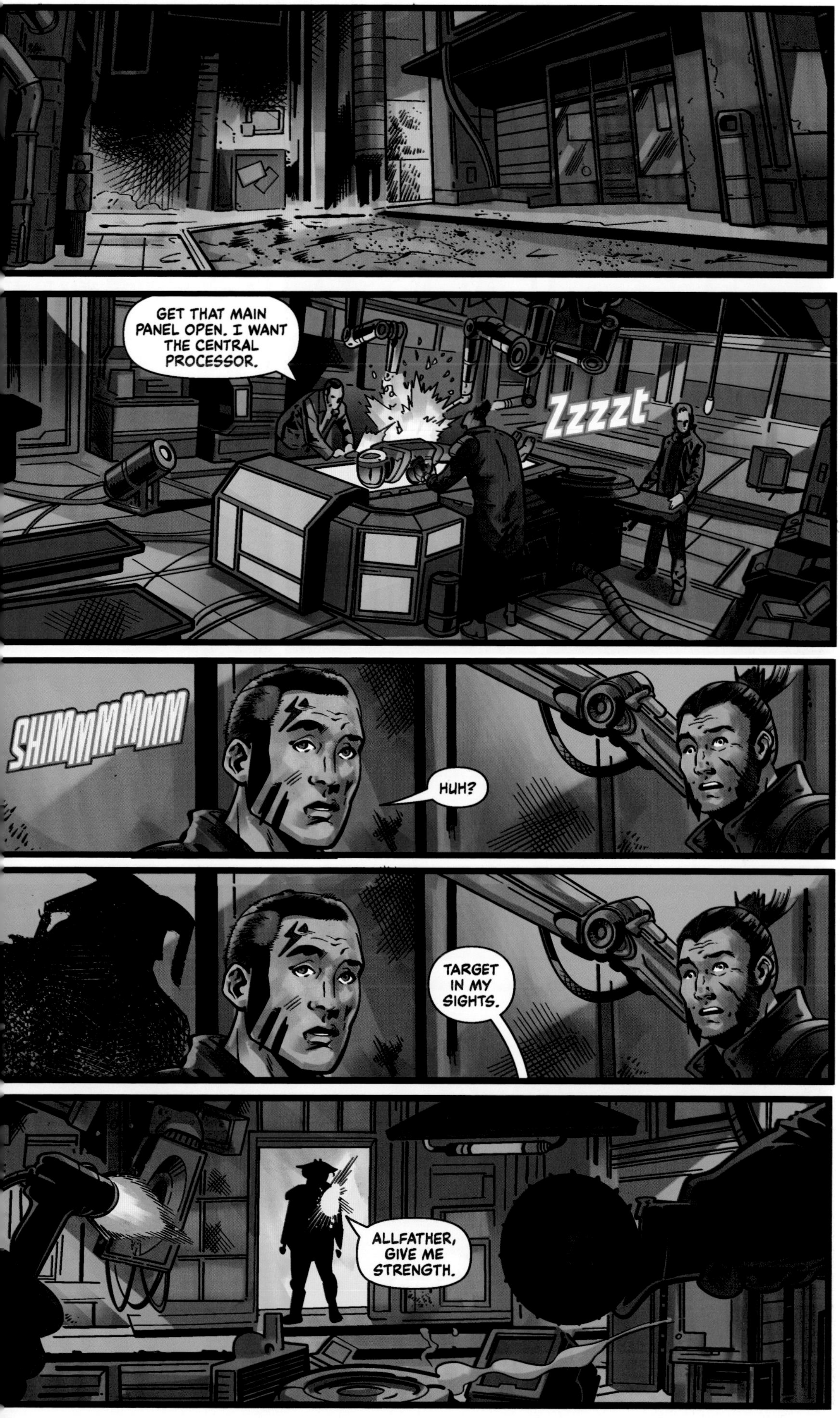
GET THAT MAIN PANEL OPEN. I WANT THE CENTRAL PROCESSOR.
Zzzzt
SHIMMMMMM
HUH?
TARGET IN MY SIGHTS.
ALLFATHER, GIVE ME STRENGTH.

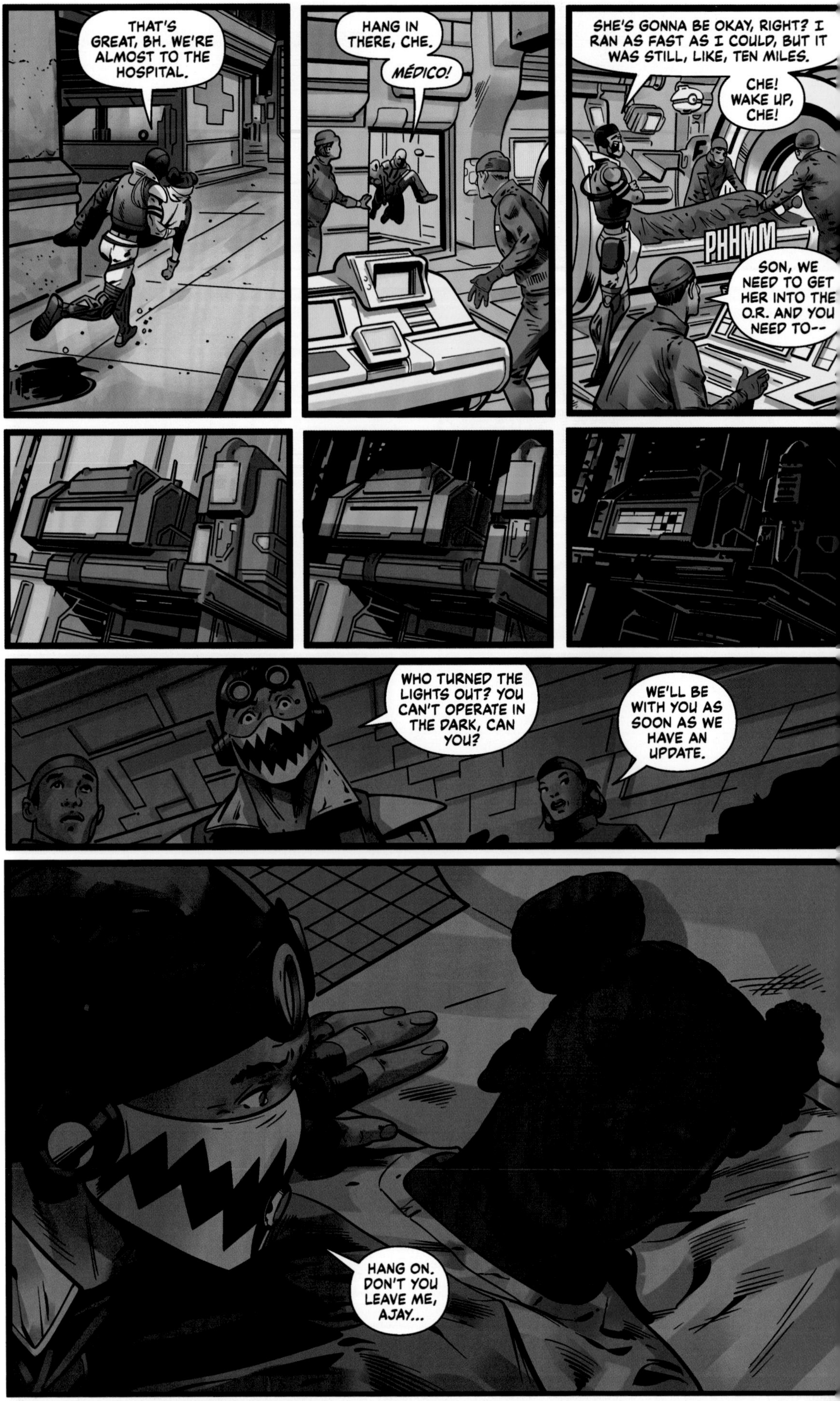
THAT'S GREAT, BH. WE'RE ALMOST TO THE HOSPITAL.
HANG IN THERE, CHE.
MÉDICO!
SHE'S GONNA BE OKAY, RIGHT? I RAN AS FAST AS I COULD, BUT IT WAS STILL, LIKE, TEN MILES.
CHE! WAKE UP, CHE!
PHHMM
SON, WE NEED TO GET HER INTO THE O.R. AND YOU NEED TO--
WHO TURNED THE LIGHTS OUT? YOU CAN'T OPERATE IN THE DARK, CAN YOU?
WE'LL BE WITH YOU AS SOON AS WE HAVE AN UPDATE.
HANG ON. DON'T YOU LEAVE ME, AJAY...

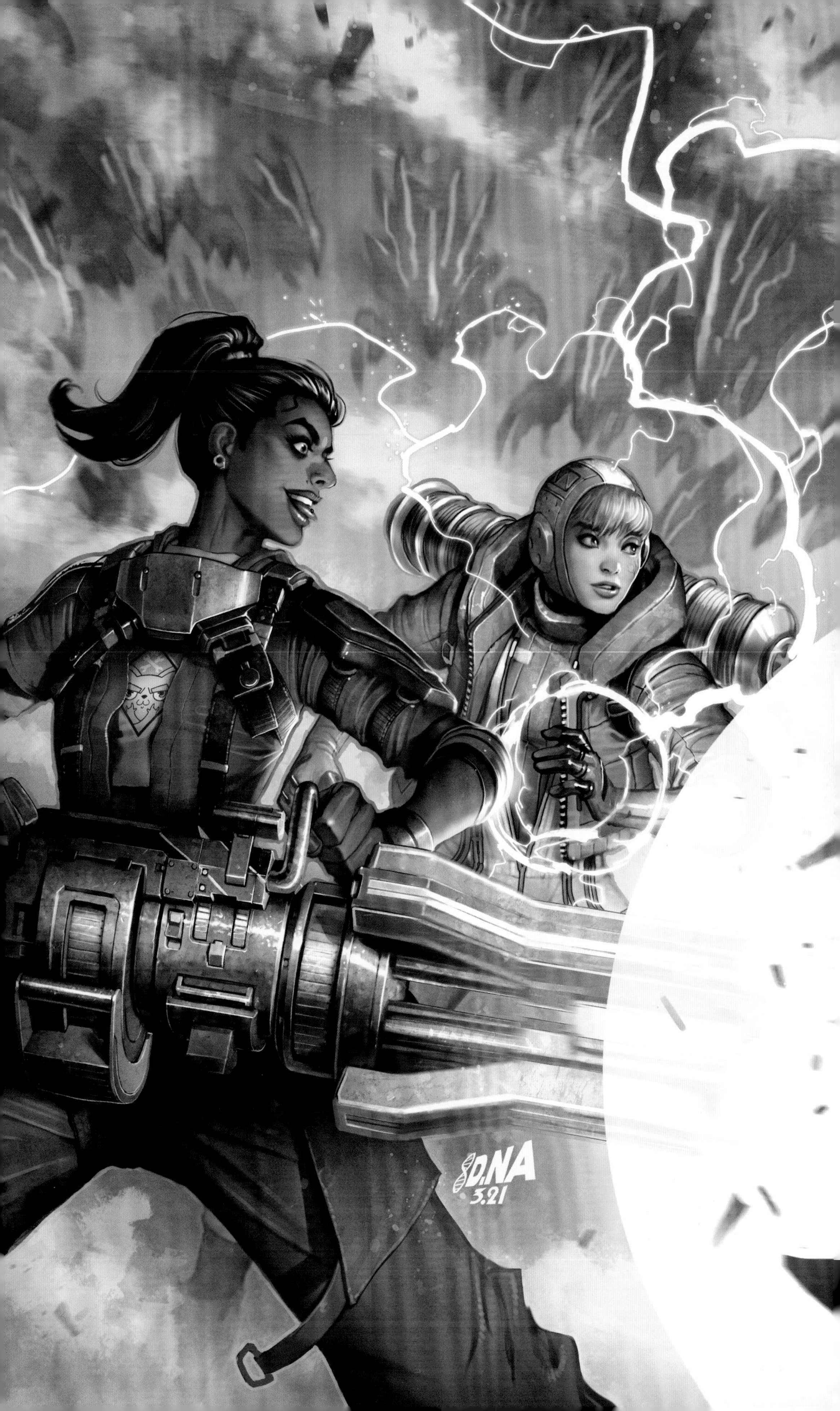
D.NA
3.21

>>

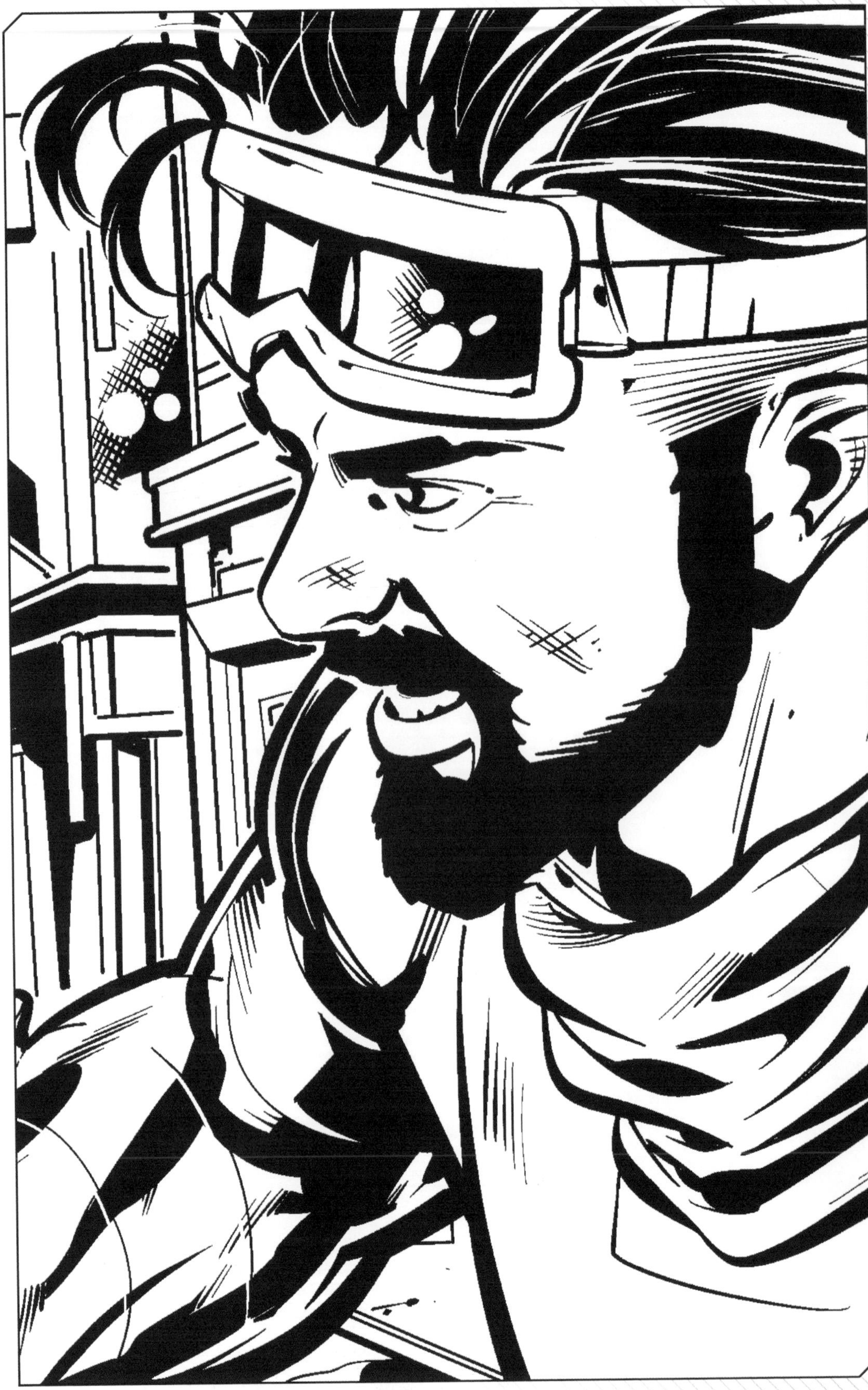

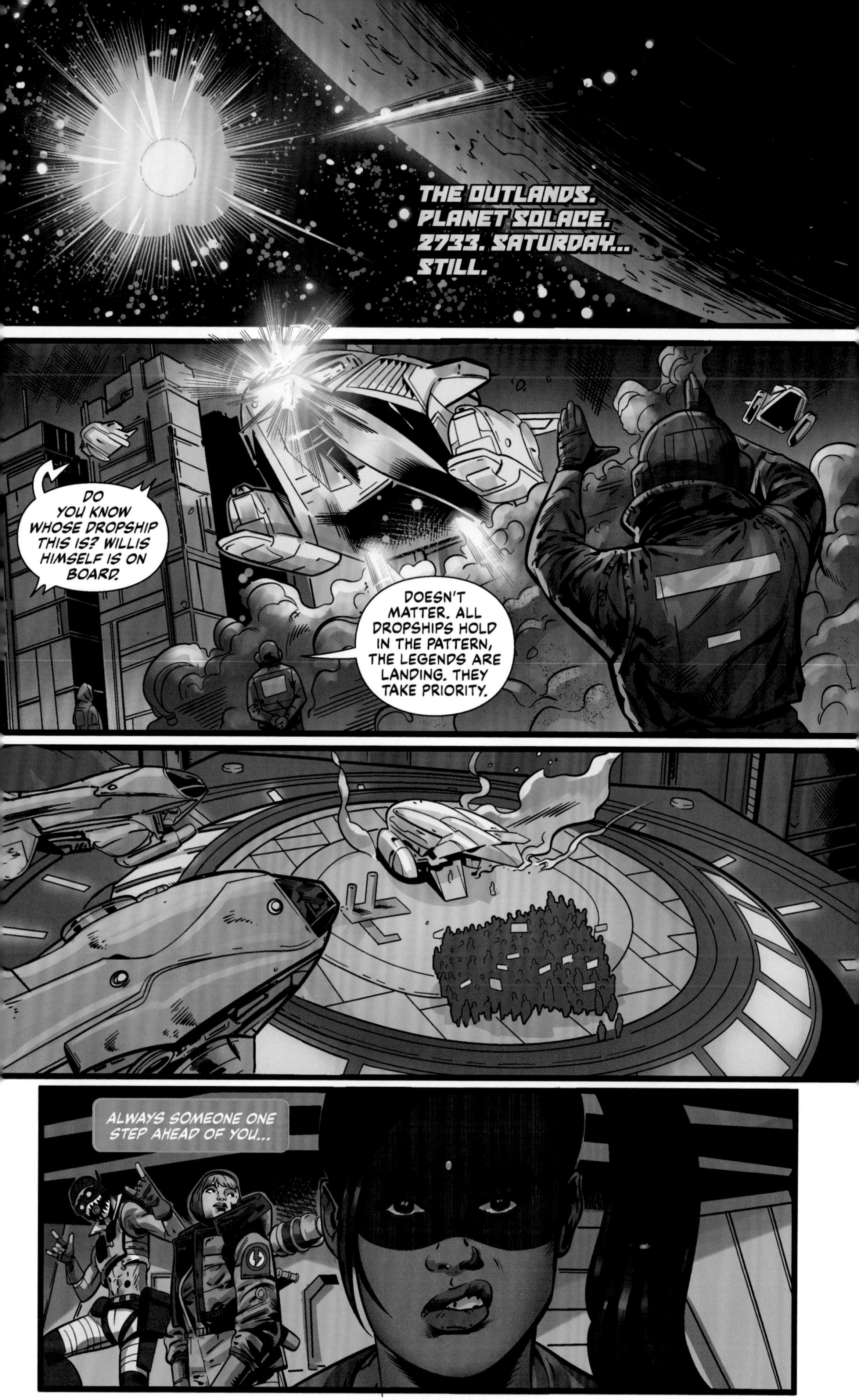
THE OUTLANDS. PLANET SOLACE. 2733. SATURDAY... STILL.
DO YOU KNOW WHOSE DROPSHIP THIS IS? WILLIS HIMSELF IS ON BOARD.
DOESN'T MATTER. ALL DROPSHIPS HOLD IN THE PATTERN, THE LEGENDS ARE LANDING. THEY TAKE PRIORITY.
ALWAYS SOMEONE ONE STEP AHEAD OF YOU...

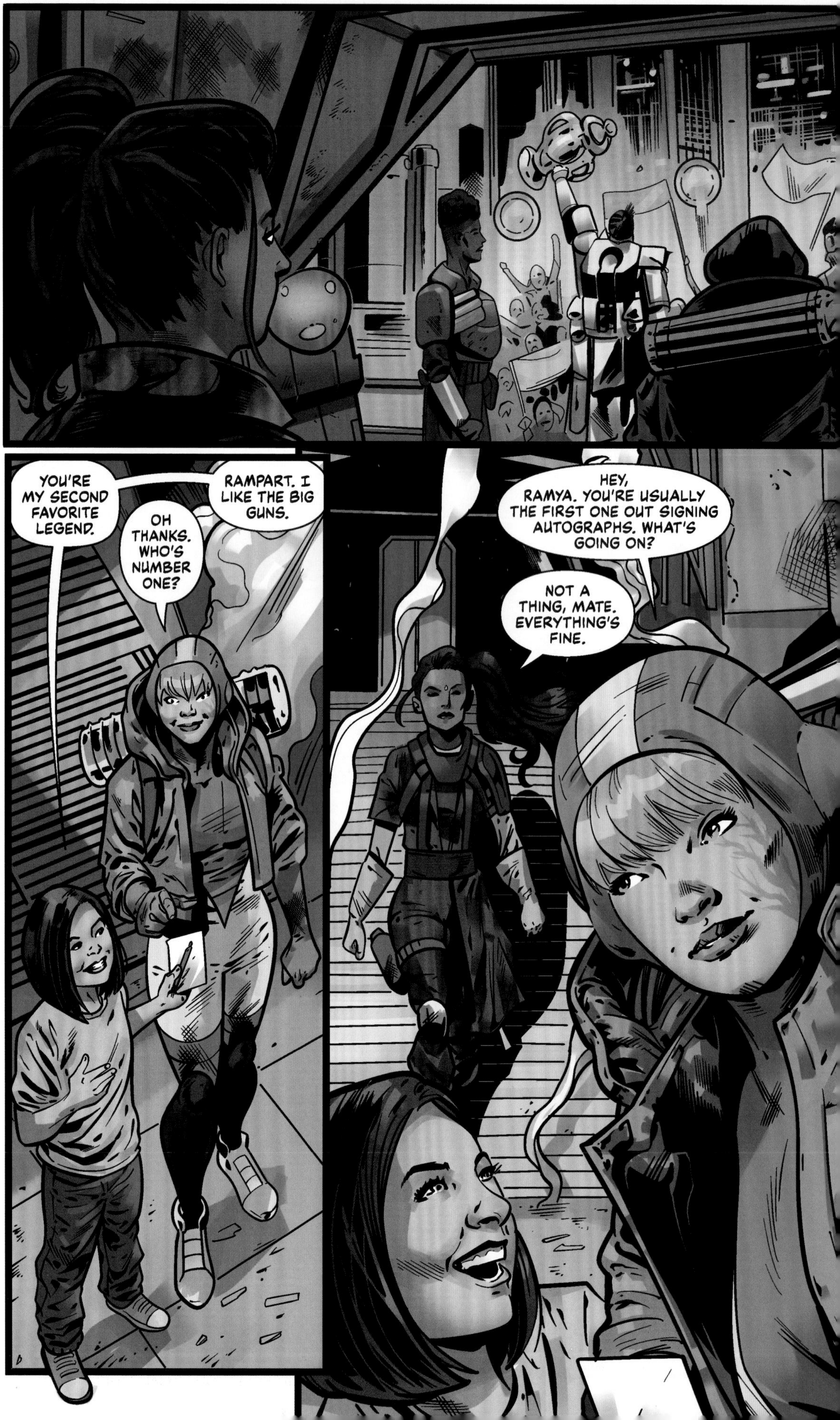
YOU'RE MY SECOND FAVORITE LEGEND.
OH THANKS. WHO'S NUMBER ONE?
RAMPART. I LIKE THE BIG GUNS.
HEY, RAMYA. YOU'RE USUALLY THE FIRST ONE OUT SIGNING AUTOGRAPHS. WHAT'S GOING ON?
NOT A THING, MATE. EVERYTHING'S FINE.

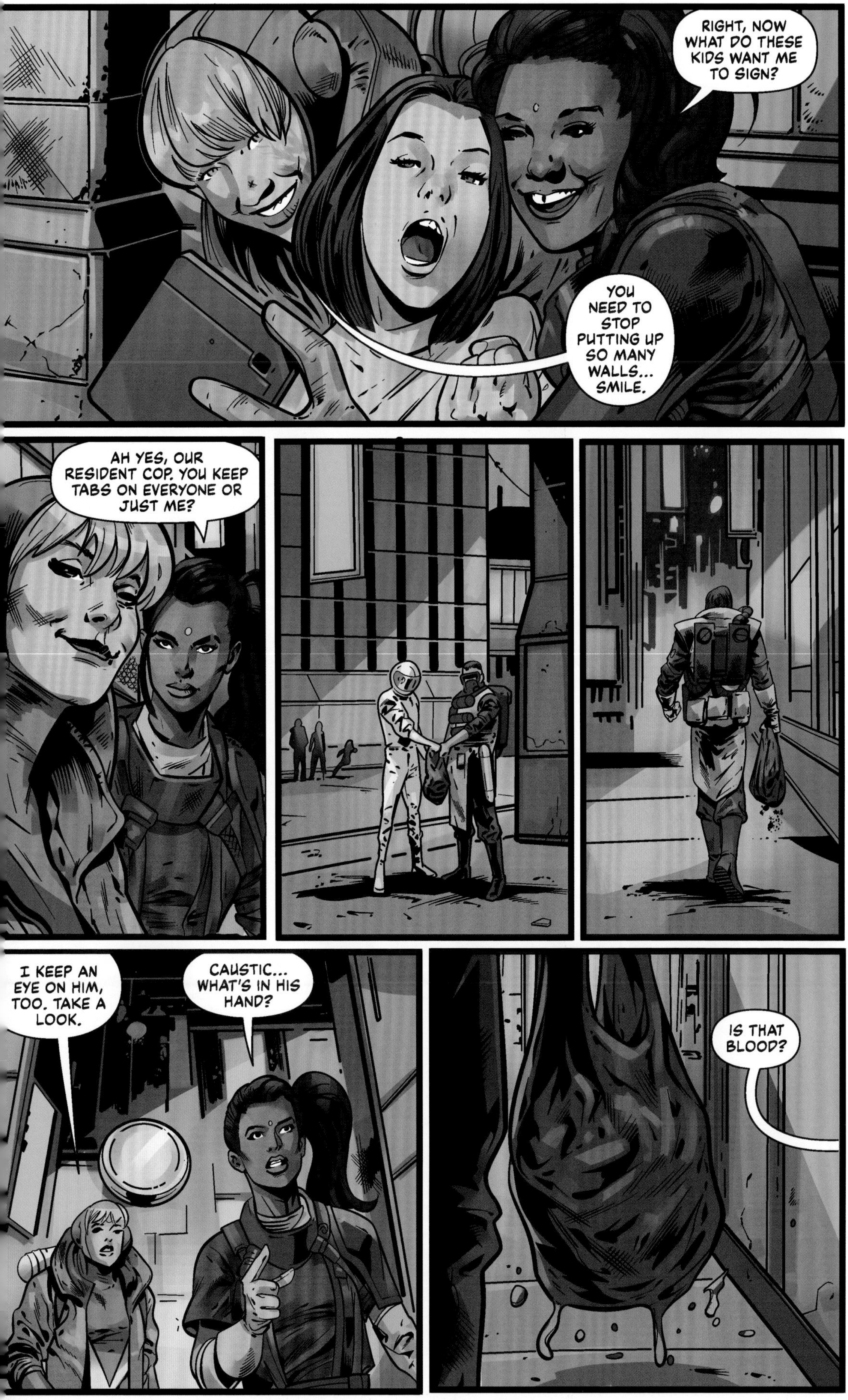
RIGHT, NOW WHAT DO THESE KIDS WANT ME TO SIGN?
YOU NEED TO STOP PUTTING UP SO MANY WALLS... SMILE.
AH YES, OUR RESIDENT COP. YOU KEEP TABS ON EVERYONE OR JUST ME?
I KEEP AN EYE ON HIM, TOO. TAKE A LOOK.
CAUSTIC... WHAT'S IN HIS HAND?
IS THAT BLOOD?

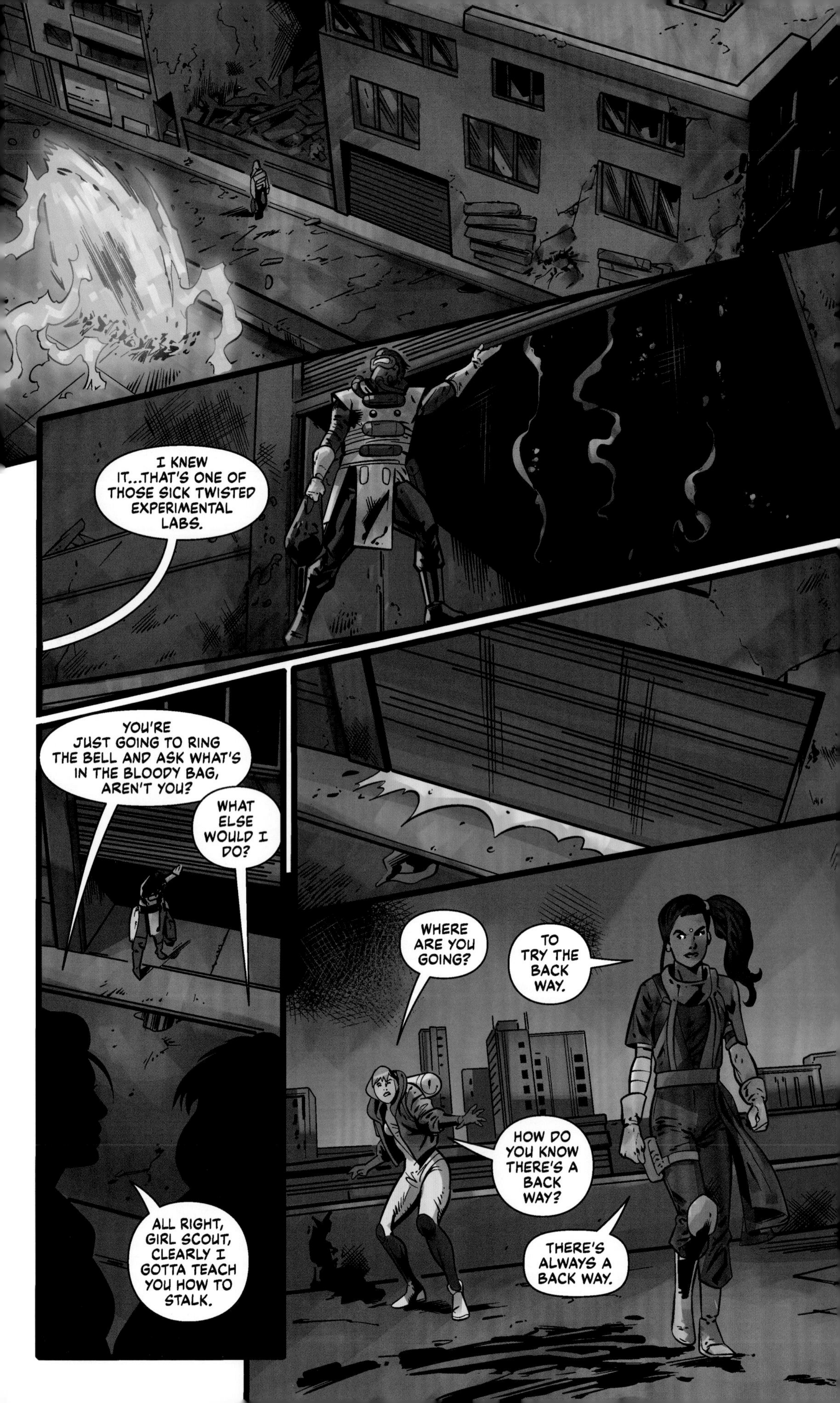
I KNEW IT...THAT'S ONE OF THOSE SICK TWISTED EXPERIMENTAL LABS.
YOU'RE JUST GOING TO RING THE BELL AND ASK WHAT'S IN THE BLOODY BAG, AREN'T YOU?
WHAT ELSE WOULD I DO?
ALL RIGHT, GIRL SCOUT, CLEARLY I GOTTA TEACH YOU HOW TO STALK.
WHERE ARE YOU GOING?
TO TRY THE BACK WAY.
HOW DO YOU KNOW THERE'S A BACK WAY?
THERE'S ALWAYS A BACK WAY.

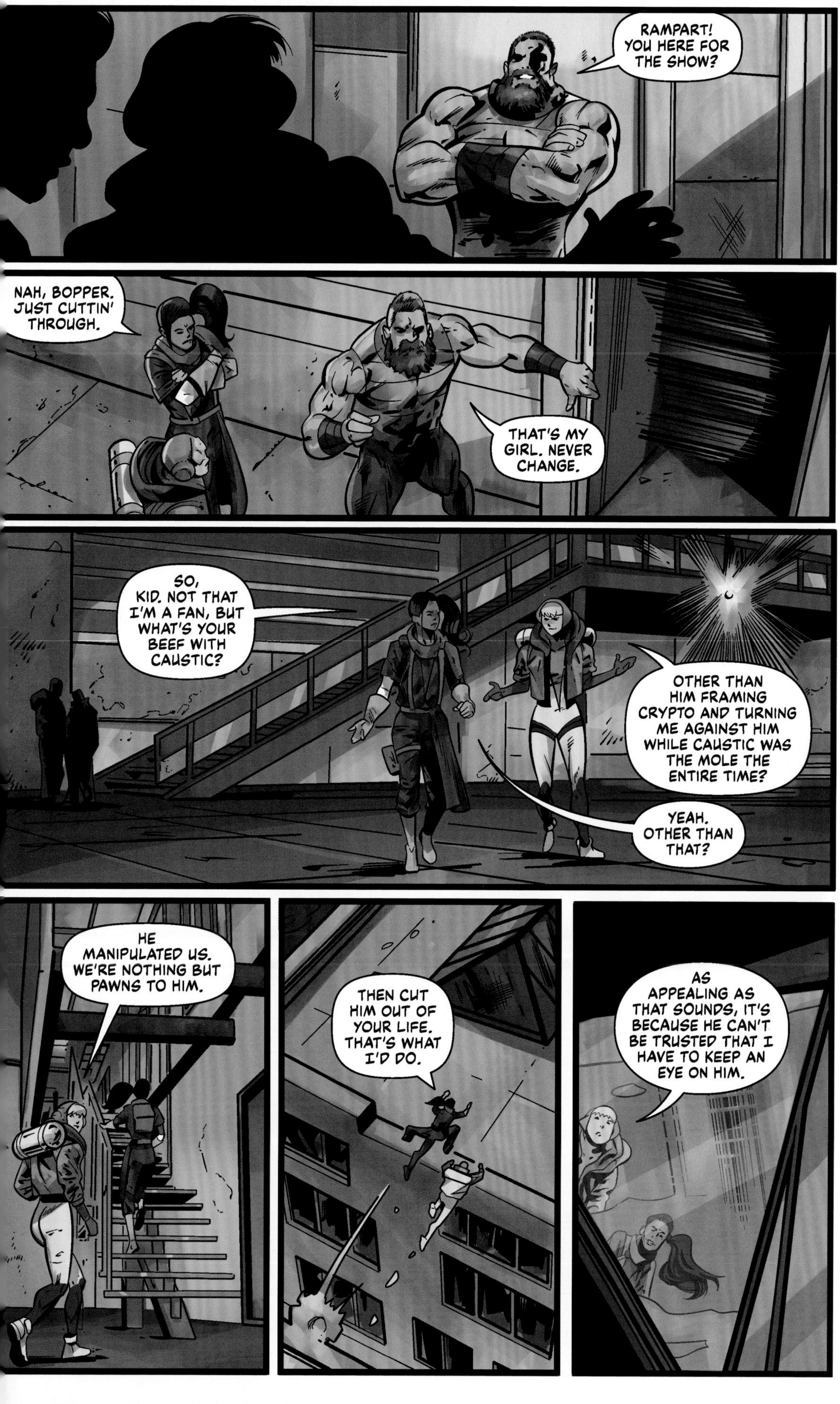
RAMPART! YOU HERE FOR THE SHOW?
NAH, BOPPER. JUST CUTTIN' THROUGH.
THAT'S MY GIRL. NEVER CHANGE.
SO, KID. NOT THAT I'M A FAN, BUT WHAT'S YOUR BEEF WITH CAUSTIC?
OTHER THAN HIM FRAMING CRYPTO AND TURNING ME AGAINST HIM WHILE CAUSTIC WAS THE MOLE THE ENTIRE TIME?
YEAH. OTHER THAN THAT?
HE MANIPULATED US. WE'RE NOTHING BUT PAWNS TO HIM.
THEN CUT HIM OUT OF YOUR LIFE. THAT'S WHAT I'D DO.
AS APPEALING AS THAT SOUNDS, IT'S BECAUSE HE CAN'T BE TRUSTED THAT I HAVE TO KEEP AN EYE ON HIM.

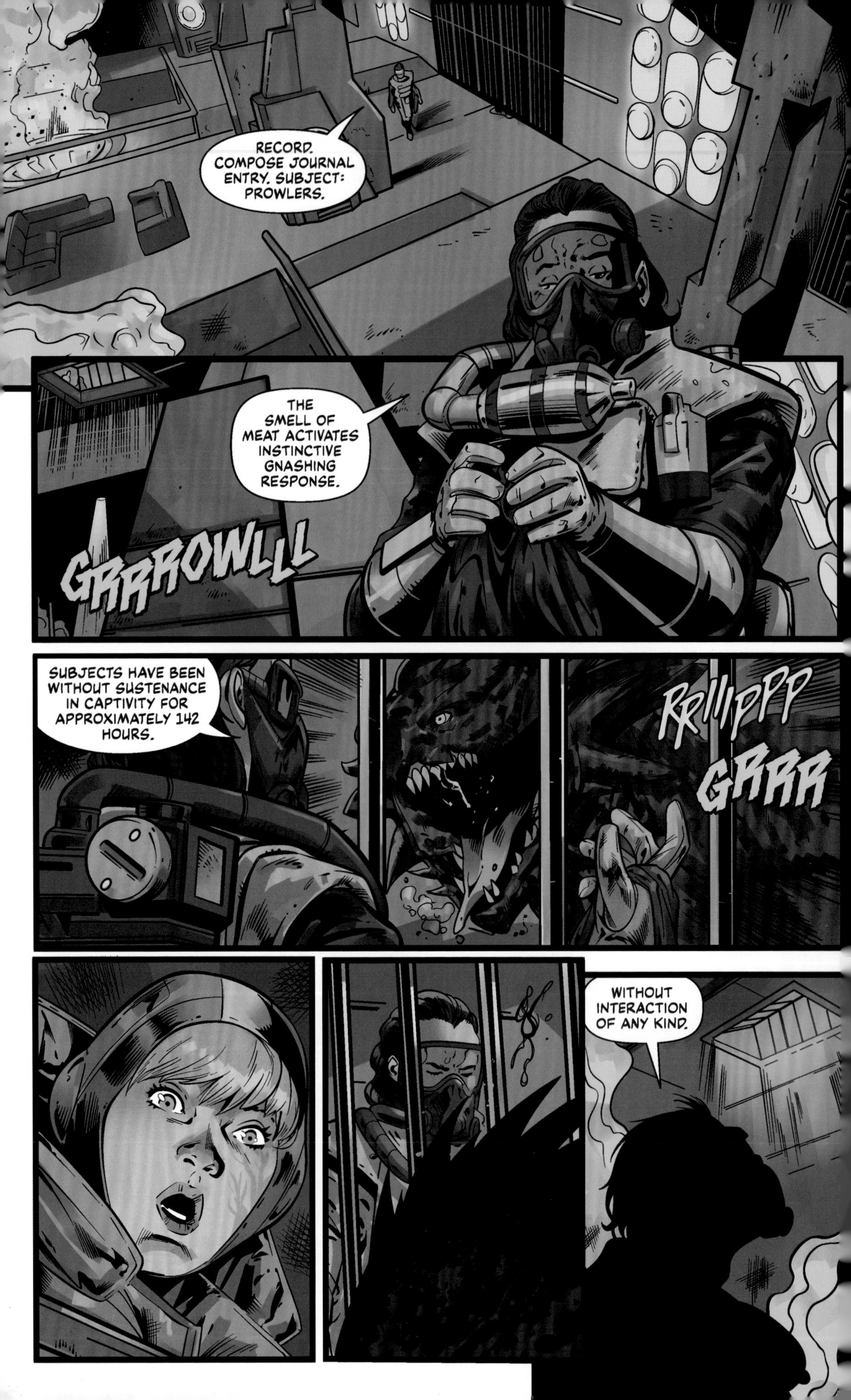
RECORD. COMPOSE JOURNAL ENTRY. SUBJECT: PROWLERS.
THE SMELL OF MEAT ACTIVATES INSTINCTIVE GNASHING RESPONSE.
GRRROWLLL
SUBJECTS HAVE BEEN WITHOUT SUSTENANCE IN CAPTIVITY FOR APPROXIMATELY 142 HOURS.
RRIIIPPP
GRRR
WITHOUT INTERACTION OF ANY KIND.

SNIFF
SNIFF

BARK
BARK
BARK

SPYING ON ME, MS. PAQUETTE? WHO SENT YOU?

UH, NO ONE. I, UH, JUST WANTED TO ASK YOU SOME MATH QUESTIONS.

WHY DON'T YOU JUST ASK...THE ENGINEER?

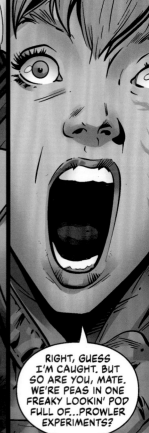

RIGHT, GUESS I'M CAUGHT. BUT SO ARE YOU, MATE. WE'RE PEAS IN ONE FREAKY LOOKIN' POD FULL OF...PROWLER EXPERIMENTS?

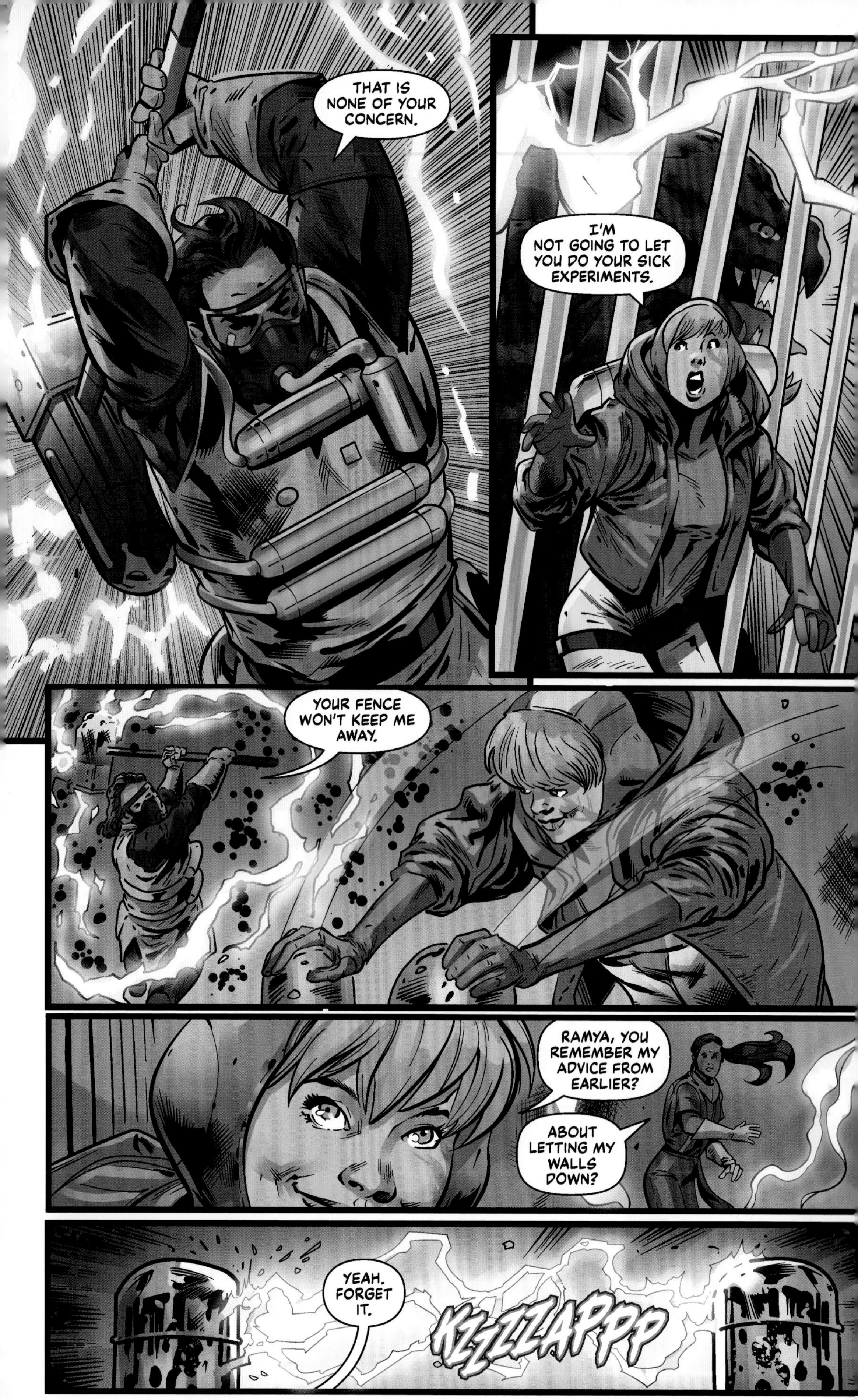
THAT IS NONE OF YOUR CONCERN.
I'M NOT GOING TO LET YOU DO YOUR SICK EXPERIMENTS.
YOUR FENCE WON'T KEEP ME AWAY.
RAMYA, YOU REMEMBER MY ADVICE FROM EARLIER?
ABOUT LETTING MY WALLS DOWN?
YEAH. FORGET IT.
KZZZZZAPPPP

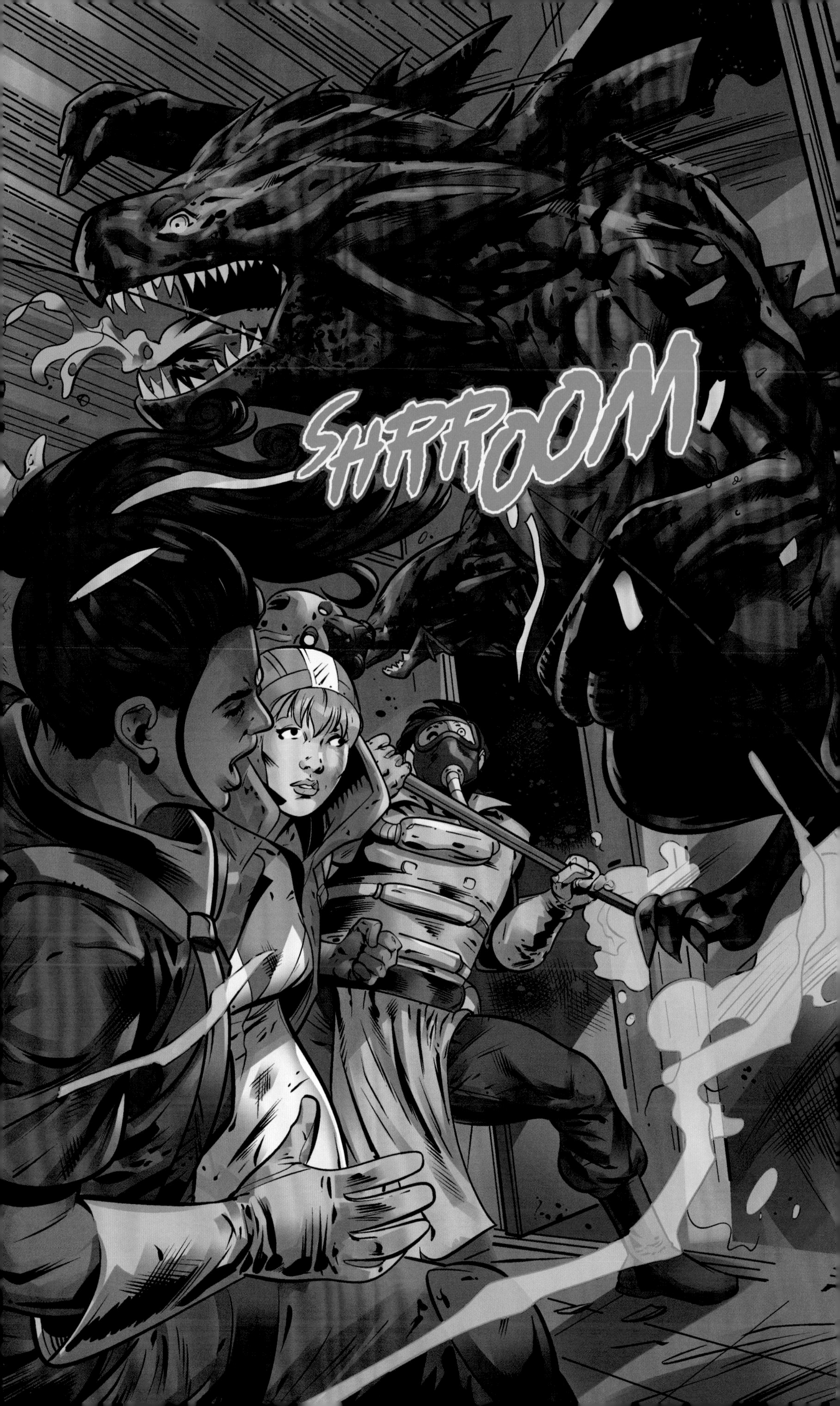
SHRROOM

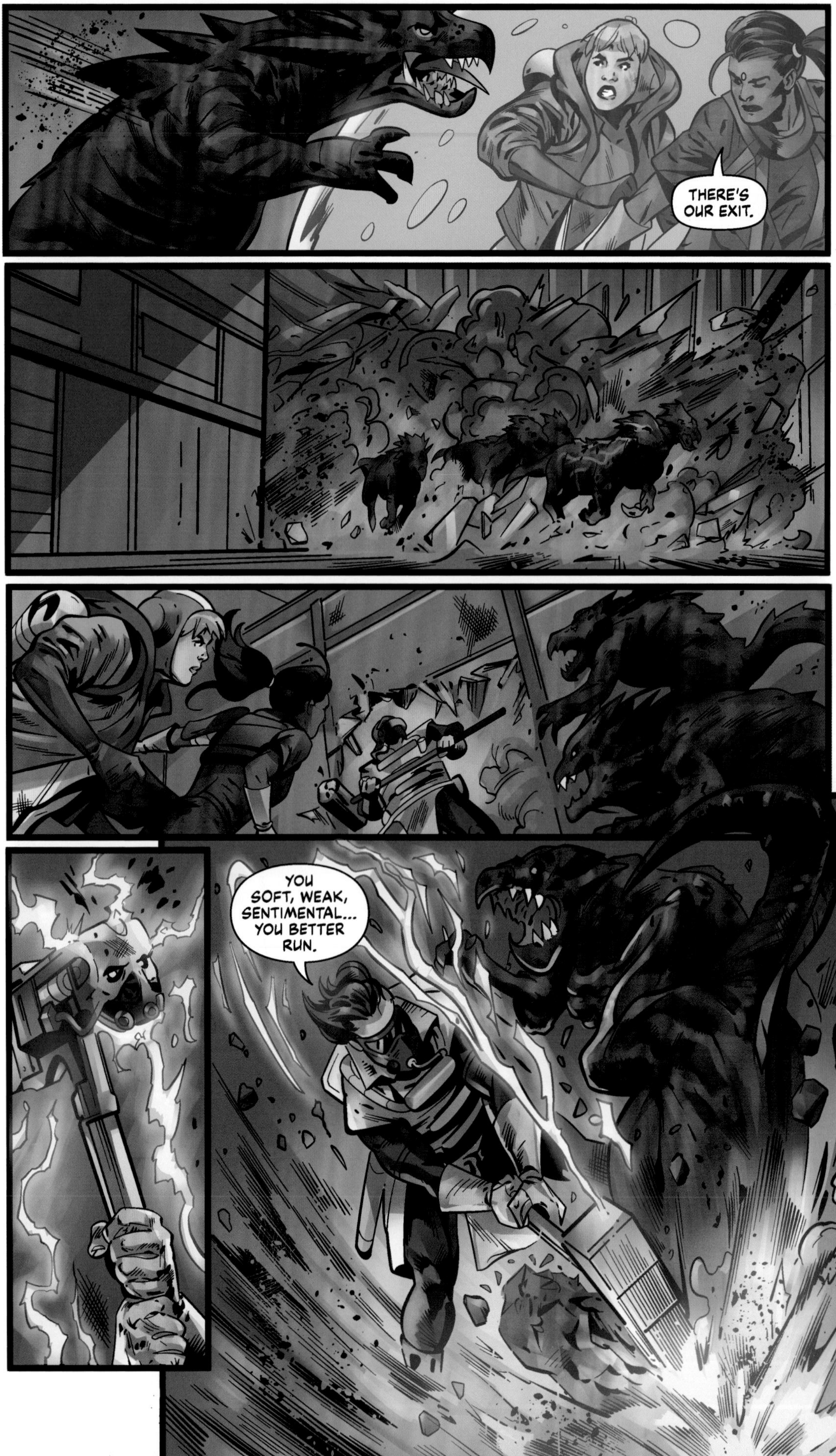
THERE'S OUR EXIT.
YOU SOFT, WEAK, SENTIMENTAL... YOU BETTER RUN.

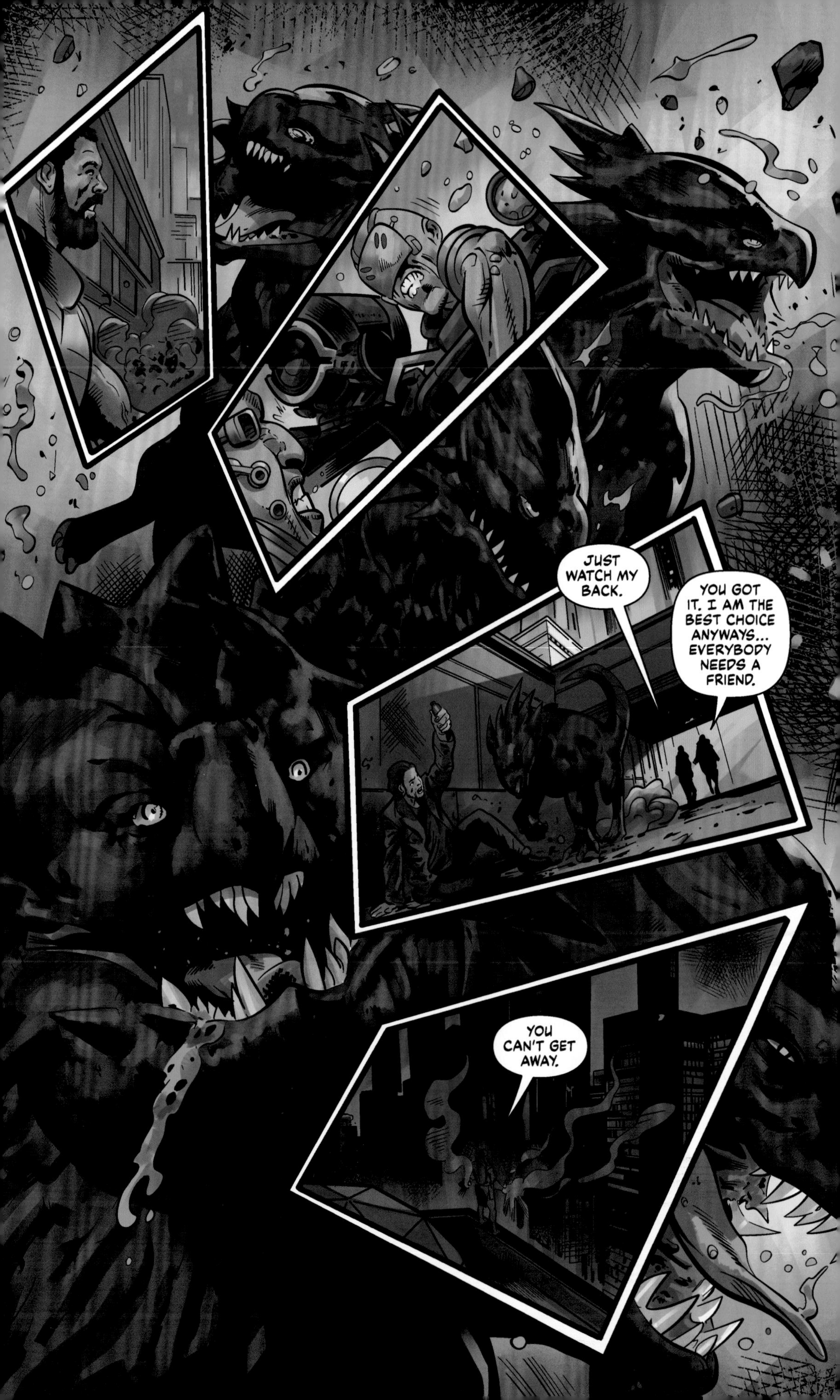
JUST WATCH MY BACK.
YOU GOT IT. I AM THE BEST CHOICE ANYWAYS... EVERYBODY NEEDS A FRIEND.
YOU CAN'T GET AWAY.

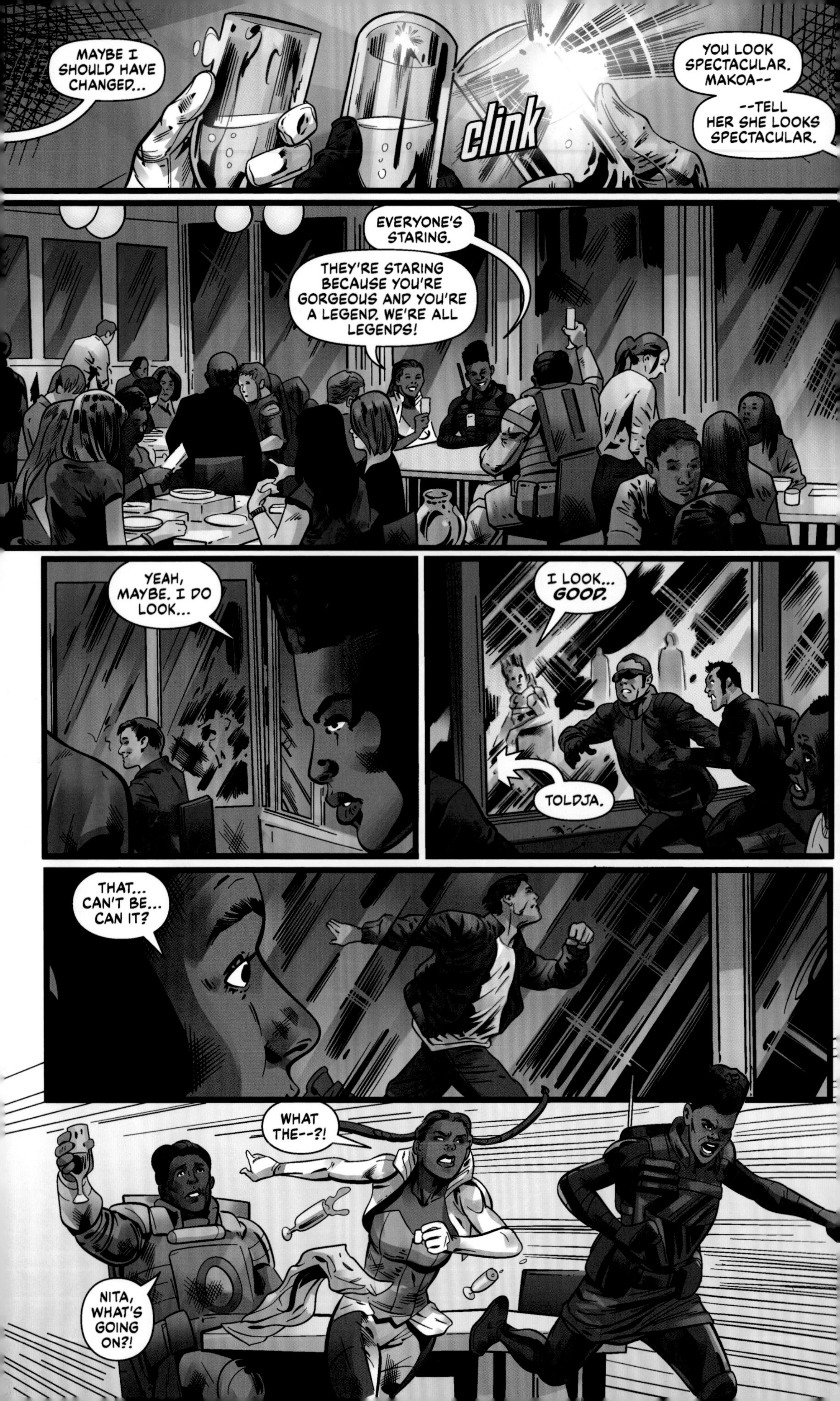
MAYBE I SHOULD HAVE CHANGED...
clink
YOU LOOK SPECTACULAR. MAKOA--
--TELL HER SHE LOOKS SPECTACULAR.
EVERYONE'S STARING.
THEY'RE STARING BECAUSE YOU'RE GORGEOUS AND YOU'RE A LEGEND. WE'RE ALL LEGENDS!
YEAH, MAYBE. I DO LOOK...
I LOOK... GOOD.
TOLDJA.
THAT... CAN'T BE... CAN IT?
WHAT THE--?!
NITA, WHAT'S GOING ON?!

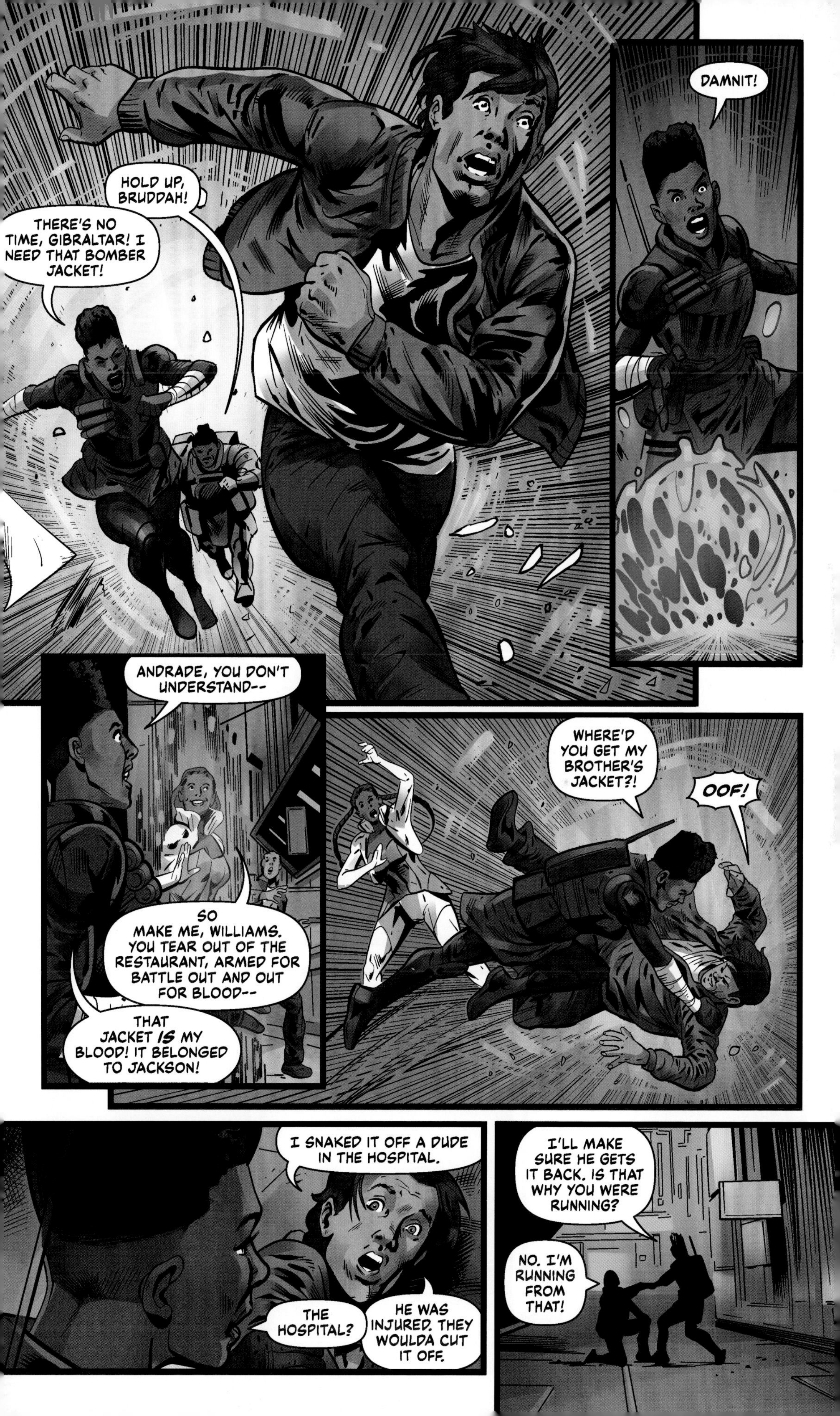
HOLD UP, BRUDDAH!
THERE'S NO TIME, GIBRALTAR! I NEED THAT BOMBER JACKET!
DAMNIT!
ANDRADE, YOU DON'T UNDERSTAND--
SO MAKE ME, WILLIAMS. YOU TEAR OUT OF THE RESTAURANT, ARMED FOR BATTLE OUT AND OUT FOR BLOOD--
THAT JACKET *IS* MY BLOOD! IT BELONGED TO JACKSON!
WHERE'D YOU GET MY BROTHER'S JACKET?!
OOF!
I SNAKED IT OFF A DUDE IN THE HOSPITAL.
THE HOSPITAL?
HE WAS INJURED. THEY WOULDA CUT IT OFF.
I'LL MAKE SURE HE GETS IT BACK. IS THAT WHY YOU WERE RUNNING?
NO. I'M RUNNING FROM THAT!

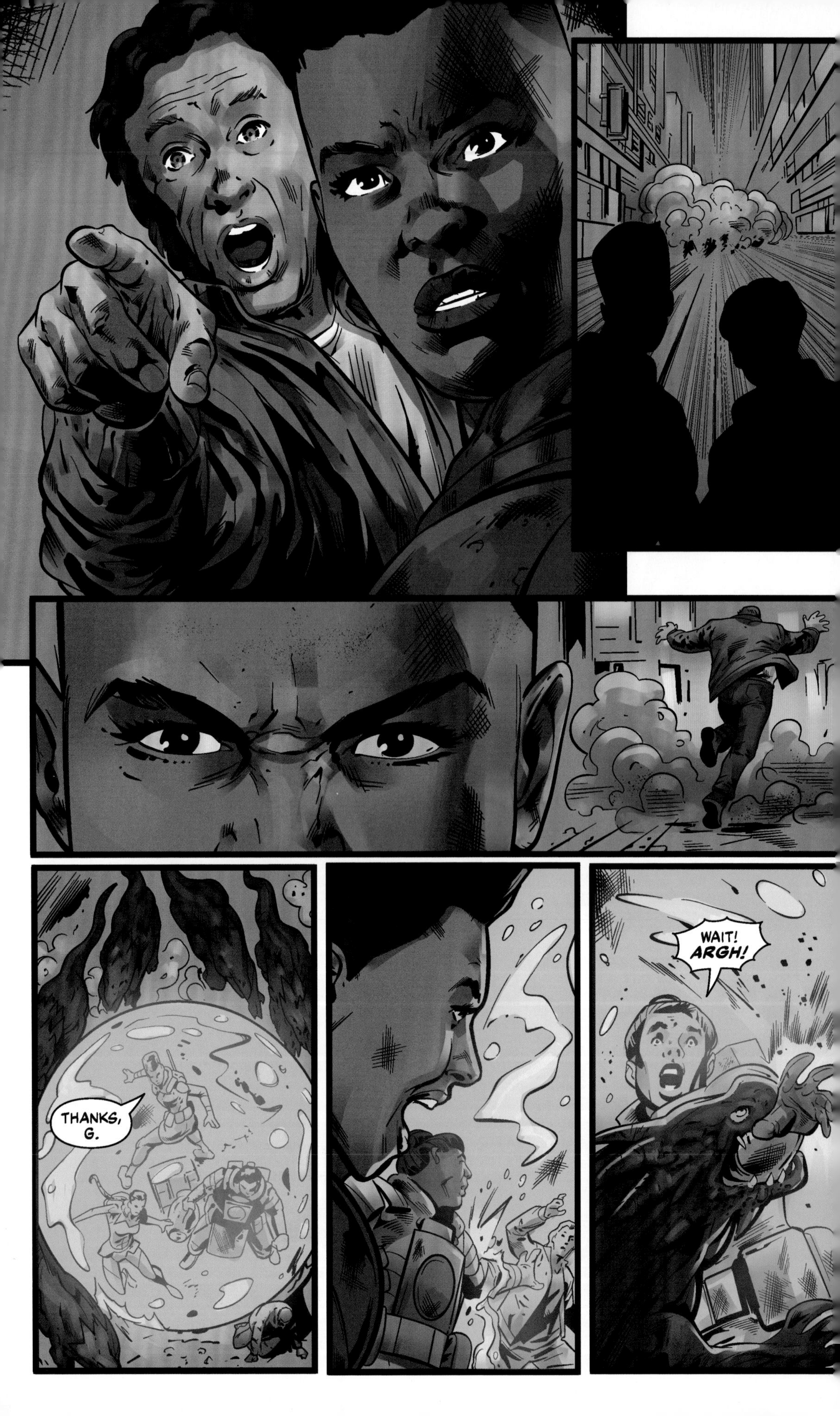
THANKS, G.
WAIT! ARGH!

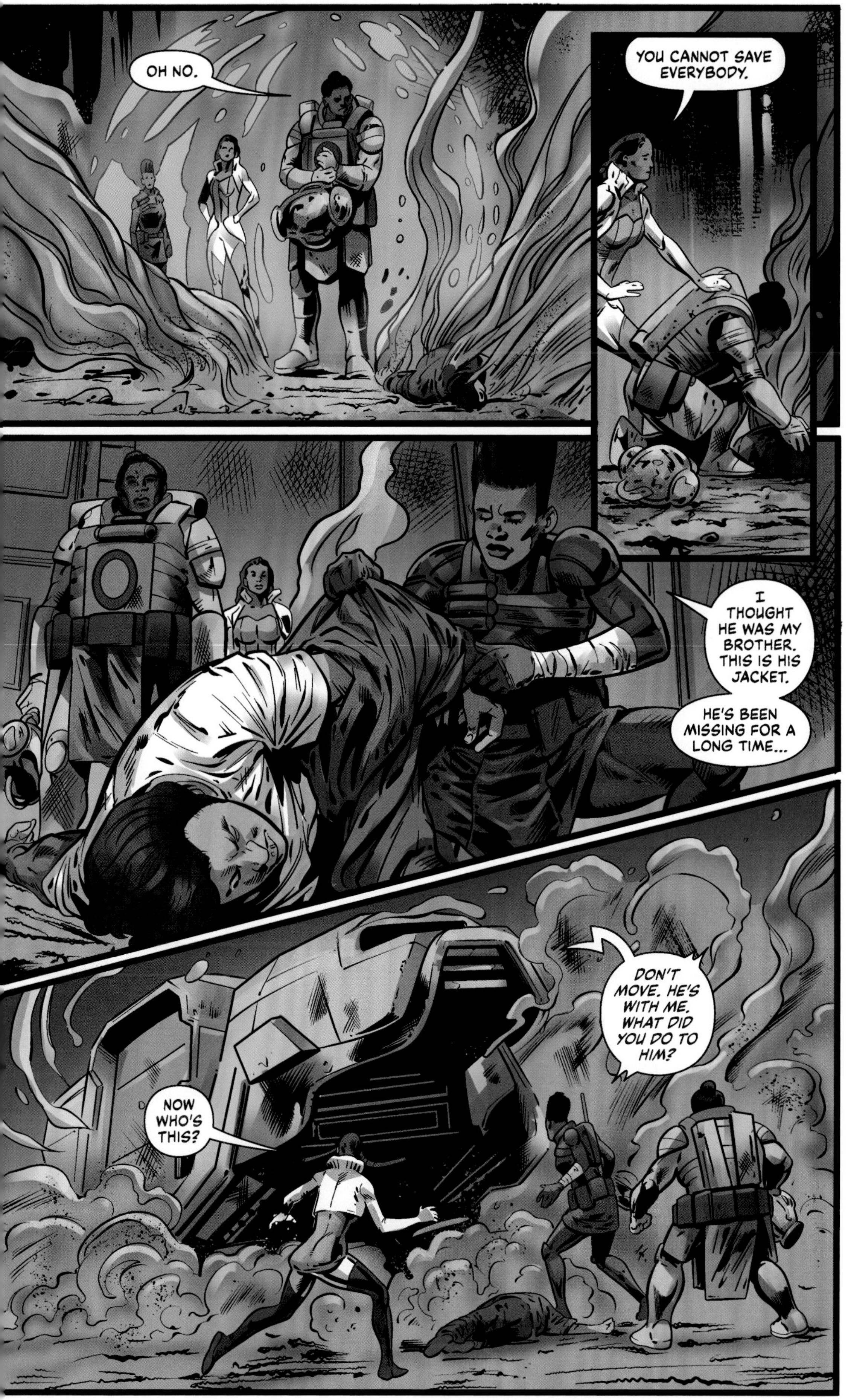
OH NO.
YOU CANNOT SAVE EVERYBODY.
I THOUGHT HE WAS MY BROTHER. THIS IS HIS JACKET.
HE'S BEEN MISSING FOR A LONG TIME...
DON'T MOVE. HE'S WITH ME. WHAT DID YOU DO TO HIM?
NOW WHO'S THIS?

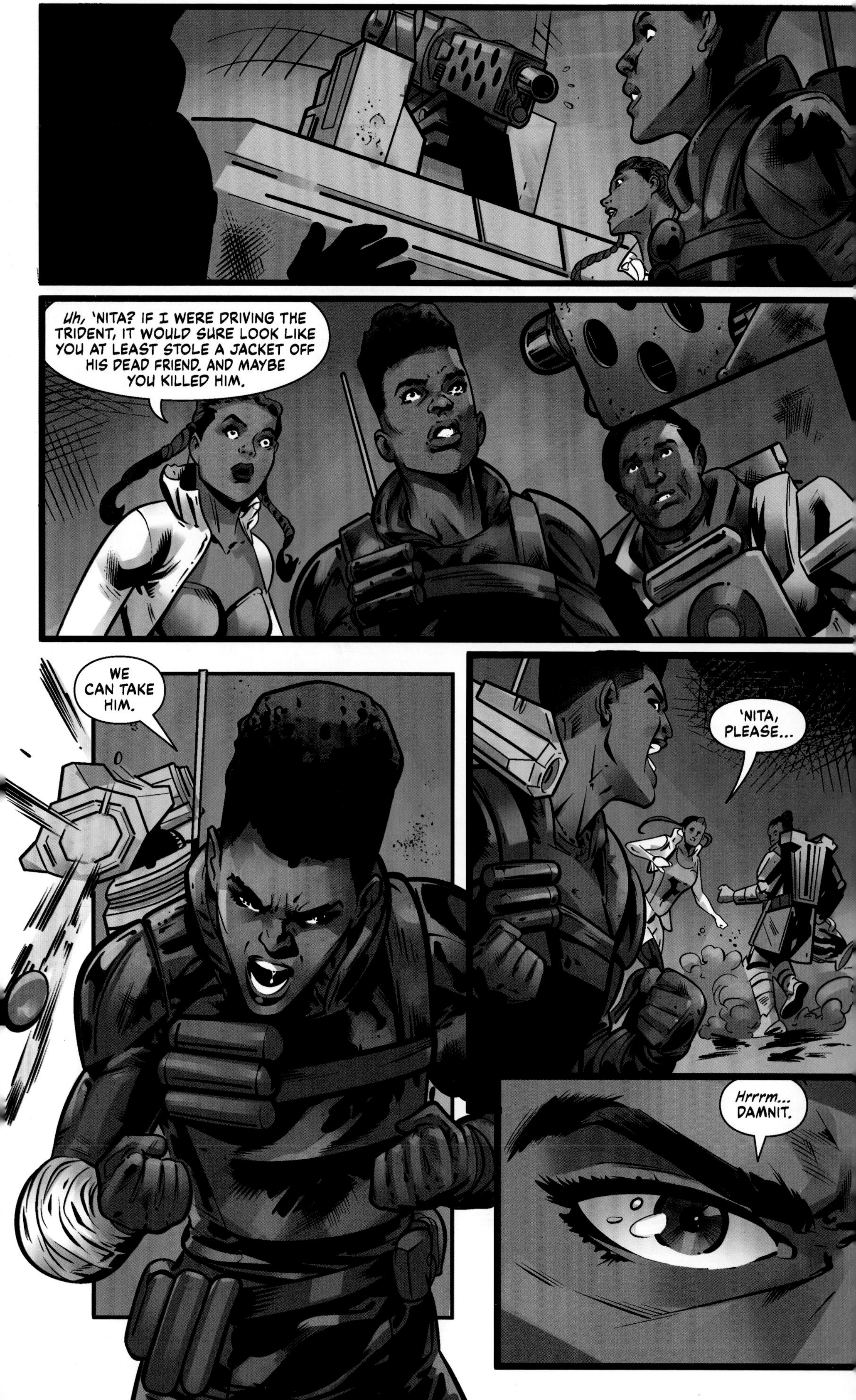
Uh, 'NITA? IF I WERE DRIVING THE TRIDENT, IT WOULD SURE LOOK LIKE YOU AT LEAST STOLE A JACKET OFF HIS DEAD FRIEND. AND MAYBE YOU KILLED HIM.
WE CAN TAKE HIM.
'NITA, PLEASE...
Hrrrm... DAMNIT.

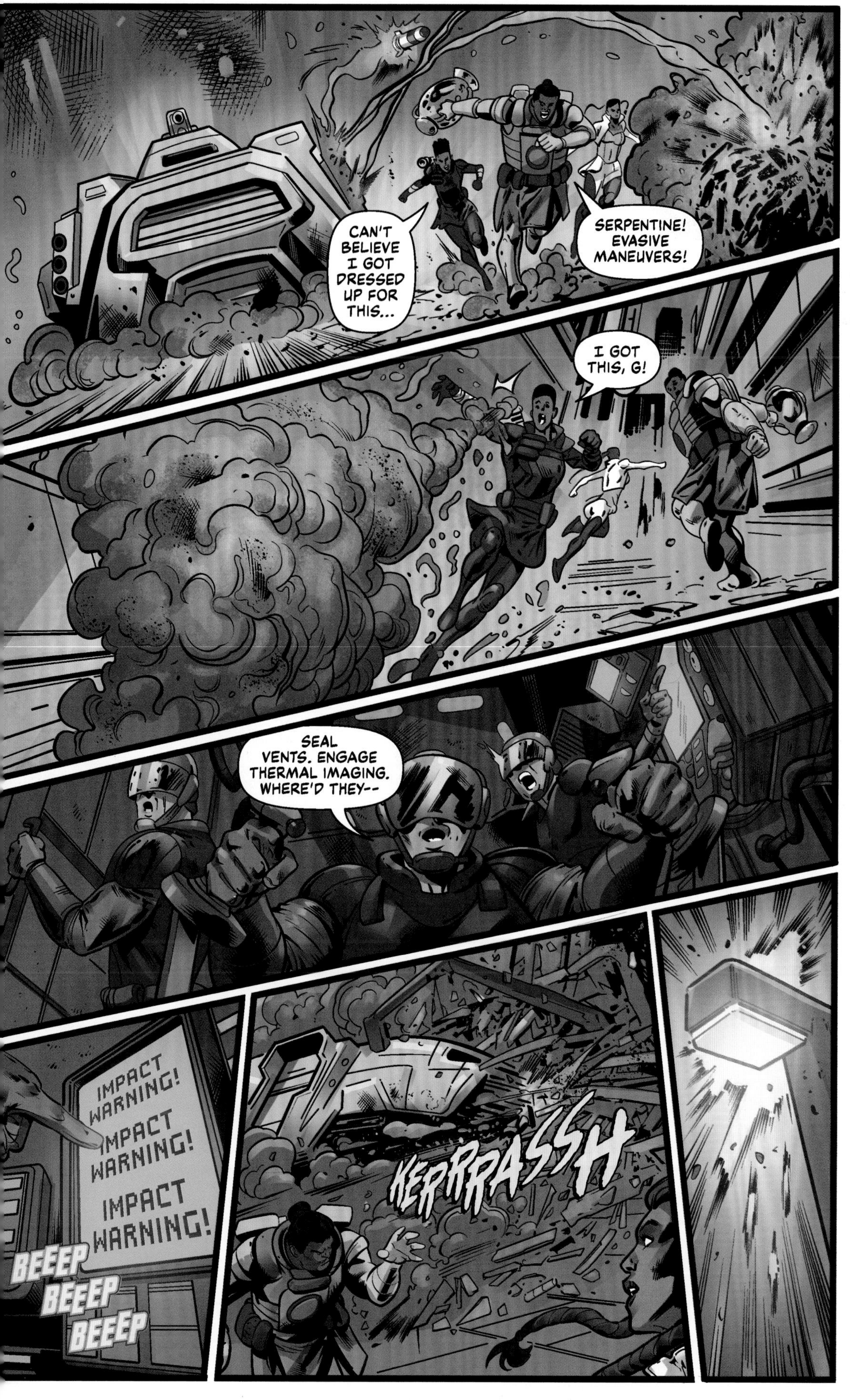
CAN'T BELIEVE I GOT DRESSED UP FOR THIS...
SERPENTINE! EVASIVE MANEUVERS!
I GOT THIS, G!
SEAL VENTS. ENGAGE THERMAL IMAGING. WHERE'D THEY--
IMPACT WARNING! IMPACT WARNING! IMPACT WARNING!
BEEEP BEEEP BEEEP
KERRRASSH

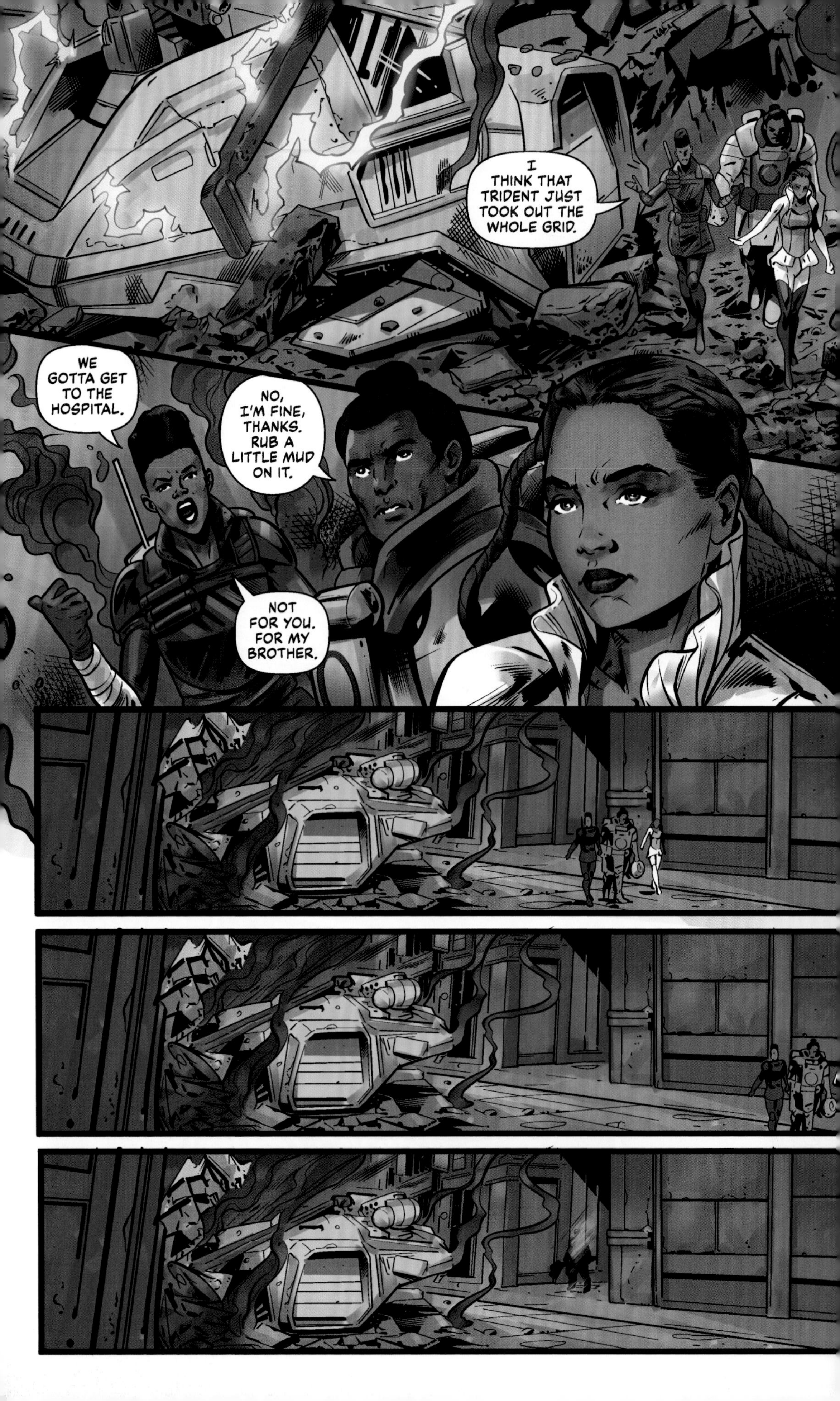
I THINK THAT TRIDENT JUST TOOK OUT THE WHOLE GRID.
WE GOTTA GET TO THE HOSPITAL.
NO, I'M FINE, THANKS. RUB A LITTLE MUD ON IT.
NOT FOR YOU. FOR MY BROTHER.

LOOK AT THIS. LEGENDS COMING THROUGH.

YOU LOOK LIKE YOU'RE HIDING.

YOU LOOK LIKE YOU'RE SEEKING.

OCTANE? WHAT'S HAPPENING HERE?

CHE'S IN THE MIDDLE OF SURGERY, WE'RE IN THE MIDDLE OF A BLACKOUT...

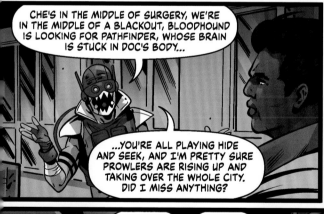

CHE'S IN THE MIDDLE OF SURGERY, WE'RE IN THE MIDDLE OF A BLACKOUT, BLOODHOUND IS LOOKING FOR PATHFINDER, WHOSE BRAIN IS STUCK IN DOC'S BODY...

...YOU'RE ALL PLAYING HIDE AND SEEK, AND I'M PRETTY SURE PROWLERS ARE RISING UP AND TAKING OVER THE WHOLE CITY. DID I MISS ANYTHING?

I HAVE FOUND PATHFINDER'S CHASSIS, BUT I BELIEVE OUR PRESENCE HERE IS ONLY THE BEGINNING...I SENSE DESTRUCTION IN THE WIND.

WOOOOOOOOOOO

WHAT IS THAT WEIRD SOUND?

OH NO, AMIGOS!

CLEAR THE LZ! REPEAT CLEAR THE LZ! DROPSHIP COMING IN HOT.

INCOMING!

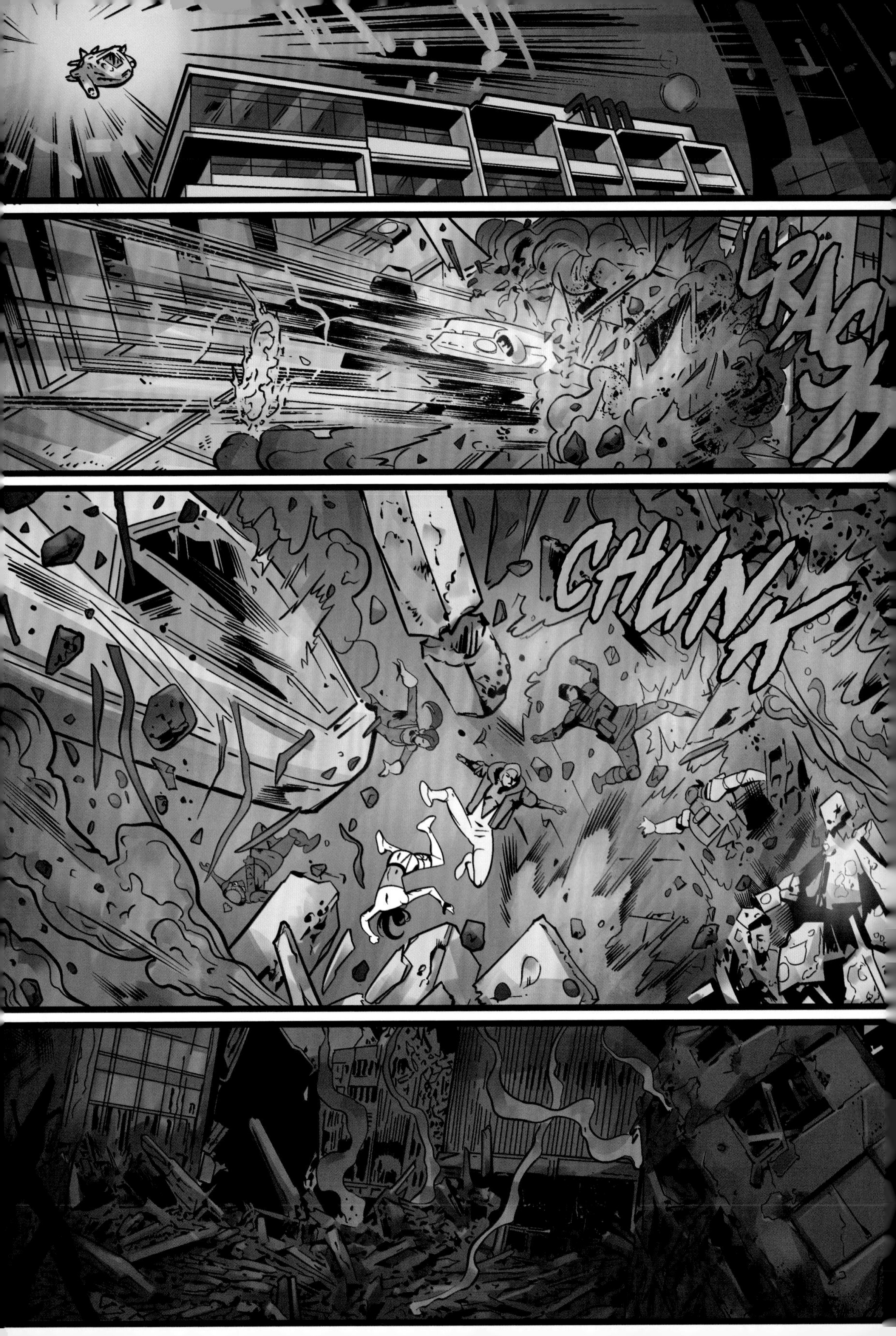
CRACK
CHUNK

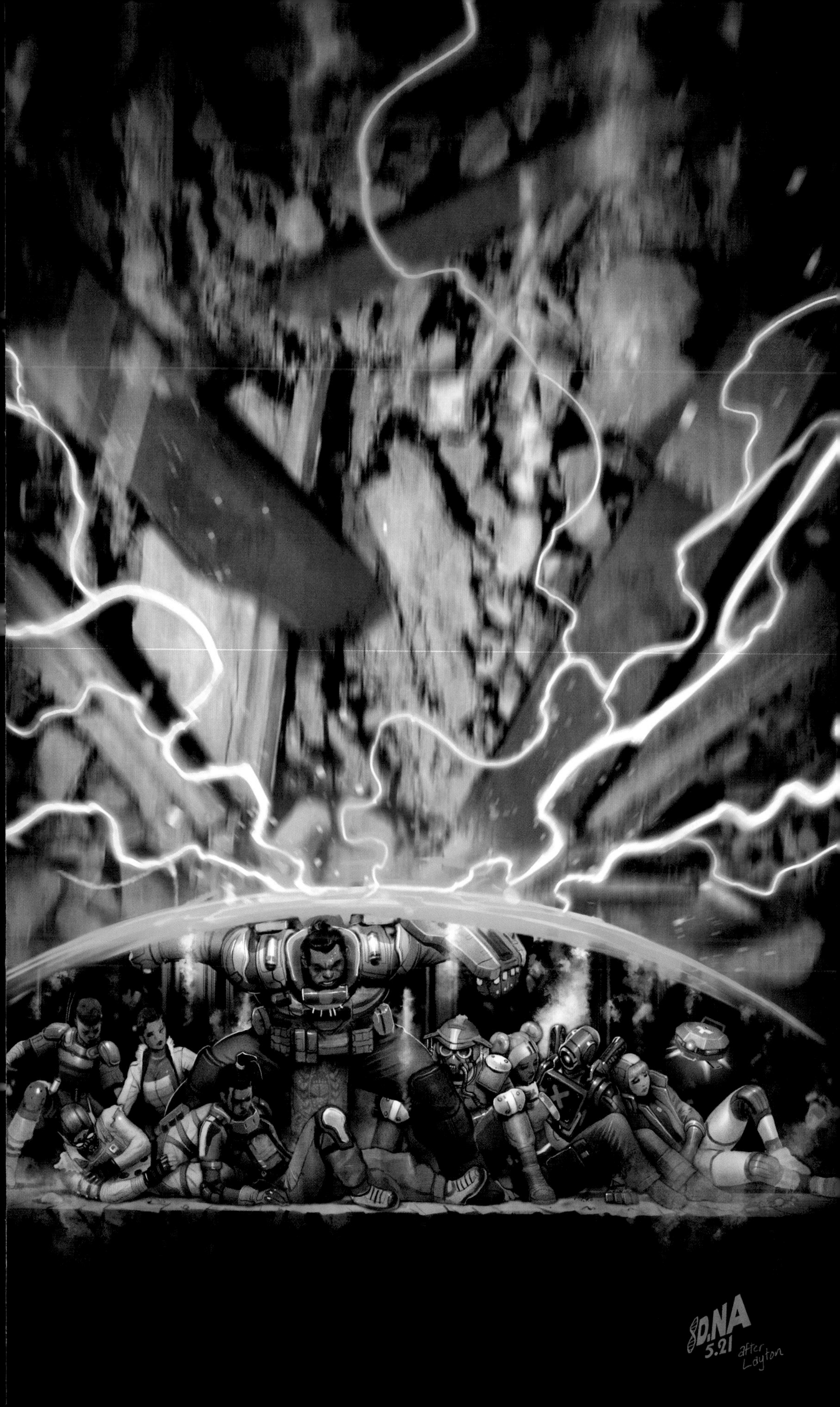
D.NA
5.21
after Layton

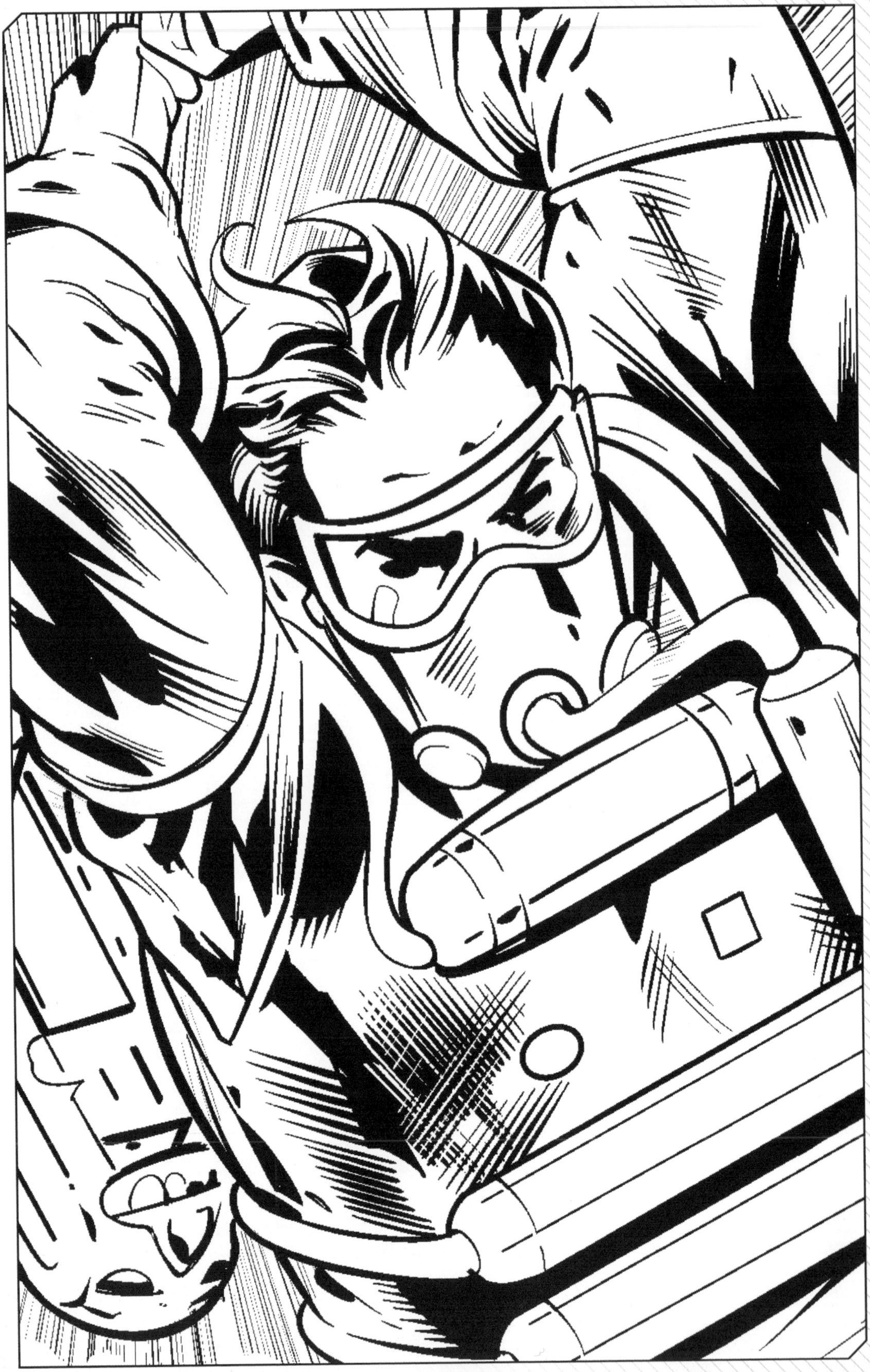

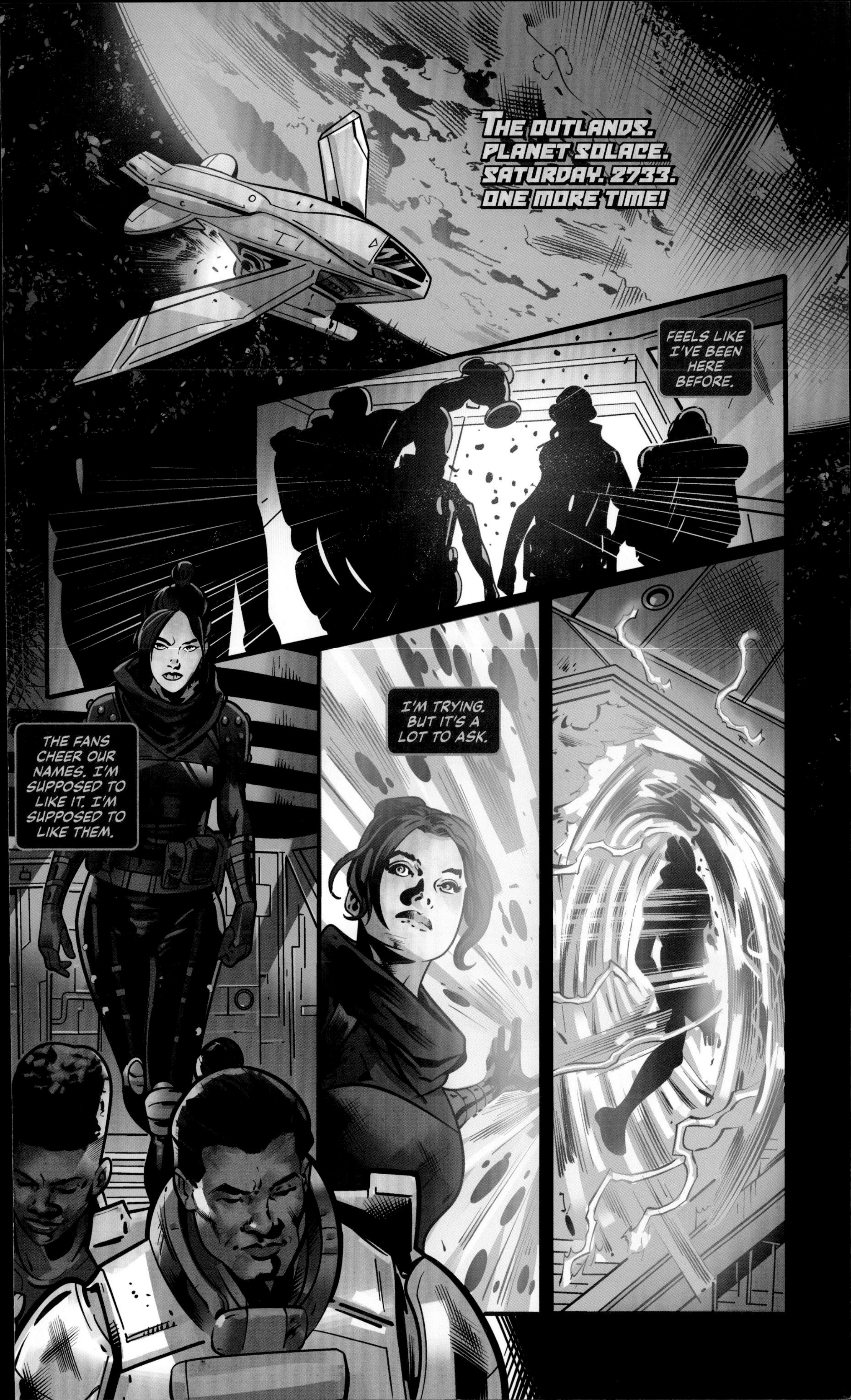
THE OUTLANDS. PLANET SOLACE. SATURDAY. 2733. ONE MORE TIME!
FEELS LIKE I'VE BEEN HERE BEFORE.
THE FANS CHEER OUR NAMES. I'M SUPPOSED TO LIKE IT. I'M SUPPOSED TO LIKE THEM.
I'M TRYING. BUT IT'S A LOT TO ASK.

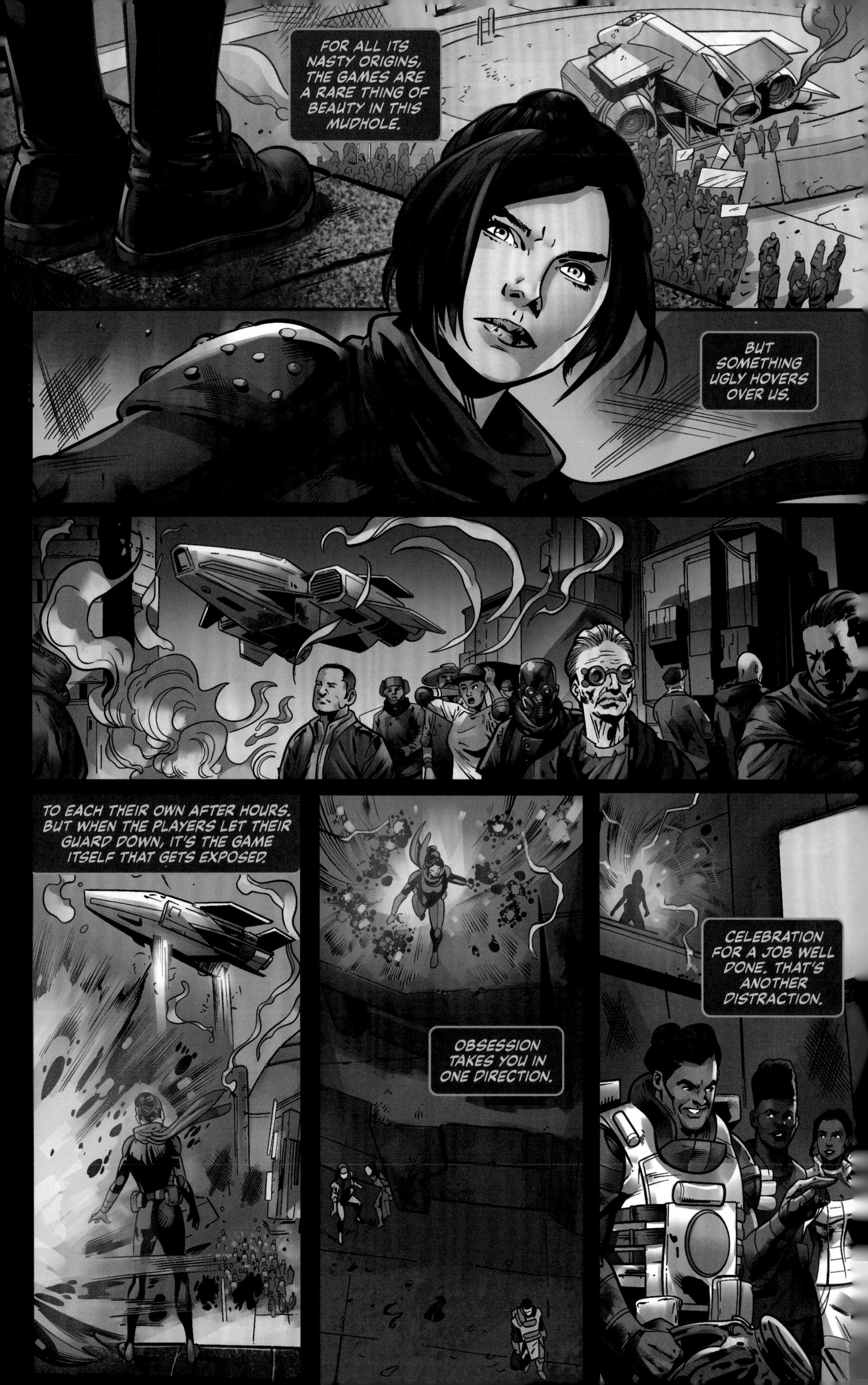
FOR ALL ITS NASTY ORIGINS, THE GAMES ARE A RARE THING OF BEAUTY IN THIS MUDHOLE.
BUT SOMETHING UGLY HOVERS OVER US.
TO EACH THEIR OWN AFTER HOURS. BUT WHEN THE PLAYERS LET THEIR GUARD DOWN, IT'S THE GAME ITSELF THAT GETS EXPOSED.
OBSESSION TAKES YOU IN ONE DIRECTION.
CELEBRATION FOR A JOB WELL DONE. THAT'S ANOTHER DISTRACTION.

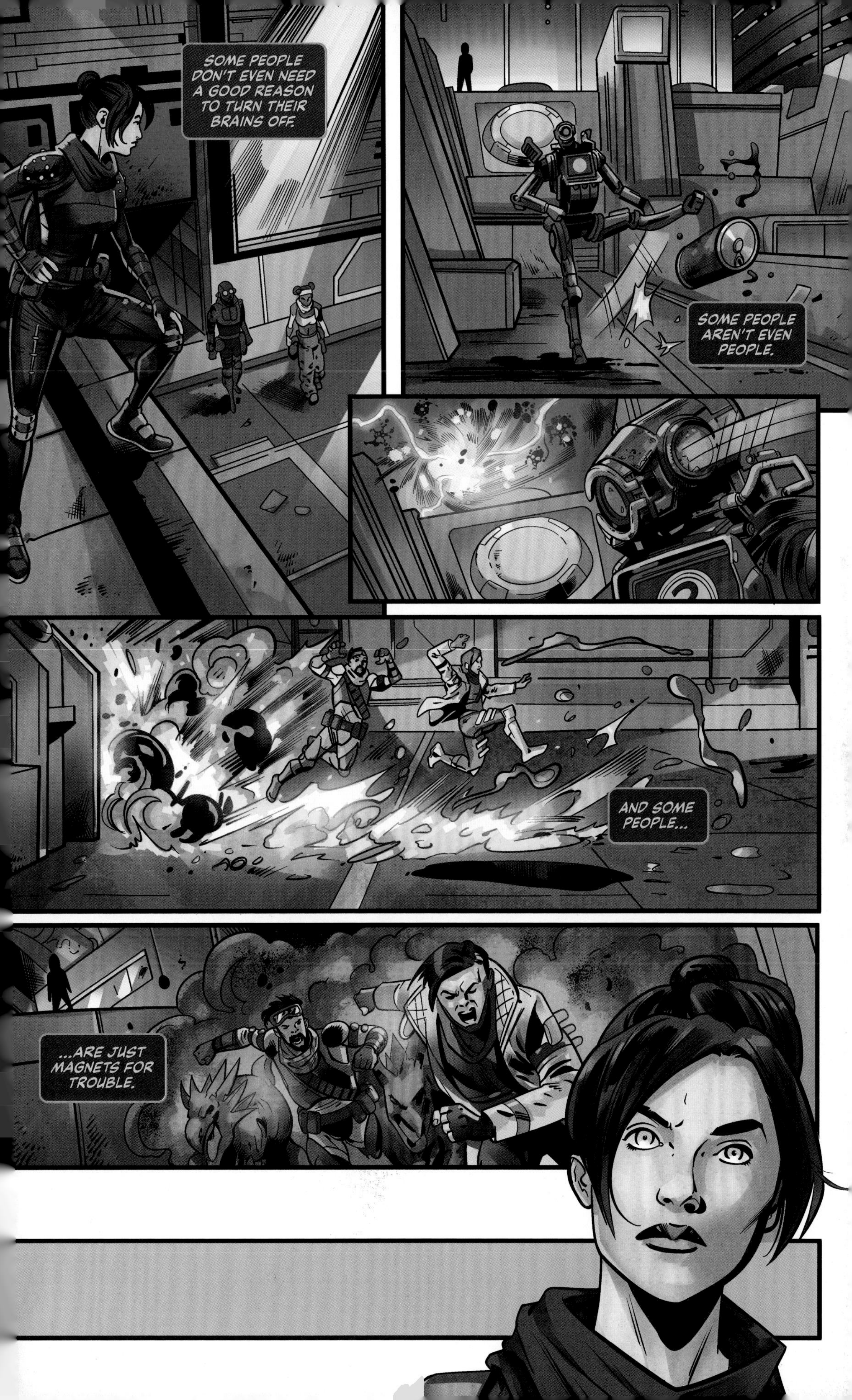
SOME PEOPLE DON'T EVEN NEED A GOOD REASON TO TURN THEIR BRAINS OFF.
SOME PEOPLE AREN'T EVEN PEOPLE.
AND SOME PEOPLE...
...ARE JUST MAGNETS FOR TROUBLE.

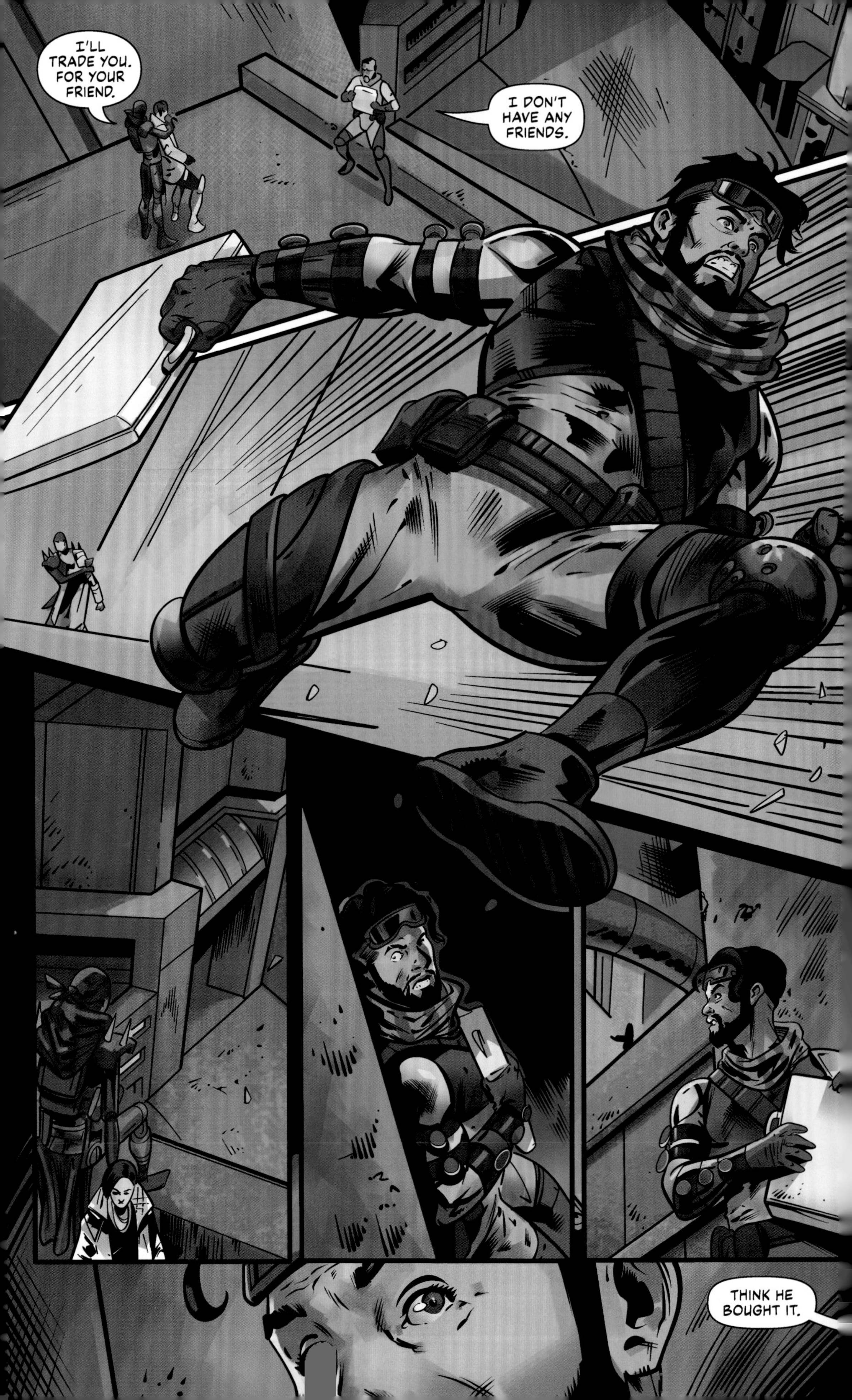
I'LL TRADE YOU. FOR YOUR FRIEND.
I DON'T HAVE ANY FRIENDS.
THINK HE BOUGHT IT.

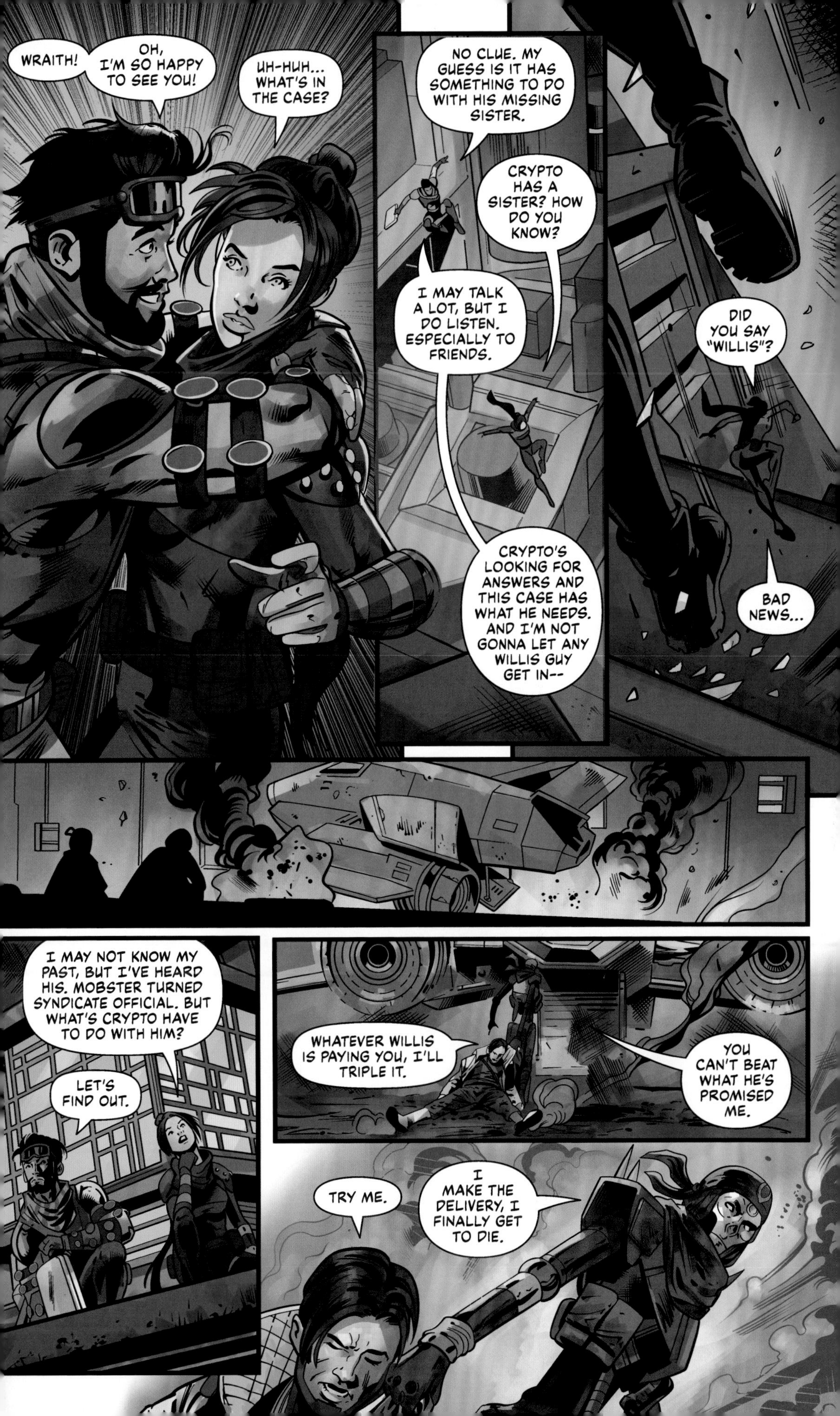
WRAITH!
OH, I'M SO HAPPY TO SEE YOU!
UH-HUH... WHAT'S IN THE CASE?
NO CLUE. MY GUESS IS IT HAS SOMETHING TO DO WITH HIS MISSING SISTER.
CRYPTO HAS A SISTER? HOW DO YOU KNOW?
I MAY TALK A LOT, BUT I DO LISTEN. ESPECIALLY TO FRIENDS.
CRYPTO'S LOOKING FOR ANSWERS AND THIS CASE HAS WHAT HE NEEDS. AND I'M NOT GONNA LET ANY WILLIS GUY GET IN--
DID YOU SAY "WILLIS"?
BAD NEWS...
I MAY NOT KNOW MY PAST, BUT I'VE HEARD HIS. MOBSTER TURNED SYNDICATE OFFICIAL. BUT WHAT'S CRYPTO HAVE TO DO WITH HIM?
LET'S FIND OUT.
WHATEVER WILLIS IS PAYING YOU, I'LL TRIPLE IT.
YOU CAN'T BEAT WHAT HE'S PROMISED ME.
TRY ME.
I MAKE THE DELIVERY, I FINALLY GET TO DIE.

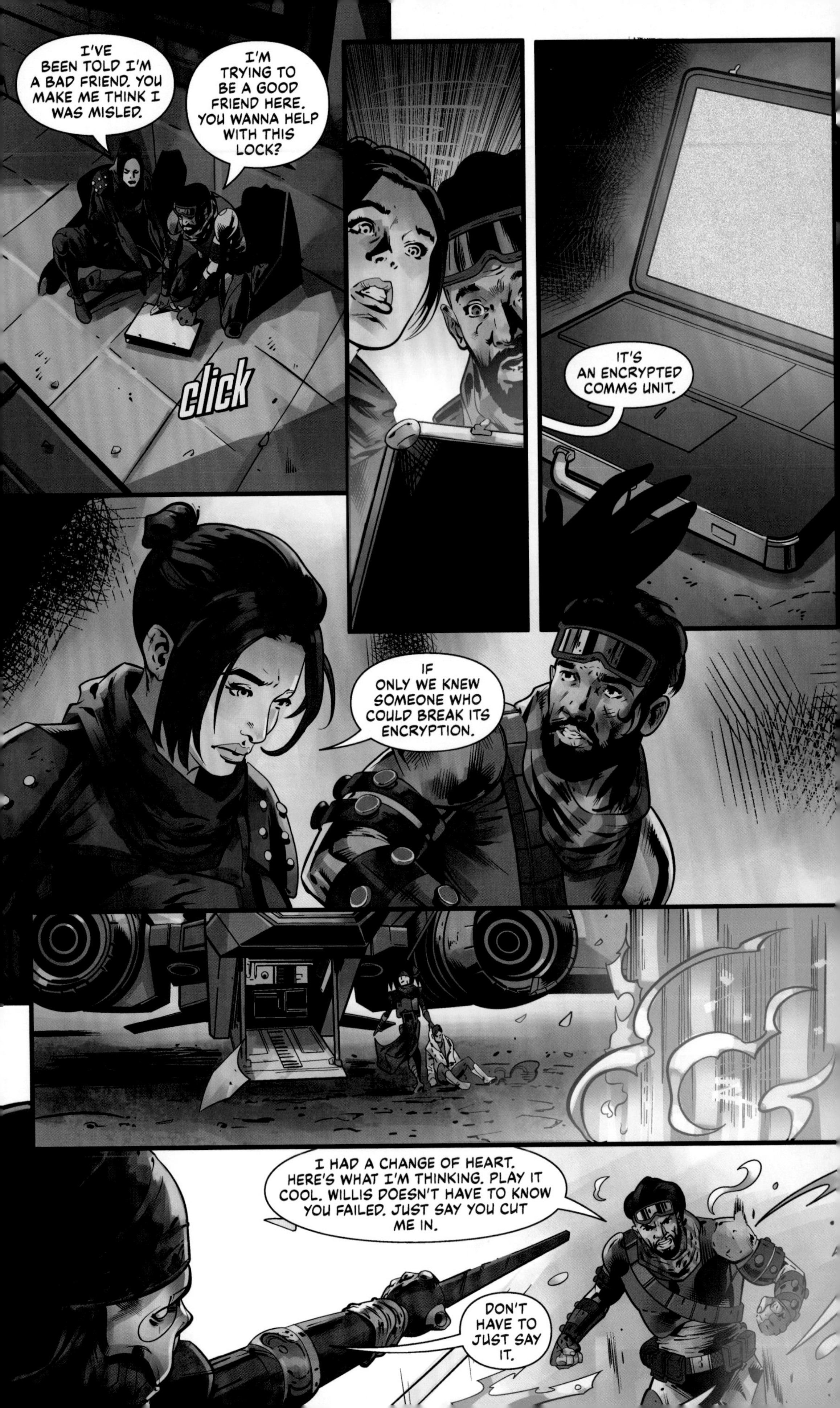

I'VE BEEN TOLD I'M A BAD FRIEND. YOU MAKE ME THINK I WAS MISLED.
I'M TRYING TO BE A GOOD FRIEND HERE. YOU WANNA HELP WITH THIS LOCK?
click
IT'S AN ENCRYPTED COMMS UNIT.
IF ONLY WE KNEW SOMEONE WHO COULD BREAK ITS ENCRYPTION.
I HAD A CHANGE OF HEART. HERE'S WHAT I'M THINKING. PLAY IT COOL. WILLIS DOESN'T HAVE TO KNOW YOU FAILED. JUST SAY YOU CUT ME IN.
DON'T HAVE TO JUST SAY IT.

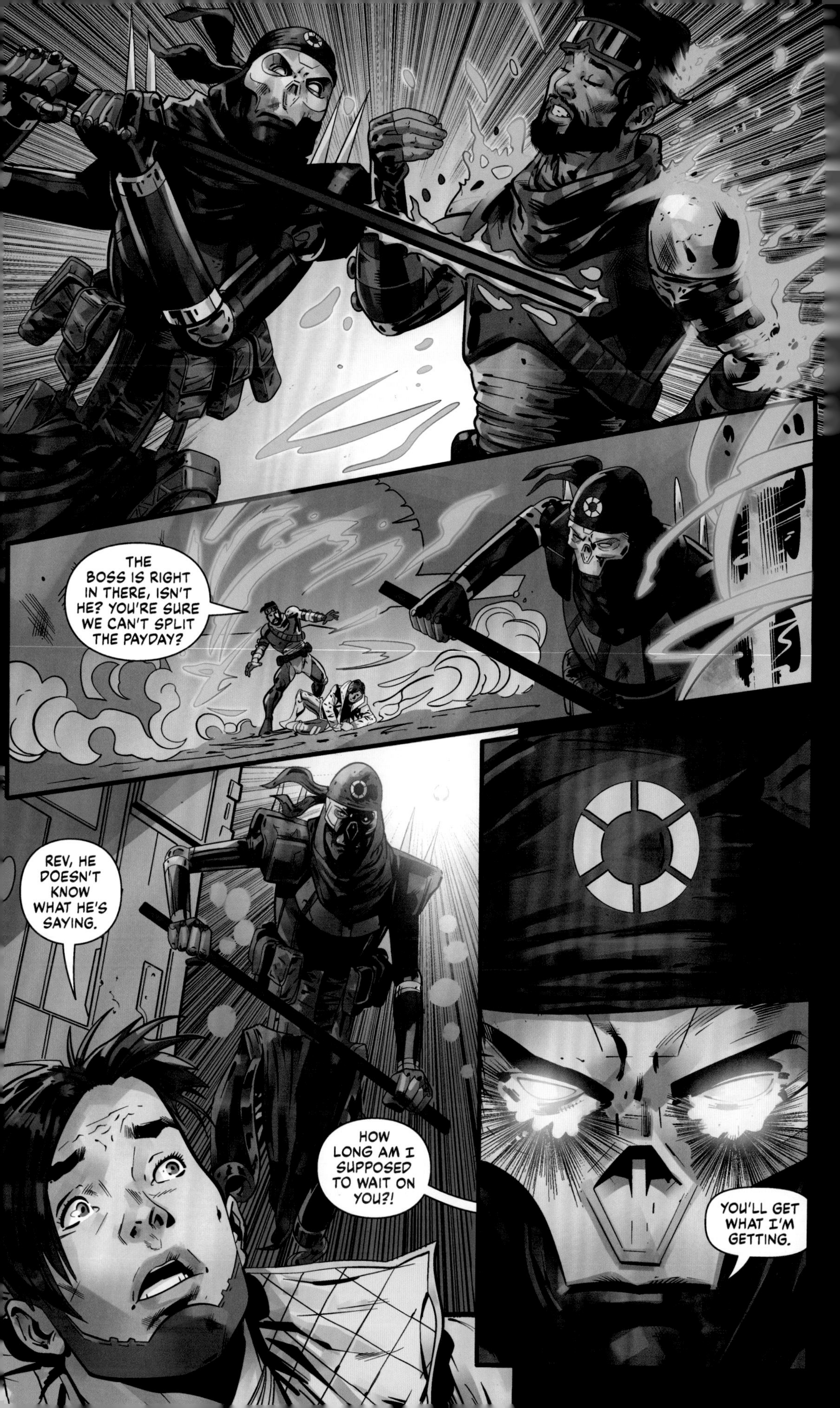
THE BOSS IS RIGHT IN THERE, ISN'T HE? YOU'RE SURE WE CAN'T SPLIT THE PAYDAY?
REV, HE DOESN'T KNOW WHAT HE'S SAYING.
HOW LONG AM I SUPPOSED TO WAIT ON YOU?!
YOU'LL GET WHAT I'M GETTING.

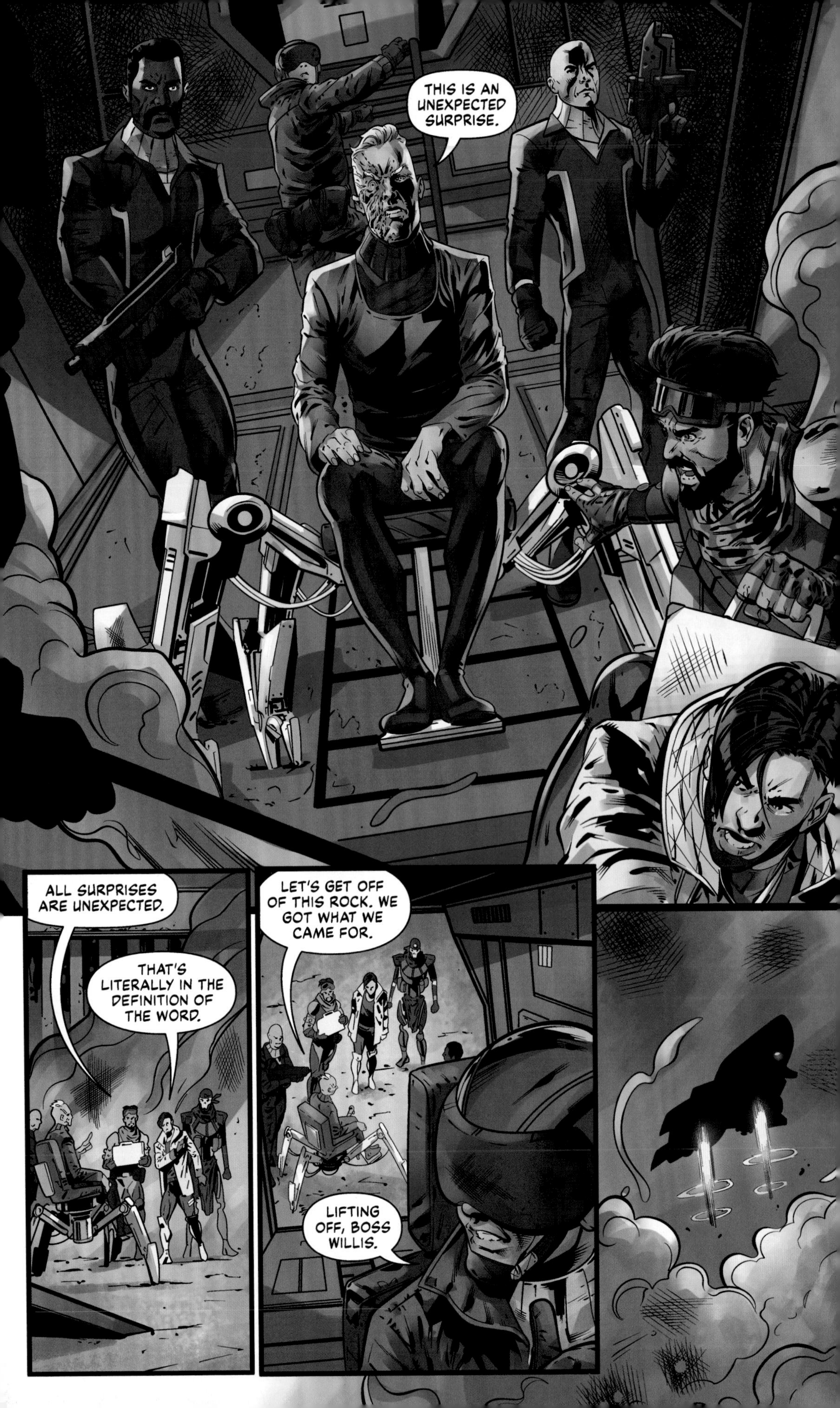
THIS IS AN UNEXPECTED SURPRISE.
ALL SURPRISES ARE UNEXPECTED.
THAT'S LITERALLY IN THE DEFINITION OF THE WORD.
LET'S GET OFF OF THIS ROCK. WE GOT WHAT WE CAME FOR.
LIFTING OFF, BOSS WILLIS.

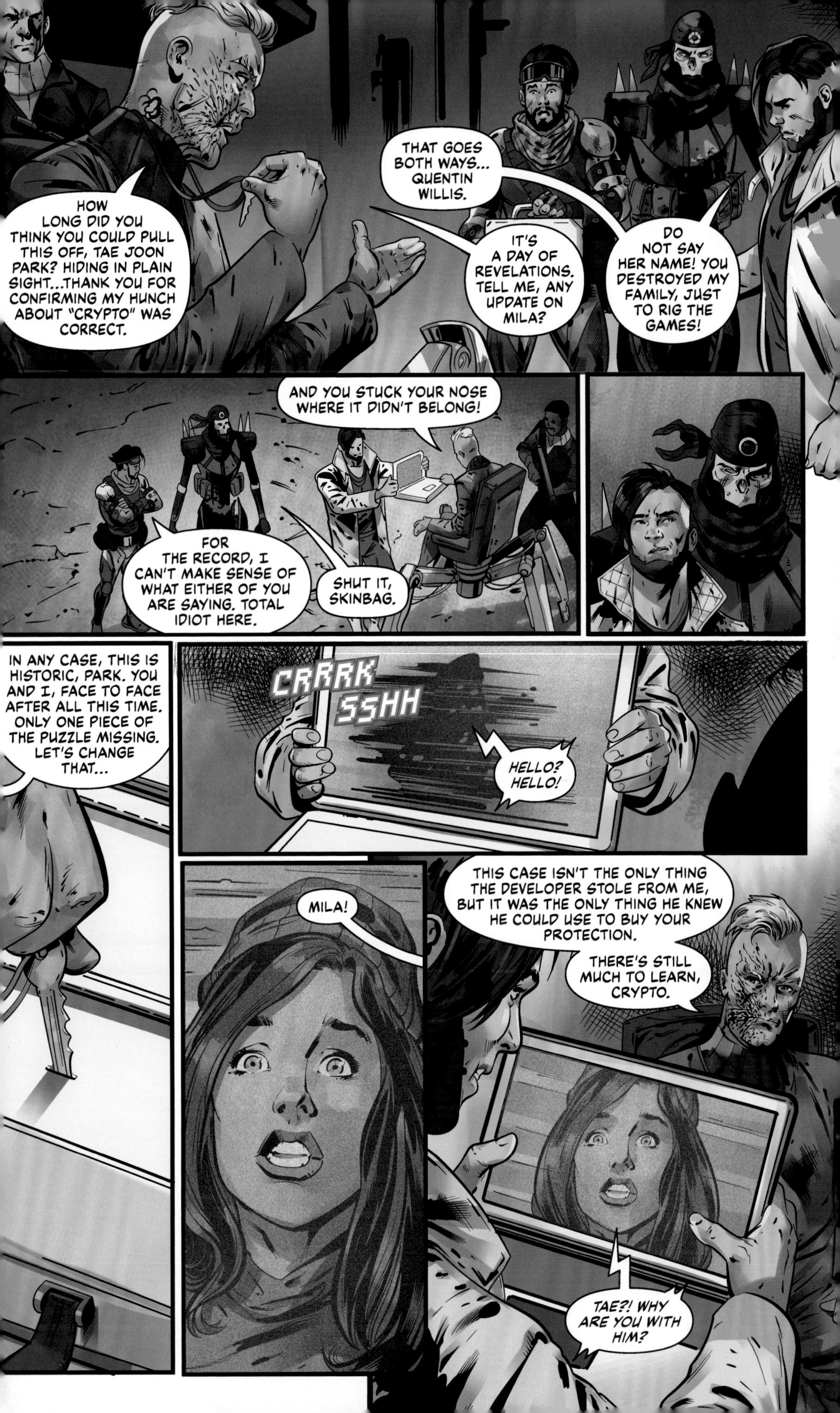
HOW LONG DID YOU THINK YOU COULD PULL THIS OFF, TAE JOON PARK? HIDING IN PLAIN SIGHT...THANK YOU FOR CONFIRMING MY HUNCH ABOUT "CRYPTO" WAS CORRECT.
THAT GOES BOTH WAYS... QUENTIN WILLIS.
IT'S A DAY OF REVELATIONS. TELL ME, ANY UPDATE ON MILA?
DO NOT SAY HER NAME! YOU DESTROYED MY FAMILY, JUST TO RIG THE GAMES!
AND YOU STUCK YOUR NOSE WHERE IT DIDN'T BELONG!
FOR THE RECORD, I CAN'T MAKE SENSE OF WHAT EITHER OF YOU ARE SAYING. TOTAL IDIOT HERE.
SHUT IT, SKINBAG.
IN ANY CASE, THIS IS HISTORIC, PARK. YOU AND I, FACE TO FACE AFTER ALL THIS TIME. ONLY ONE PIECE OF THE PUZZLE MISSING. LET'S CHANGE THAT...
CRRRK SSHH
HELLO? HELLO!
MILA!
THIS CASE ISN'T THE ONLY THING THE DEVELOPER STOLE FROM ME, BUT IT WAS THE ONLY THING HE KNEW HE COULD USE TO BUY YOUR PROTECTION.
THERE'S STILL MUCH TO LEARN, CRYPTO.
TAE?! WHY ARE YOU WITH HIM?

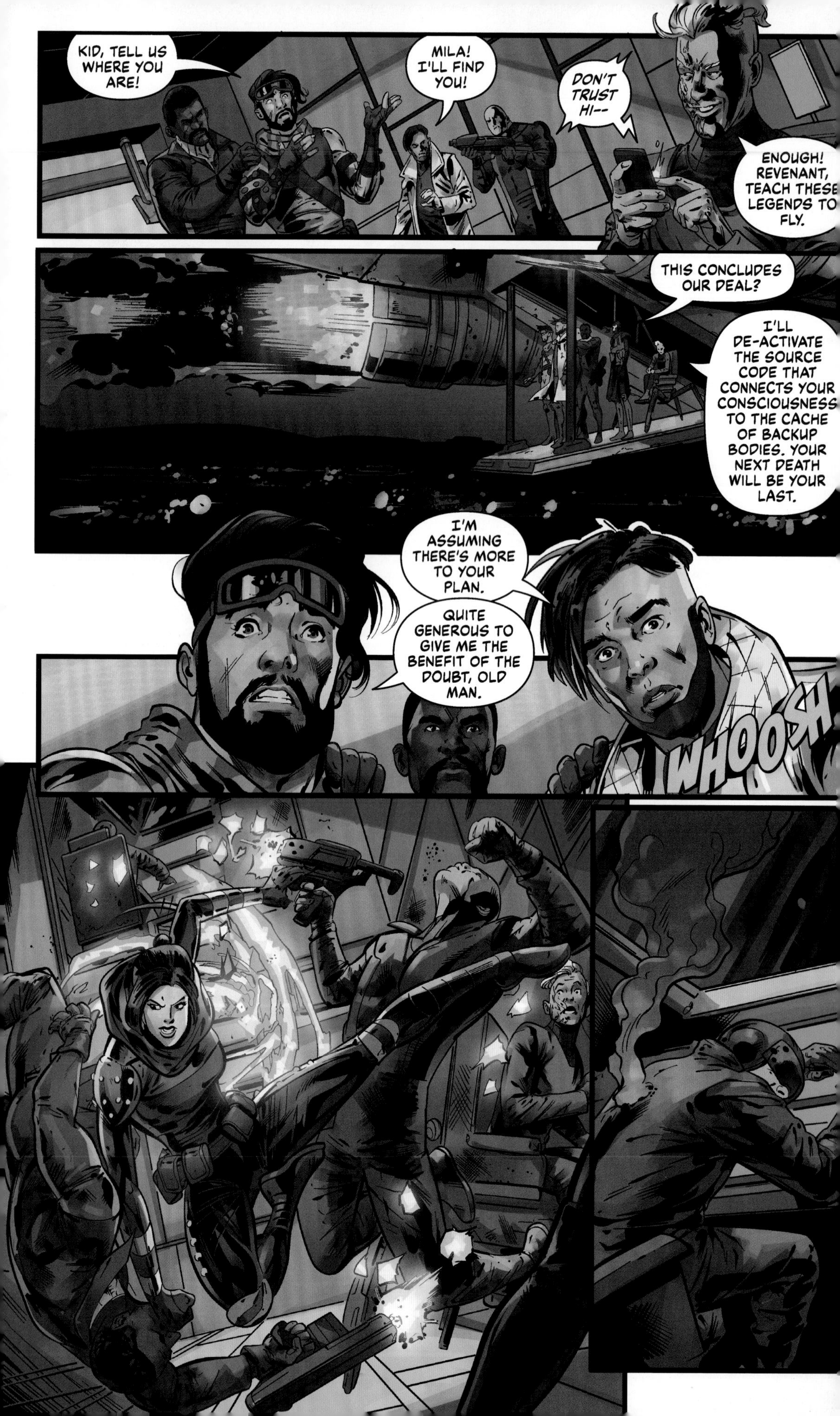
KID, TELL US WHERE YOU ARE!
MILA! I'LL FIND YOU!
DON'T TRUST HI--
ENOUGH! REVENANT, TEACH THESE LEGENDS TO FLY.
THIS CONCLUDES OUR DEAL?
I'LL DE-ACTIVATE THE SOURCE CODE THAT CONNECTS YOUR CONSCIOUSNESS TO THE CACHE OF BACKUP BODIES. YOUR NEXT DEATH WILL BE YOUR LAST.
I'M ASSUMING THERE'S MORE TO YOUR PLAN.
QUITE GENEROUS TO GIVE ME THE BENEFIT OF THE DOUBT, OLD MAN.
WHOOSH

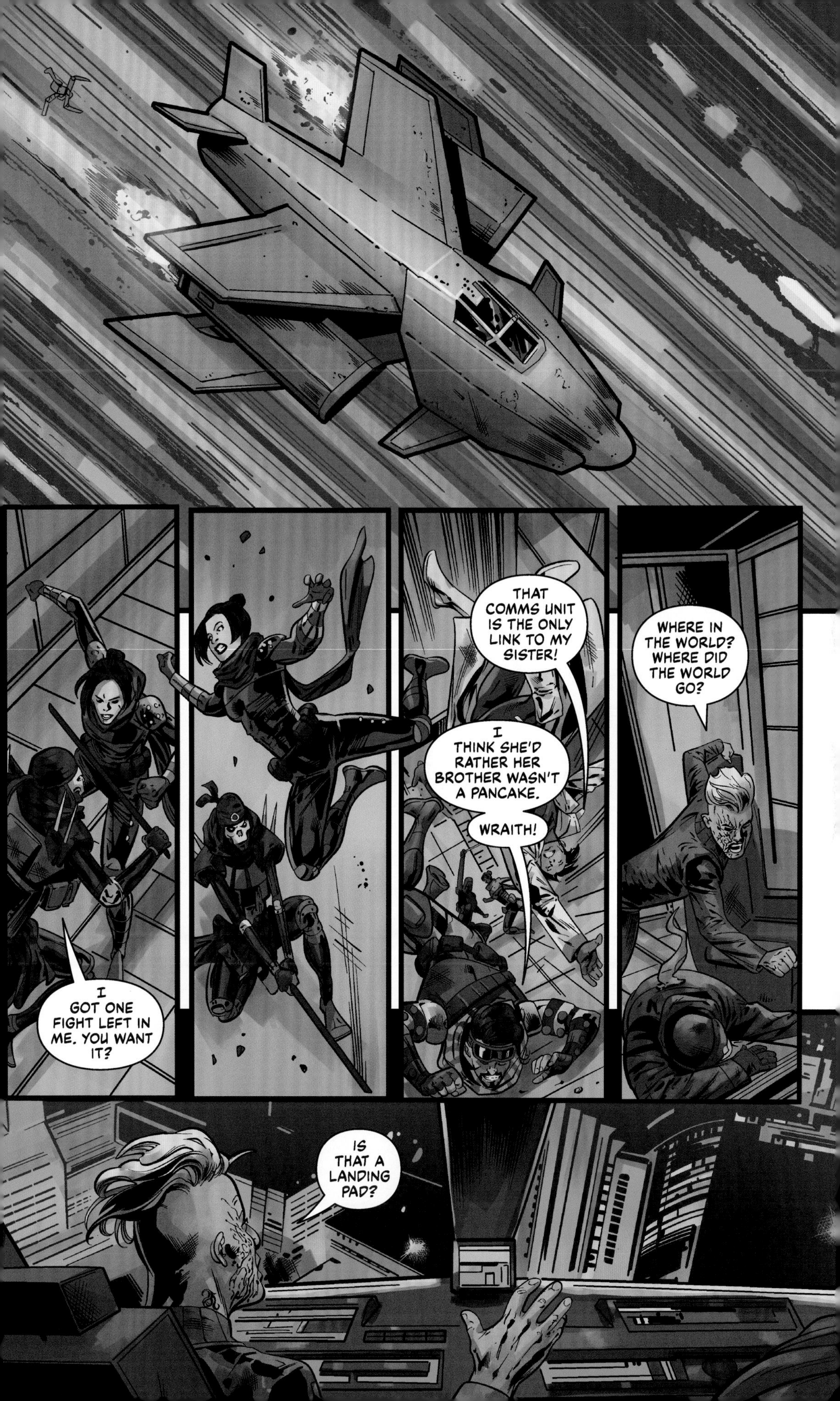
I GOT ONE FIGHT LEFT IN ME. YOU WANT IT?
THAT COMMS UNIT IS THE ONLY LINK TO MY SISTER!
I THINK SHE'D RATHER HER BROTHER WASN'T A PANCAKE.
WRAITH!
WHERE IN THE WORLD? WHERE DID THE WORLD GO?
IS THAT A LANDING PAD?

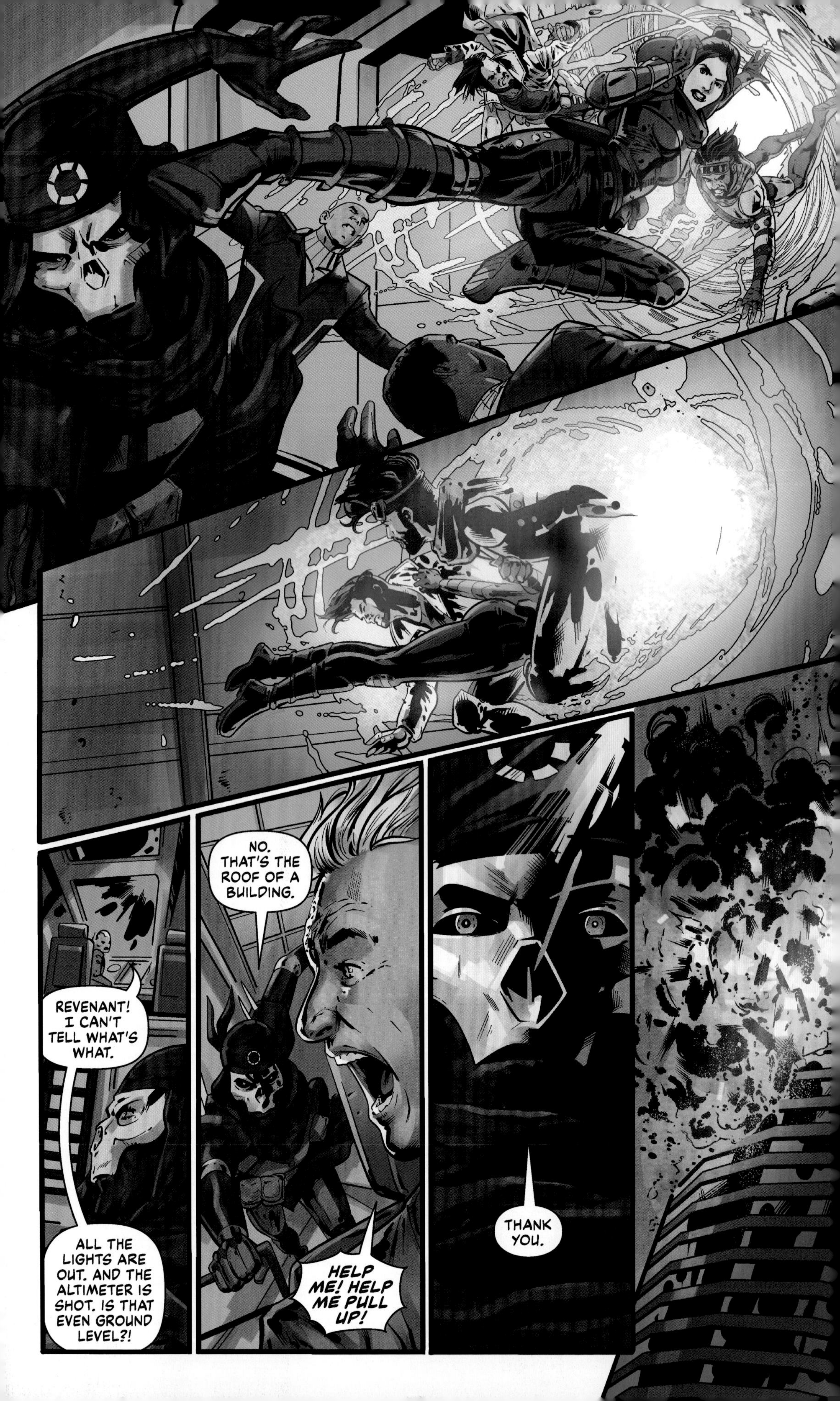
REVENANT! I CAN'T TELL WHAT'S WHAT.
ALL THE LIGHTS ARE OUT. AND THE ALTIMETER IS SHOT. IS THAT EVEN GROUND LEVEL?!
NO. THAT'S THE ROOF OF A BUILDING.
HELP ME! HELP ME PULL UP!
THANK YOU.

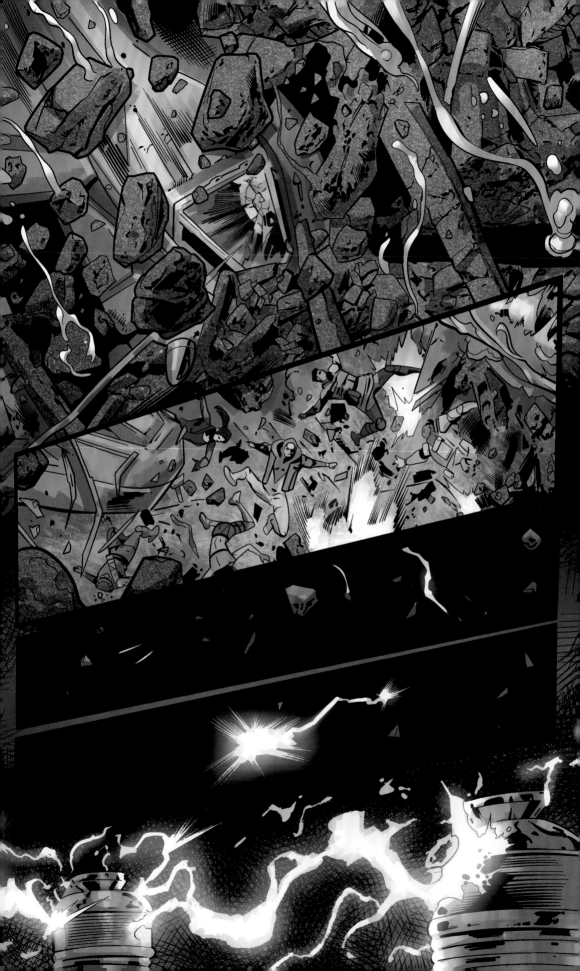

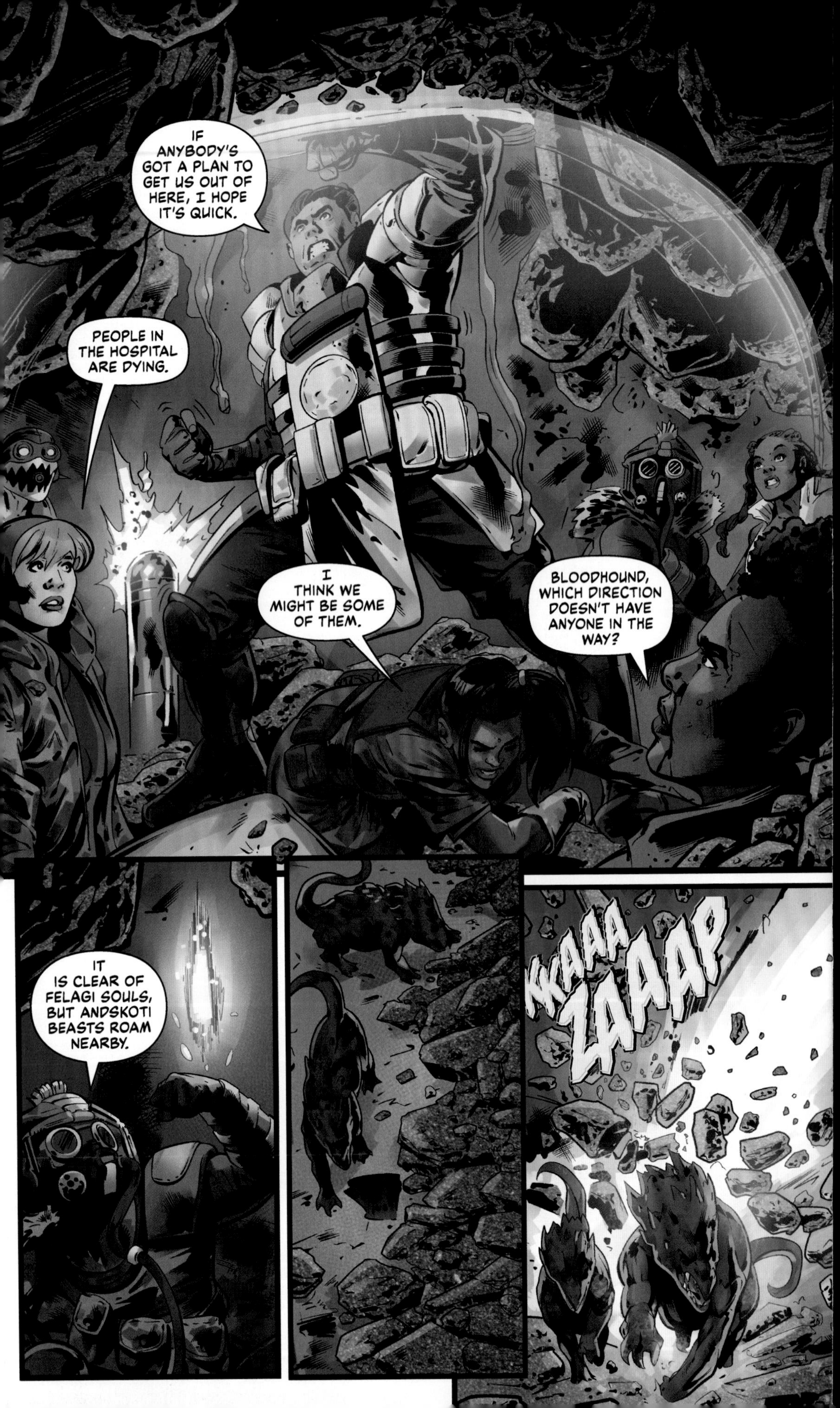
IF ANYBODY'S GOT A PLAN TO GET US OUT OF HERE, I HOPE IT'S QUICK.
PEOPLE IN THE HOSPITAL ARE DYING.
I THINK WE MIGHT BE SOME OF THEM.
BLOODHOUND, WHICH DIRECTION DOESN'T HAVE ANYONE IN THE WAY?
IT IS CLEAR OF FELAGI SOULS, BUT ANDSKOTI BEASTS ROAM NEARBY.
KKAAAA ZAAAAP

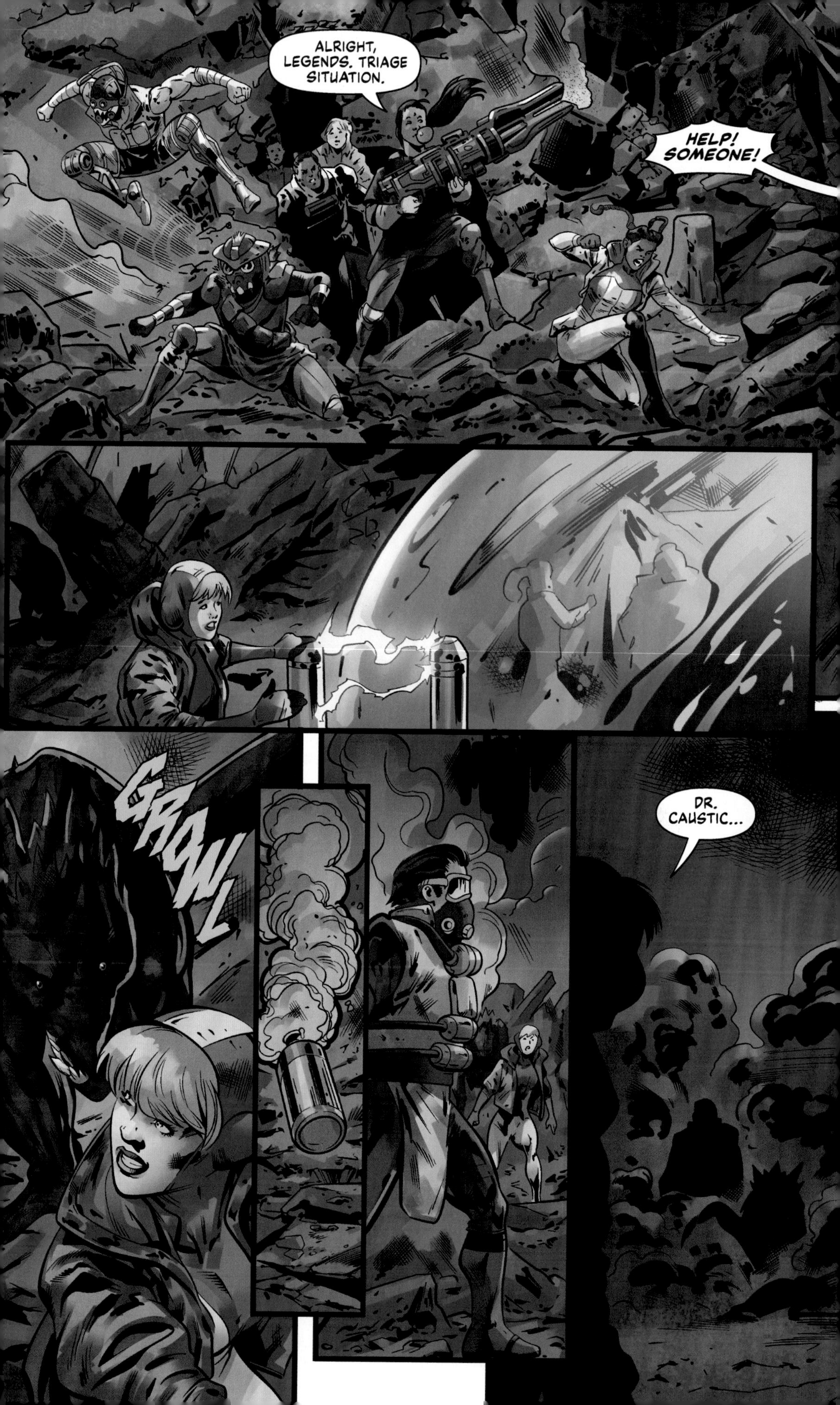
ALRIGHT, LEGENDS. TRIAGE SITUATION.
HELP! SOMEONE!
GROWL
DR. CAUSTIC...

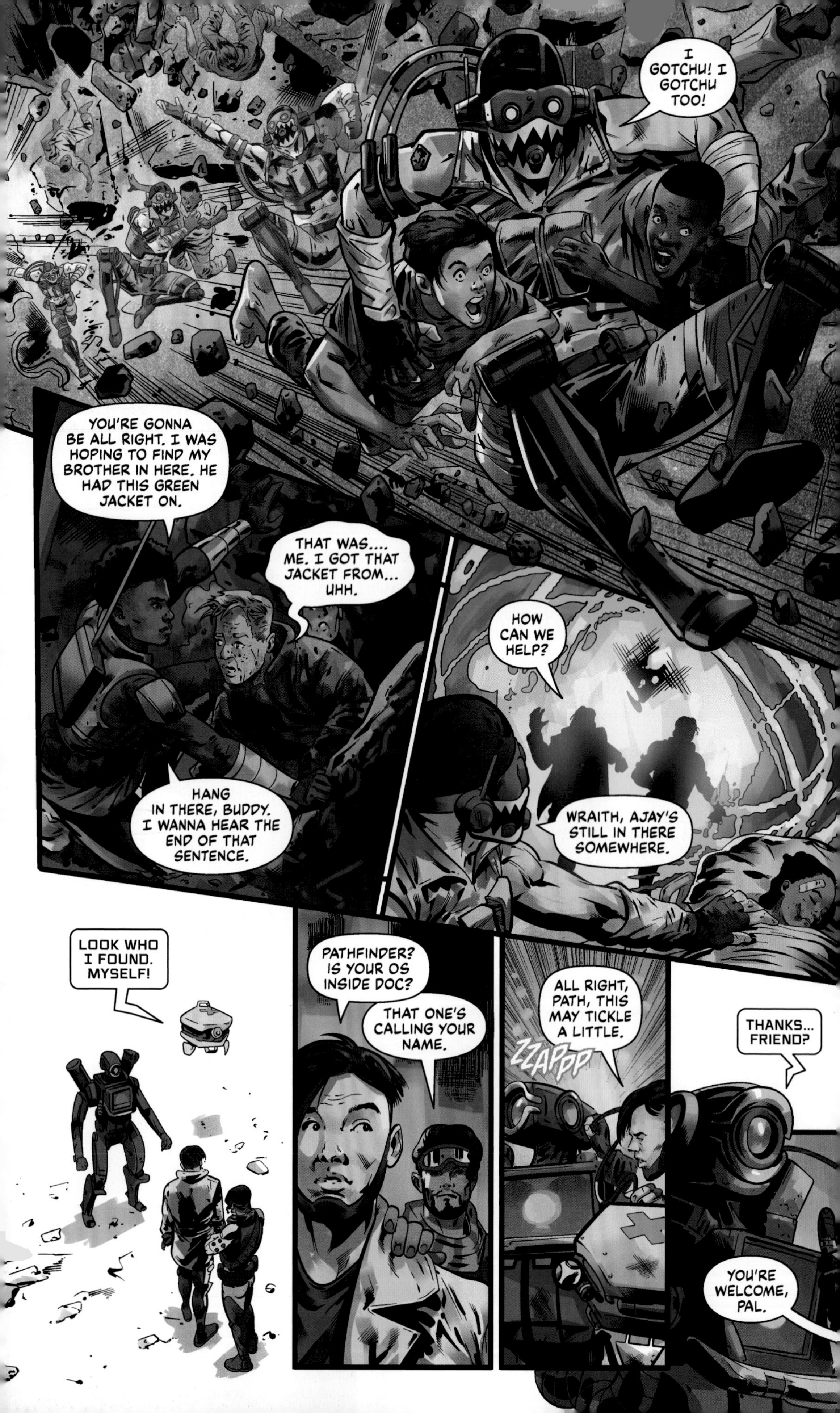
I GOTCHU! I GOTCHU TOO!
YOU'RE GONNA BE ALL RIGHT. I WAS HOPING TO FIND MY BROTHER IN HERE. HE HAD THIS GREEN JACKET ON.
THAT WAS.... ME. I GOT THAT JACKET FROM... UHH.
HANG IN THERE, BUDDY. I WANNA HEAR THE END OF THAT SENTENCE.
HOW CAN WE HELP?
WRAITH, AJAY'S STILL IN THERE SOMEWHERE.
LOOK WHO I FOUND. MYSELF!
PATHFINDER? IS YOUR OS INSIDE DOC?
THAT ONE'S CALLING YOUR NAME.
ALL RIGHT, PATH, THIS MAY TICKLE A LITTLE.
ZZAPPP
THANKS... FRIEND?
YOU'RE WELCOME, PAL.

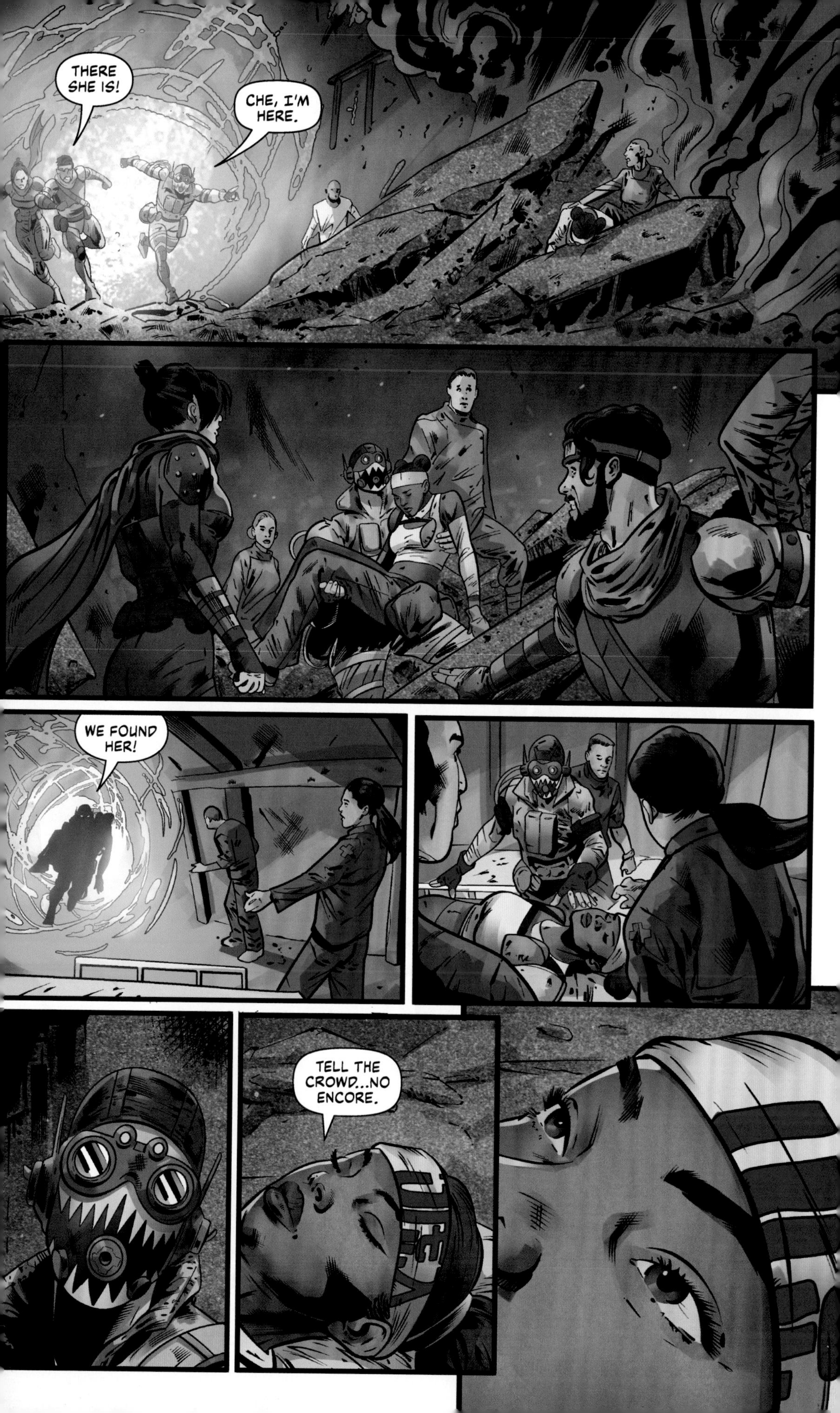
THERE SHE IS!
CHE, I'M HERE.
WE FOUND HER!
TELL THE CROWD...NO ENCORE.

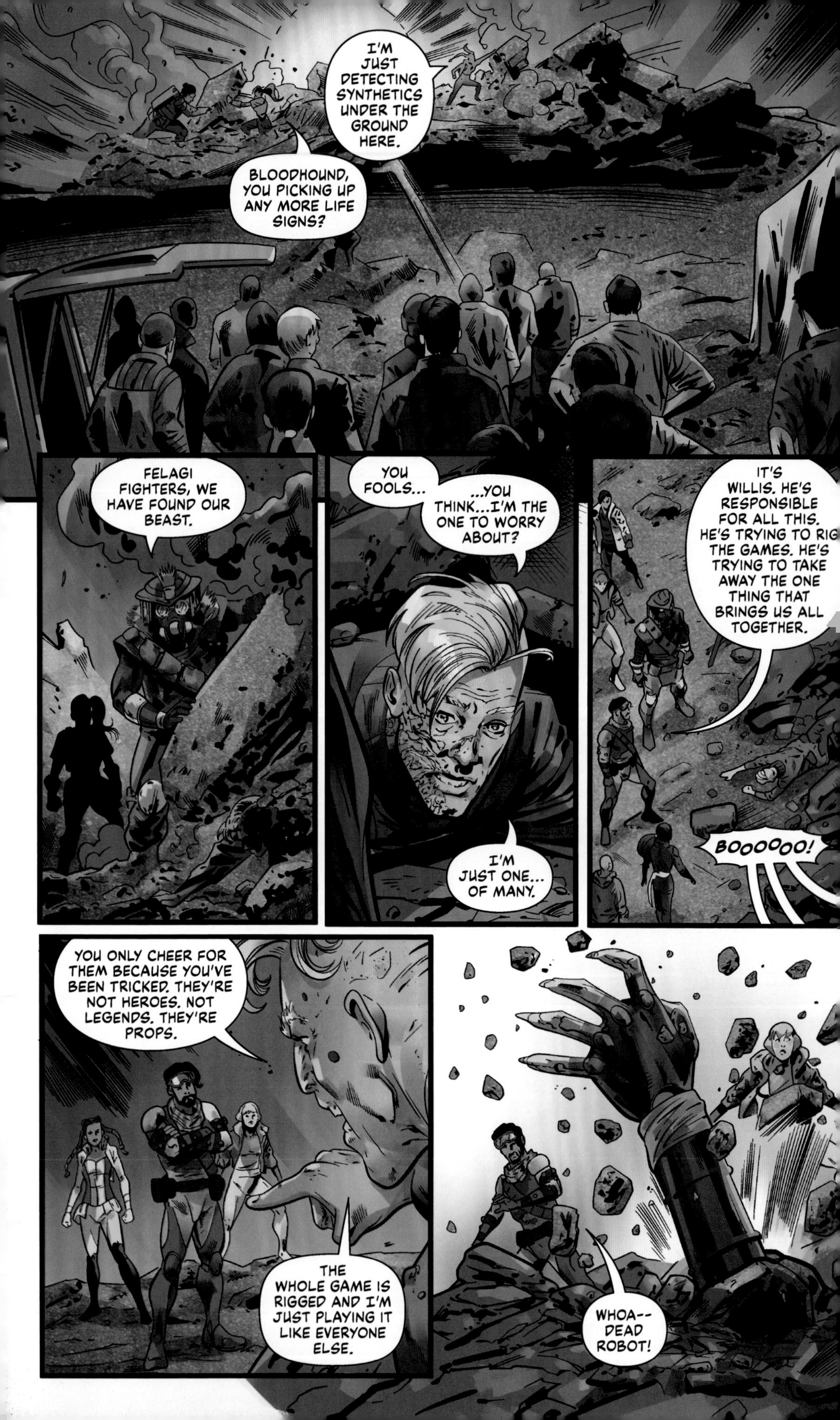
BLOODHOUND, YOU PICKING UP ANY MORE LIFE SIGNS?
I'M JUST DETECTING SYNTHETICS UNDER THE GROUND HERE.
FELAGI FIGHTERS, WE HAVE FOUND OUR BEAST.
YOU FOOLS...
...YOU THINK...I'M THE ONE TO WORRY ABOUT?
I'M JUST ONE... OF MANY.
IT'S WILLIS. HE'S RESPONSIBLE FOR ALL THIS. HE'S TRYING TO RIG THE GAMES. HE'S TRYING TO TAKE AWAY THE ONE THING THAT BRINGS US ALL TOGETHER.
BOOOOOO!
YOU ONLY CHEER FOR THEM BECAUSE YOU'VE BEEN TRICKED. THEY'RE NOT HEROES. NOT LEGENDS. THEY'RE PROPS.
THE WHOLE GAME IS RIGGED AND I'M JUST PLAYING IT LIKE EVERYONE ELSE.
WHOA-- DEAD ROBOT!

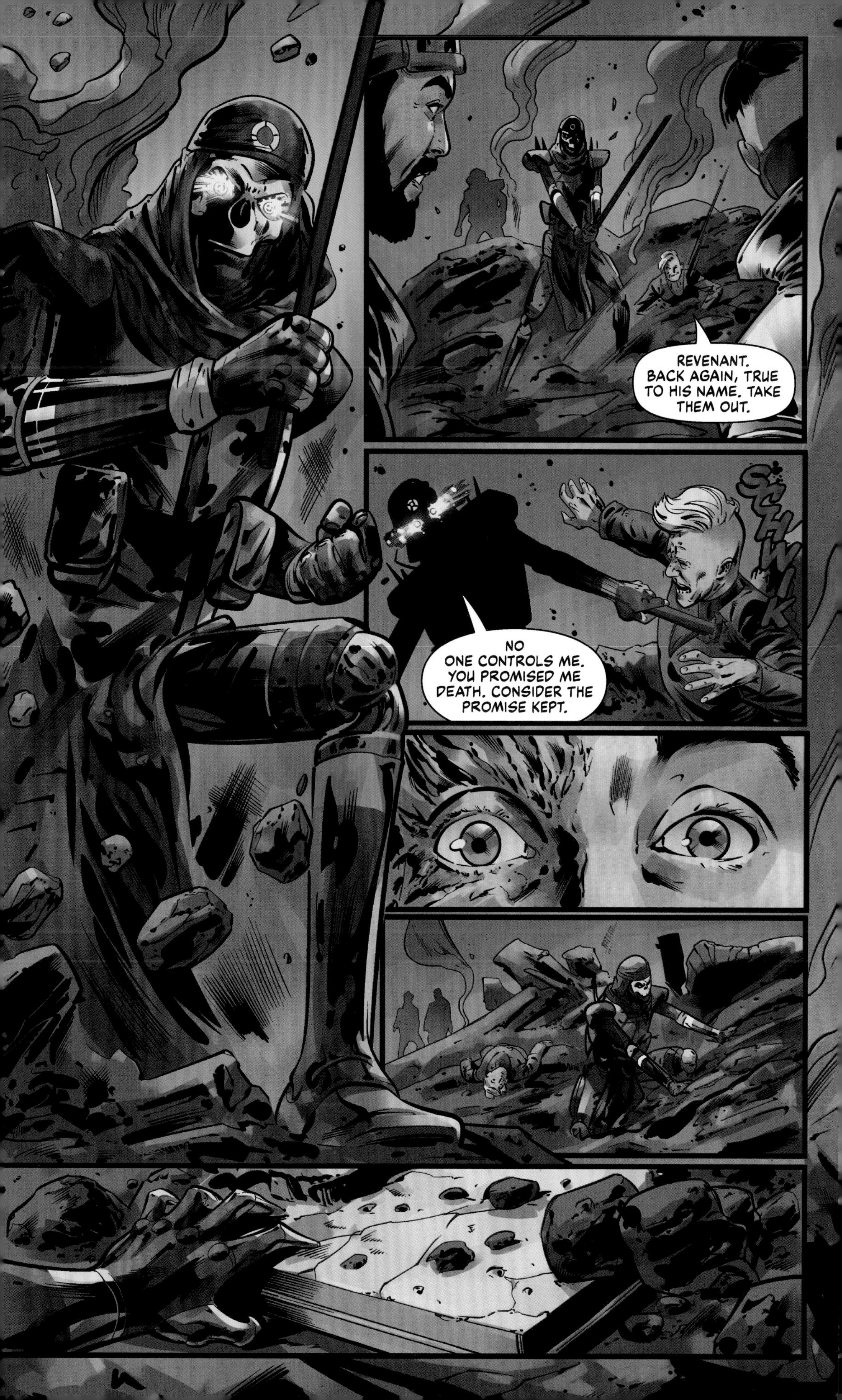
REVENANT. BACK AGAIN, TRUE TO HIS NAME. TAKE THEM OUT.
SCHWIK
NO ONE CONTROLS ME. YOU PROMISED ME DEATH. CONSIDER THE PROMISE KEPT.

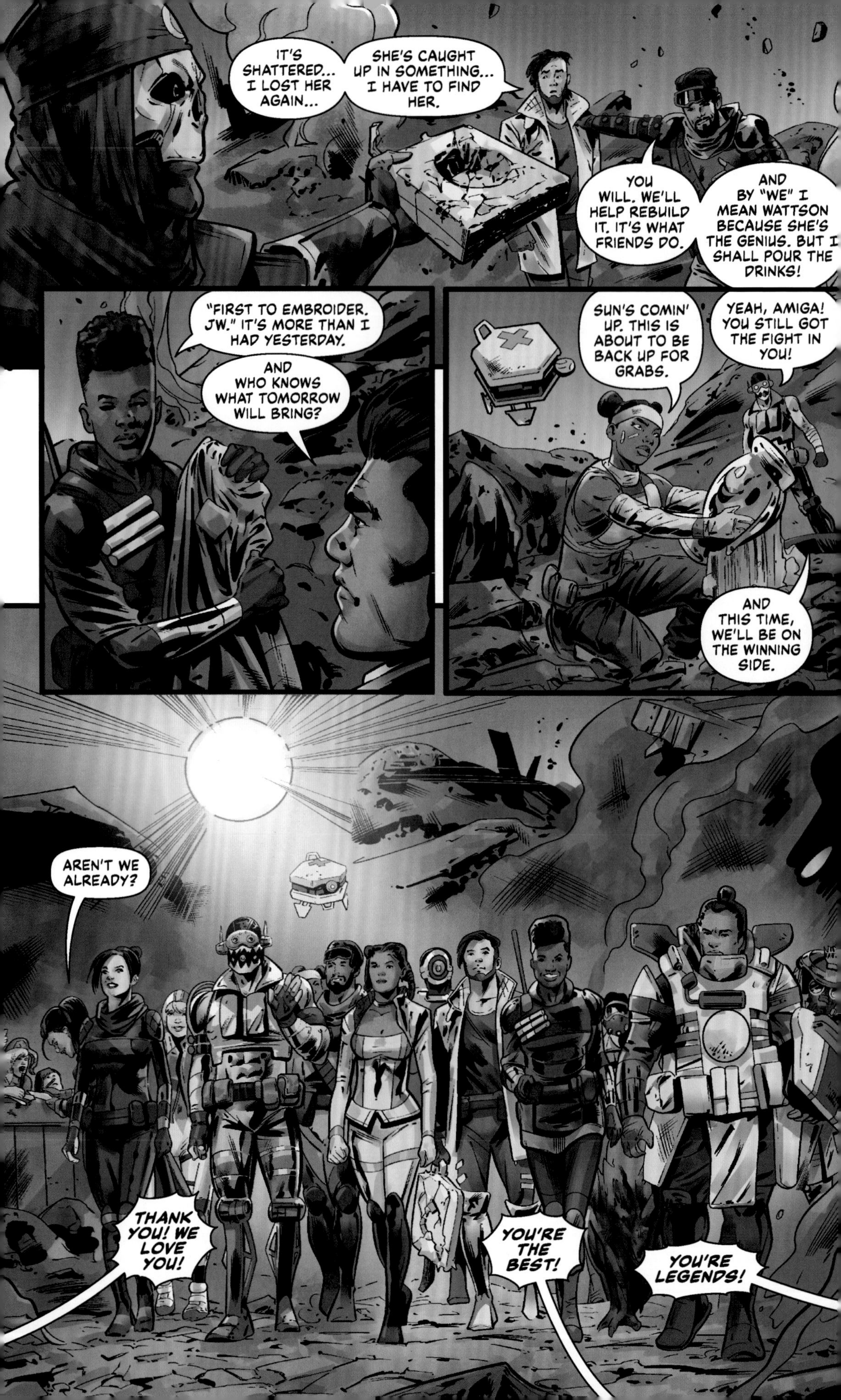
IT'S SHATTERED... I LOST HER AGAIN...
SHE'S CAUGHT UP IN SOMETHING... I HAVE TO FIND HER.
YOU WILL. WE'LL HELP REBUILD IT. IT'S WHAT FRIENDS DO.
AND BY "WE" I MEAN WATTSON BECAUSE SHE'S THE GENIUS. BUT I SHALL POUR THE DRINKS!
"FIRST TO EMBROIDER. JW." IT'S MORE THAN I HAD YESTERDAY.
AND WHO KNOWS WHAT TOMORROW WILL BRING?
SUN'S COMIN' UP. THIS IS ABOUT TO BE BACK UP FOR GRABS.
YEAH, AMIGA! YOU STILL GOT THE FIGHT IN YOU!
AND THIS TIME, WE'LL BE ON THE WINNING SIDE.
AREN'T WE ALREADY?
THANK YOU! WE LOVE YOU!
YOU'RE THE BEST!
YOU'RE LEGENDS!

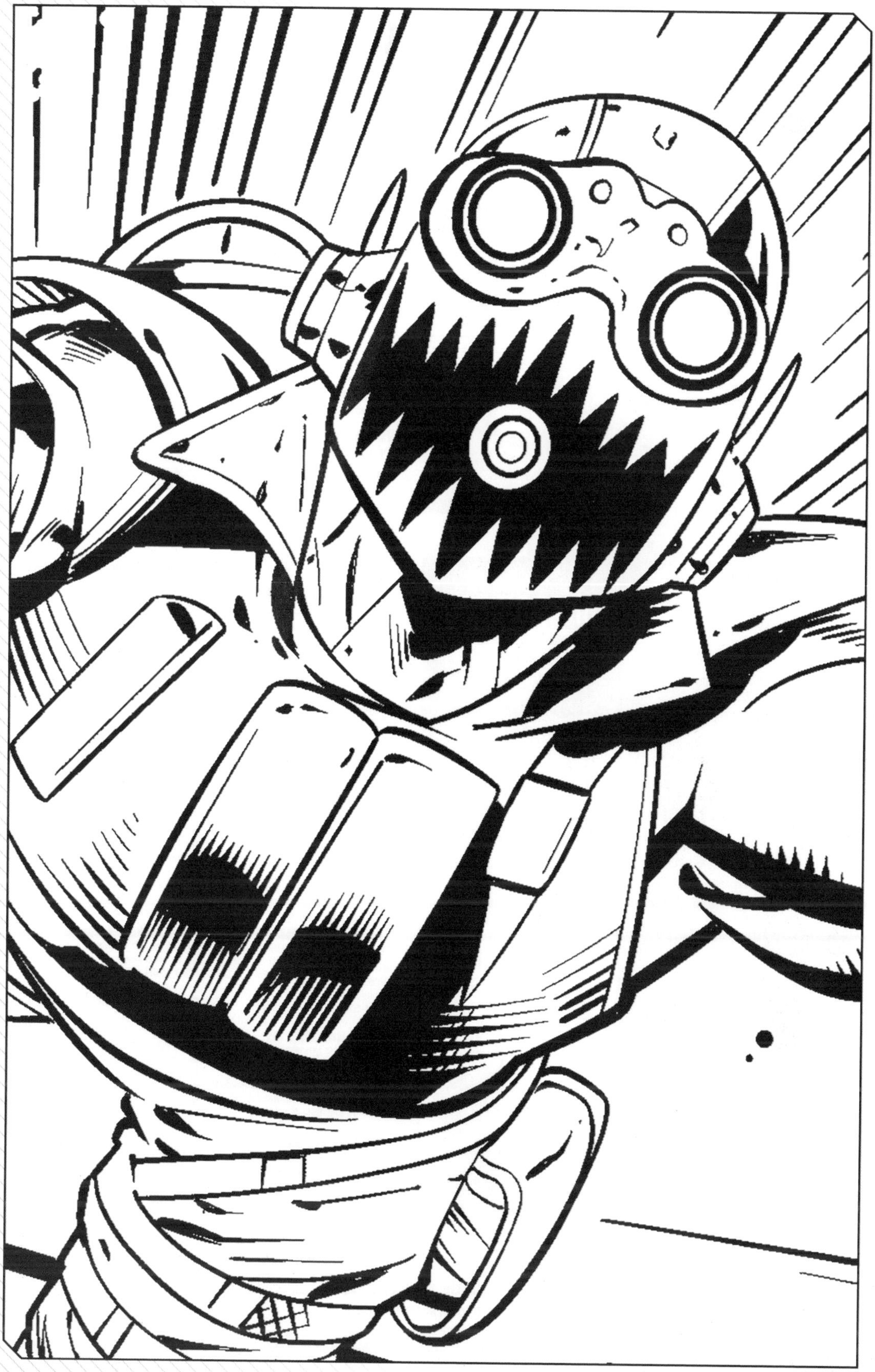

"If you think there's no room left in your life for another superhero comic, *Black Hammer* might just prove you wrong."—IGN

BLACK HAMMER™

ONCE THEY WERE HEROES, but the age of heroes has long since passed. Banished from existence by a multiversal crisis, the old champions of Spiral City—Abraham Slam, Golden Gail, Colonel Weird, Madame Dragonfly, and Barbalien—now lead simple lives in an idyllic, timeless farming village from which there is no escape! And yet, the universe isn't done with them—it's time for one last grand adventure.

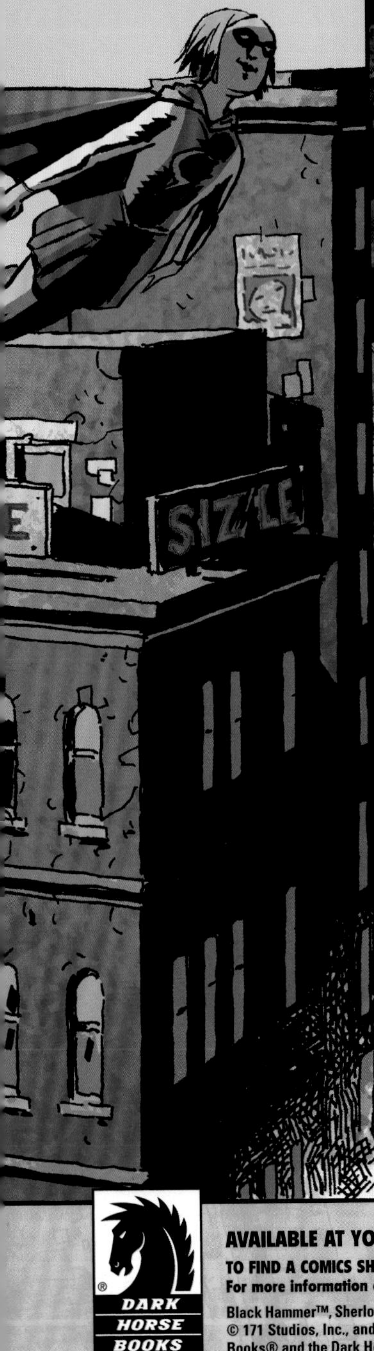

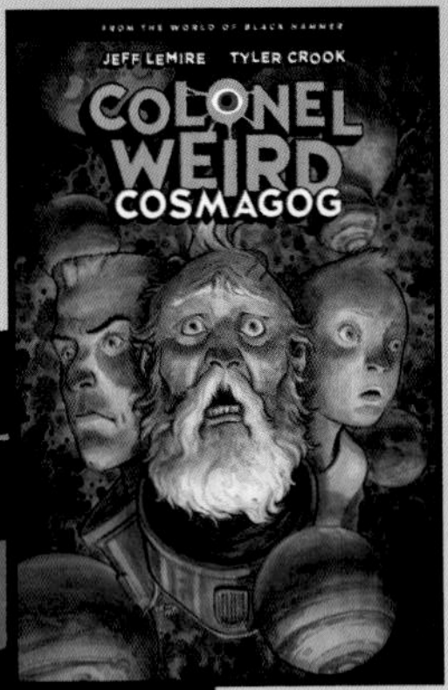
FROM THE WORLD OF BLACK HAMMER
JEFF LEMIRE
TYLER CROOK
COLONEL WEIRD
COSMAGOG

BLACK HAMMER
Written by Jeff Lemire • Art by Dean Ormston

LIBRARY EDITION VOLUME 1
978-1-50671-073-0 • $49.99

LIBRARY EDITION VOLUME 2
978-1-50671-185-0 • $49.99

THE WORLD OF BLACK HAMMER
LIBRARY EDITION VOLUME 1
978-1-50671-995-5 • $49.99

LIBRARY EDITION VOLUME 2
978-1-50671-996-2 • $49.99

VOLUME 1: SECRET ORIGINS
978-1-61655-786-7 • $14.99

VOLUME 2: THE EVENT
978-1-50670-198-1 • $19.99

VOLUME 3: AGE OF DOOM
PART ONE
978-1-50670-389-3 • $19.99

VOLUME 4: AGE OF DOOM
PART TWO
978-1-50670-816-4 • $19.99

VOLUME 5:
BLACK HAMMER REBORN
PART ONE
Art by Caitlin Yarsky
978-1-50671-426-4 • $19.99

VOLUME 6:
BLACK HAMMER REBORN
PART TWO
Written by Jeff Lemire
Art by Malachi Ward
and Matthew Sheean
978-1-50671-515-5 • $19.99

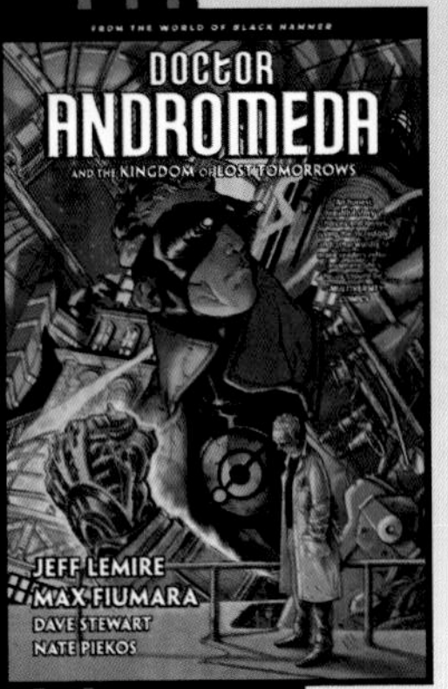
FROM THE WORLD OF BLACK HAMMER
DOCTOR
ANDROMEDA
AND THE KINGDOM OF LOST TOMORROWS
JEFF LEMIRE
MAX FIUMARA
DAVE STEWART
NATE PIEKOS

SHERLOCK FRANKENSTEIN & THE LEGION OF EVIL
Written by Jeff Lemire
Art by David Rubín
978-1-50670-526-2 • $17.99

DOCTOR ANDROMEDA & THE KINGDOM OF LOST TOMORROWS
Written by Jeff Lemire
Art by Max Fiumara
978-1-50672-329-7 • $19.99

THE UNBELIEVABLE UNTEENS: FROM THE WORLD OF BLACK HAMMER
VOLUME 1
Written by Jeff Lemire
Art by Tyler Crook, Tonci Zonjic, Ray Fawkes, and others
978-1-50672-436-2 • $19.99

THE QUANTUM AGE: FROM THE WORLD OF BLACK HAMMER
VOLUME 1
Written by Jeff Lemire
Art by Wilfredo Torres
978-1-50670-841-6 • $19.99

BLACK HAMMER '45: FROM THE WORLD OF BLACK HAMMER
Written by Jeff Lemire and Ray Fawkes
Art by Matt Kindt and Sharlene Kindt
978-1-50670-850-8 • $17.99

COLONEL WEIRD—COSMAGOG: FROM THE WORLD OF BLACK HAMMER
Written by Jeff Lemire
Art by Tyler Crook
978-1-50671-516-2 • $19.99

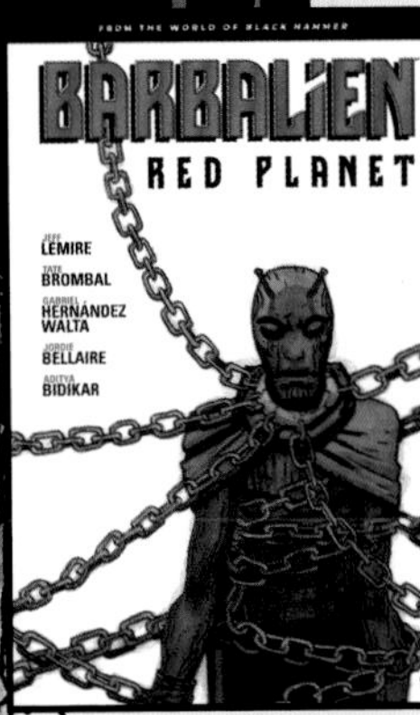
FROM THE WORLD OF BLACK HAMMER
BARBALIEN
RED PLANET
JEFF LEMIRE
TATE BROMBAL
GABRIEL HERNANDEZ WALTA
JORDIE BELLAIRE
ADITYA BIDIKAR

BLACK HAMMER: STREETS OF SPIRAL
Written by Jeff Lemire, Tate Brombal, and Ray Fawkes
Art by Dean Ormston, Matt Kindt, Tyler Crook, and others
978-1-50670-941-3 • $19.99

BLACK HAMMER/ JUSTICE LEAGUE: HAMMER OF JUSTICE!
Written by Jeff Lemire
Art by Michael Walsh
978-1-50671-099-0 • $29.99

BARBALIEN: RED PLANET
Written by Jeff Lemire and Tate Brombal
Art by Gabriel Hernández Walta and Jordie Bellaire
978-1-50671-580-3 • $19.99

SKULLDIGGER AND SKELETON BOY
Written by Jeff Lemire
Art by Tonci Zonjic
978-1-50671-033-4 • $19.99

BLACK HAMMER VISIONS
VOLUME 1
Written by Patton Oswalt, Geoff Johns, Chip Zdarsky, and Mariko Tamaki
Art by Johnnie Christmas, Scott Kollins, and Diego Olortegui
978-1-50672-326-6 • $24.99

VOLUME 2
Written by Kelly Thompson, Scott Snyder, Cecil Castelluci, and Cullen Bunn
Art by David Rubín, Matthew Sheean, Melissa Duffy, and others
978-1-50672-551-2 • $24.99

DARK HORSE BOOKS

AVAILABLE AT YOUR LOCAL COMICS SHOP OR BOOKSTORE
TO FIND A COMICS SHOP IN YOUR AREA, VISIT COMICSHOPLOCATOR.COM.
For more information or to order direct, visit darkhorse.com.

THE UMBRELLA ACADEMY™

Written by **GERARD WAY**
Art by **GABRIEL BÁ**
Featuring covers by **JAMES JEAN**

"...[F]lawless... stylish, imaginative..." —NEWSARAMA

"It's the X-Men for cool people." —GRANT MORRISON (*ALL STAR SUPERMAN*)

**VOLUME 1:
APOCALYPSE SUITE**
$17.99
ISBN 978-1-59307-978-9

**VOLUME 1: APOCALYPSE SUITE
LIBRARY EDITION HARDCOVER**
$39.99
ISBN 978-1-50671-547-6

**VOLUME 2:
DALLAS**
$17.99
ISBN 978-1-59582-345-8

**THE UMBRELLA ACADEMY: DALLAS
LIBRARY EDITION HARDCOVER**
$39.99
ISBN 978-1-50671-548-3

**VOLUME 3:
HOTEL OBLIVION**
$17.99
ISBN 978-1-50671-142-3

**THE UMBRELLA ACADEMY:
HOTEL OBLIVION LIBRARY
EDITION HARDCOVER**
$39.99
ISBN 978-1-50671-646-6

**THE UMBRELLA ACADEMY
PLAYING CARDS**
$4.99
DEC180427

**THE UMBRELLA ACADEMY
MAGNET 4-PACK**
$9.99
NOV180279

**THE UMBRELLA ACADEMY
"WHEN EVIL RAINS" MUG**
$12.99
NOV180282

**THE UMBRELLA ACADEMY
HAZEL AND CHA CHA MUG**
$12.99
APR190333

**THE UMBRELLA ACADEMY
ENAMEL PIN SET**
$14.99
NOV180281

**THE UMBRELLA ACADEMY
COASTER SET**
$9.99
NOV180280

**TALES FROM THE
UMBRELLA ACADEMY:
YOU LOOK LIKE DEATH**
$19.99
ISBN 978-1-50671-910-8

**THE UMBRELLA ACADEMY
CREST KEYCHAIN**
$9.99
DEC190328

**THE UMBRELLA ACADEMY
UMBRELLA KEYCHAIN**
$9.99
DEC190332

**THE UMBRELLA ACADEMY
HAZEL AND CHA CHA MAGNET**
$9.99
DEC190333

**THE UMBRELLA ACADEMY
UMBRELLA LOGO PATCH**
$6.99
JUN190394

**THE UMBRELLA ACADEMY
CREST LOGO PATCH**
$7.99
JUN190395

**THE UMBRELLA ACADEMY
HAZEL AND CHA CHA KEYCHAIN**
$9.99
DEC190329

**THE UMBRELLA ACADEMY
HOTEL OBLIVION KEYCHAIN**
$7.99
JUN190391

**THE UMBRELLA ACADEMY
CREST MAGNET**
$9.99
DEC190330

**THE UMBRELLA ACADEMY
THE RUMOR R LOGO PATCH**
$6.99
JUN190393

**THE UMBRELLA ACADEMY THE
KRAKEN SKULL LOGO PATCH**
$6.99
JUN190392

**THE UMBRELLA ACADEMY
UMBRELLA**
$29.99
JUL080073

**THE UMBRELLA
ACADEMY JOURNAL**
$19.99
NOV180283

**THE UMBRELLA
ACADEMY COMPOSITION
NOTEBOOK**
$9.99
SEP190324

**THE UMBRELLA
ACADEMY KNIT HAT**
$12.99
JUN190390

**THE UMBRELLA ACADEMY
HAZEL AND CHA CHA PINT GLASS SET**
$19.99
APR190334

**THE UMBRELLA ACADEMY
WRAPPING PAPER**
$9.99
AUG190333

**THE UMBRELLA ACADEMY:
HOTEL OBLIVION DELUXE
EDITION HARDCOVER**
$79.99
ISBN 978-1-50671-645-9

**THE UMBRELLA ACADEMY:
APOCALYPSE SUITE
DELUXE EDITION HARDCOVER**
$79.99
ISBN 978-1-50671-804-0

**THE UMBRELLA ACADEMY:
DALLAS DELUXE EDITION
HARDCOVER**
$79.99
ISBN 978-1-50671-805-7

STRANGER THINGS
THE OTHER SIDE

STRANGER THINGS
SIX

STRANGER THINGS
INTO THE FIRE

STRANGER THINGS VOLUME 1: THE OTHER SIDE
Jody Houser, Stefano Martino, Keith Champagne, Lauren Affe
ISBN 978-1-50670-976-5 • $19.99

STRANGER THINGS VOLUME 2: SIX
Jody Houser, Edgar Salazar, Keith Champagne, Marissa Louise
ISBN 978-1-50671-232-1 • $17.99

STRANGER THINGS VOLUME 3: INTO THE FIRE
Jody Houser, Ryan Kelly, Le Beau Underwood, Triona Farrell
ISBN 978-1-50671-308-3 • $19.99

STRANGER THINGS VOLUME 4: SCIENCE CAMP
Jody Houser, Edgar Salazar, Keith Champagne, Marissa Louise
ISBN 978-1-50671-576-6 • $19.99

STRANGER THINGS VOLUME 5: THE TOMB OF YBWEN
Greg Pak, Diego Galindo, Francesco Segala
ISBN 978-1-50672-554-3 • $19.99

STRANGER THINGS
SCIENCE CAMP

STRANGER THINGS
TOMB OF YBWEN

STRANGER THINGS and
DUNGEONS & DRAGONS

STRANGER THINGS AND DUNGEONS & DRAGONS
Jody Houser, Jim Zub, Diego Gallindo, MsassyK
ISBN 978-1-50672-107-1 • $19.99

STRANGER THINGS: ZOMBIE BOYS
Greg Pak, Valeria Favoccia, Dan Jackson
ISBN 978-1-50671-309-0 • $10.99

STRANGER THINGS: THE BULLY
Greg Pak, Valeria Favoccia, Dan Jackson, Nate Piekos
ISBN 978-1-50671-453-0 • $12.99

STRANGER THINGS: ERICA THE GREAT
Greg Pak, Danny Lore, Valeria Favoccia, Dan Jackson
ISBN 978-1-50671-454-7 • $12.99

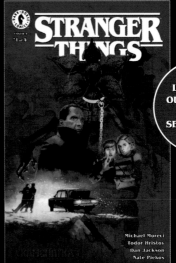

STRANGER THINGS
ZOMBIE BOYS

STRANGER THINGS
THE BULLY

STRANGER THINGS
ERICA THE GREAT

STRANGER THINGS
LIBRARY EDITION
VOLUME ONE

STRANGER THINGS
LIBRARY EDITION
VOLUME TWO

STRANGER THINGS LIBRARY EDITIONS

VOLUME 1
An oversized hardcover collecting *Stranger Things: The Other Side* and *Stranger Things: Science Camp.*
ISBN 978-1-50672-762-2 • $39.99

VOLUME 2
An oversized hardcover collecting *Stranger Things: Six* and *Stranger Things: Into the Fire.*
ISBN 978-1-50672-763-9 • $39.99

STRANGER THINGS
#1 of 4
Michael Moreci
Todor Hristov
Dan Jackson
Nate Piekos

LOOK FOR OUR NEWEST COMICS SERIES NOW!

STRANGER THINGS KAMCHATKA #1
Michael Moreci, Todor Hristov, Dan Jackson
$3.99

DARKHORSE.COM • AVAILABLE AT YOUR LOCAL COMICS SHOP OR BOOKSTORE
To find a comics shop near you, visit comicshoplocator.com
For more information or to order direct, visit darkhorse.com